Anonymous

The Barnet Book of Photography

A collection of practical articles

Anonymous

The Barnet Book of Photography
A collection of practical articles

ISBN/EAN: 9783337218171

Printed in Europe, USA, Canada, Australia, Japan

Cover: Foto ©Thomas Meinert / pixelio.de

More available books at **www.hansebooks.com**

THE BARNET BOOK OF PHOTOGRAPHY.

A COLLECTION OF PRACTICAL ARTICLES

BY

CAPT. W. DE W. ABNEY, C.B., F.R.S., ETC.
CHARLES H. BOTHAMLEY, F.C.S., F.I.C.
CHAPMAN JONES, F.C.S., F.I.C.
HAROLD BAKER
A. HORSLEY HINTON
JOHN H. AVERY
W. THOMAS
ANDREW PRINGLE
JOHN A. HODGES, F.R.P.S.
REV. F. C. LAMBERT, M A.
W. ETHELBERT HENRY, C.E.
JAMES PACKHAM, F.R.P.S.
THOS. S. SKELTON

THIRD EDITION.

PUBLISHED BY
ELLIOTT & SON, BARNET, HERTS.

PERCY LUND, HUMPHRIES & CO., LTD.,
3, AMEN CORNER, LONDON, E.C.

1898.

CONTENTS OF THE BOOK.

	PAGE.
ALPINE PHOTOGRAPHY. *W. de W. Abney, C.B., F.R.S.*	9
NEGATIVE MAKING. *C. H. Bothamley, F.C.S., F.I.C.*	23
LENSES. *Chapman Jones, F.C.S., F.I.C.*	57
PORTRAITURE. *Harold Baker*	77
PICTORIAL PHOTOGRAPHY. *A. Horsley Hinton*	87
ARCHITECTURAL PHOTOGRAPHY. *John H. Avery*	117
THE HAND CAMERA AND ITS USE. *W. Thomas*	131
LANTERN SLIDES. *Andrew Pringle*	141
HOW TO MAKE ENLARGEMENTS. *John A. Hodges, F.R.P.S.*	155
P.O.P. *Rev. F. C. Lambert, M.A.*	177
PLATINOTYPE PRINTING. *A. Horsley Hinton*	197
CONTACT PRINTING ON BROMIDE PAPER. *W. Ethelbert Henry, C.E.*	225
THE GUM-BICHROMATE PROCESS. *Jas. Packham, F.R.P.S.*	241
AN INTRODUCTION TO CARBON PRINTING FOR BEGINNERS	253
THE CARBON PROCESS. *Thomas S. Skelton*	261

ILLUSTRATIONS.

HOMEWARDS. KARL GREGER	16
AMONG THE ALPS. W. DE W. ABNEY	24
WINTER TIME ON THE ALPS. W. DE W. ABNEY	40
MELTON MEADOWS. A. HORSLEY HINTON	72
MISS LILY HANBURY—A PORTRAIT. HAROLD BAKER	88
GATHER THE ROSES WHILE YE MAY. ALEX. KEIGHLEY	120
BIRCH AND BRACKEN. W. THOMAS	136
DRIFTING STORM CLOUDS. W. THOMAS	168
STREONSALCH. W. J. WARREN	200
CUPBOARD LOVE. T. LEE SYMS	232
AT THE FOUNTAIN. J. W. WADE	264

PREFACE.

THE BARNET BOOK OF PHOTOGRAPHY.

The purpose of this book is to place in the hands of every Photographer instructive articles on essential processes and manipulations, by eminent writers who have given such subjects their especial study, and who have borne in mind that whilst the experienced Amateur and the Professional may each find much to learn from a comparatively elementary description of methods and means, it is the Beginner who stands in greatest need of help.

In the mind of every photographer the name of Barnet is inseparable from a great Photographic Industry, and now it is intended that the name shall be associated with a good and useful book, which is called the BARNET BOOK OF PHOTOGRAPHY, and it is left to the reader to say if the fulfilment of its purpose and the manner of its doing are such as to justify its existence.

To all who are interested in photography, who love it for itself and for its productions, and who desire to improve their own practice of its many processes and applications, this Book is respectfully dedicated.

Barnet, Herts.   ELLIOTT & SON.
    April, 1898.

A FAMOUS PIKE STREAM

Contact Print on

BARNET PLATINO MATT BROMIDE PAPER.

Alpine Photography.

WRITING in London on a day in winter with a murky sky and sloshy streets, the title of Alpine Photography is verily refreshing. It brings back days of sunlight and joyous experiment, and as we write the soul stirring scenery is before us called up by photographs taken under varying conditions of comfort and discomfort. That there is something different in Alpine photography to photography in our own country, we are bound to believe, since a special article is demanded for it.

The first question invariably asked is as to the nature of the outfit required. We should here like to divide our reply into two divisions. The one concerning the mountaineer, and the other the ordinary tourist. For the former we have no doubt in our minds that a hand camera to take ¼ plate or 5 × 4 pictures is the most convenient form of camera to take. It is not our business to advertise any person's wares and we shall content ourselves by saying that personally we prefer a camera which has separate slides and does not possess a magazine, more particularly when glass plates are to be used, though a form of kodak is not to be despised. But perhaps we are prejudiced in favour of glass plates, for they are simple to manipulate and have no cockles nor other drawbacks which the careless photographer may have to encounter. Probably the most useful lens to employ is a doublet of which the focal length is about a quarter more than the width of the plate, since it includes a fair angle and the margins of the photographs are not likely to be markedly different in general density to the centre, as is the case when wide-angle lenses are employed. In England a lens which will cover with a large stop, say $f/8$, is a desideratum, but in the Alps it is very rarely that such a large ratio of aperture to focal length is required. As a rule for ordinary plates a lens has to be stopped down to $f/16$ to give a negative in say $\frac{1}{50}$th of a second. Nevertheless where orthochromatic plates are to be employed it is very necessary to have a lens which will cover a plate satisfactorily with $f/8$ in order to use a colour screen for producing orthochromatic effects, since the loss of photographic light caused by the screen can only be compensated for by such an aperture even when the shutter is slowed down. The reader is therefore recommended on the whole to furnish himself with one of the modern lenses which work at $f/8$, though he must remember that the larger the aperture employed the more the margins and centre of the picture will suffer from unequal exposure. With some hand cameras there is a means of attachment to a stand, but a stand on a mountain is difficult to use and moreover has on more than one occasion been proved dangerous to carry. The mountaineer if he desires to give a time—and not an instantaneous—exposure on his excursion, would do well to have a small clip ready to attach to the head of his ice axe. The axe will form a sufficiently stable stand for the more prolonged, but still short, exposure that he may be required to give on some particular subjects such as a photograph at sunrise or near sunset.

Photographers in England are rarely afflicted with breathlessness through exertion, but it is different in mountaineering. A mountaineer may keep his wind, but it would be rare to find that his heart was beating equably after some spurt of exertion, such as rock climbing. It is often after some such exertion that he comes upon some view which he may wish to record on his photographic plate. The usual method of holding the hand camera would under such circumstances prove a failure so far as sharpness of image is concerned. Pressed against his " middle " or "upper" chest, the beatings of the heart will record themselves on the photograph. Under such circumstances resort must be had to some form of support on which to rest his camera. After many years' experience, the writer has come to the conclusion that there is no support superior to the ice axe. It is not necessary to cause it to stand upright in the ground, ice, or snow, though this should be done if possible. It will suffice to rest the point on the rock, and place the camera on the axe head, with the pick parallel to the body. We then have a firm support in one direction, and the hands, which are not affected by the automatic motion of the heart, can be trusted to keep it steady in the other direction. Photographs taken with a good lens, and with such a stand, will bear enlarging up to 22 inches, at least. It is because these photographs will bear enlarging that a small plate is recommended to the mountaineer. There is not a large proportion of Alpine views taken on the mountain side of which one would care to have anything but a memorandum, and it is such a size as that recommended which gives such a memento, and which, if desired, allows a more formidable size to be acquired at home, where we may suppose there are all the conveniences that a photographic laboratory affords. The writer has had experience on mountains with cameras varying from 12 × 10 to the ¼ plate size. When younger and more inclined to waste a few valuable minutes of day-light in putting up a camera stand, the 12 × 10 gave pictures which we often lamented having taken, whilst in his more mature years, a snap-shot has never been regretted. The cameras which require stands, require one porter at least to carry them, for although the late Mr. Donkin carried his own 7½ × 5 camera up the highest peaks, it is few men, who, even if they had the energy or the physique that he had, would imitate his example. A porter means an extra expense in fees, and an extra mouth to feed, and very likely entails slowness in a climb through having an additional man upon the rope. A quarter plate or a 5 × 4 camera the owner, however, can himself carry ; but the best form of attaching it to his body has been a difficult task to evolve. Many and many different attachments have been tried. One thing is quite certain, and that is, the camera should be in a stout case, but it cannot be carried over the shoulders by a strap as we can do in comparatively level countries. Let anyone try to come down a rock with the camera slung over his shoulders, and he will soon find it dangling in front of his stomach, or swinging like a pendulum, and threatening to displace him from what at best may be a treacherous handhold. The method of attachment we adopt now, will be readily seen from the diagram.

The shoulder strap is utilized, but a ring is attached to the back of the case as shown, and a strap or piece of whipcord comes over the strap as shown. The two shoulders are in AA and the case is carried as a knapsack. The length of the cord or strap BB is so adjusted, as is also the length of the shoulder strap, that the camera lies against the small of the back, and that it will not swing away from the body. At one time the ring was placed in front of the case, but the result was merely to cause the top of the case to rest against the

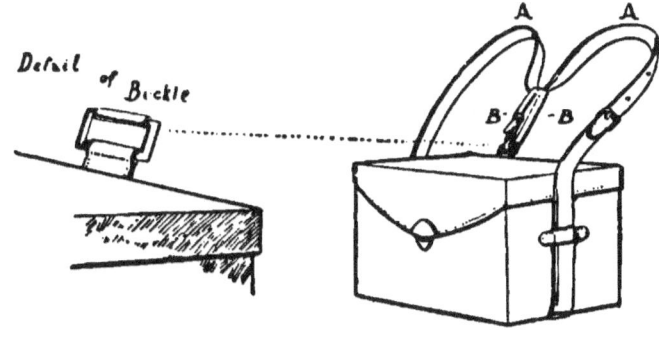

back. The plan shown above has answered under almost every variety of circumstances, and the weight is inconsiderable. (A friend has his camera attached to the bottom of a small "rücksac" and this answers, but as the writer does not carry his own provisions or change of garments he has not adopted this plan). A long day's march may be undertaken if this contrivance be employed, and the weight is scarcely felt.

For those who have not had extensive practice with hand cameras, a view finder is, if not a necessity, at all events, a great help. On the whole, perhaps the best form is that in which a miniature view falls on a ground glass. It must be recollected, however, that each view finder is adapted for some particular focal length of lens. The view in the finder and on the plate should be compared, and if the former is more extensive, the surplus ground glass should be covered up with a black mask.

If it be determined to take a camera with its stand, very few directions are required beyond those which apply to ordinary view work on the plains. It may perhaps be as well to mention that a camera stand placed on ice or snow, is not immovable until the iron shoes of the legs attain the temperature of the surrounding snow or ice. An exposure of a few seconds will often show an image which has moved on the plate.

The next point that we may call attention to is the plate to be employed. With a hand camera there is no absolute necessity to have the most rapid plate, as far as exposure is concerned, but in mountain work it must be recollected that there are very great contrasts to represent on the print. "The slower the plate the steeper the gradation" is almost axiomatic, and it must be recollected that only a certain amount of opacity will print if the deepest shadows only are to be kept of the greatest black obtainable in a print. It is evident that the greater the range of light and shade that is obtained of a printable density, the more true to nature the picture will be. For this reason a quick plate with a moderate gradation is to be preferred —as being most generally useful—but it should be a plate which is absolutely free from fog, and it should also be of as fine a grain as possible, the size of which has something to do with development. This is still more true when a camera stand and hand exposures are made. With a slow plate with feebler intensities of light, which must be the case when the lens is stopped down to admit of hand exposures, the gradation becomes more steep than if a fairly bright light be employed. A quick plate does not suffer in the same way, however small the stop may be. It has already been stated that isochromatic plates may be employed with a hand camera. For ice and snow views there is not much to commend their employment, unless to give a deeper shade to the sky and to the vast crevasses which so often form part of the foreground. The darker sky allows faint clouds to be visible in a print when they otherwise would be absent. Pictorially thus the isochromatic plate has something to recommend it. Celluloid films have often been substituted for plates by the writer, and excellent photographs have been obtained on them when they were fairly rapid. There is not much to be said in their favour as regards weight, for in most cameras the support for them weighs nearly as much as the glass plate. There is also a disadvantage in developing them, for they are not so easily manipulated as a rigid body. For convenience in travelling, however, they are to be highly commended. A gross of cut films do not weigh so much as a dozen plates and occupy much less space in the baggage. The question of the use of a Kodak camera with its roller slide, has not been brought forward, not because excellent results cannot be obtained with it, but simply because the writer prefers to use plates and films which can be got at at any time for the purposé of development.

For travelling on the continent, and to one's mountain destination, experience has shown that a small hamper is the safest receptacle of all the necessary kit. A hamper which will contain two camera cases side by side is really sufficient; but it should be a little greater in depth. It may be thought that two cameras are to be taken, but such is not the intention. If a zinc trough be made of the size of one camera case it will contain all the developing apparatus necessary, the lantern, and the plates or films, and all the few etceteras which go to make one happy. (A screwdriver, a file, and some extra screws, and gummed paper and white blotting paper cut to the size of the plates should be enough for the etceteras). The hamper may be arranged so that the camera and view finder may be taken out without any derangement of the rest of the articles in it. The developing bottles and cups, with the dishes, may be similarly extracted. This prevents undue trouble in unpacking and packing. One grand thing to remember is, pack well but not distressingly tightly, in other words don't employ an expert packer if you wish for comfort. Have the hamper a size too large rather than a size too small. Also be it remembered that it is useless to stopper the bottles with all sorts of devices at home, and have to pack in an ordinary manner when once the contents of the hamper have been brought into use. Have your bottles covered with an indiarubber cap which can easily be removed and replaced; of course we are assuming that development is to take place during one's travels, and not to be left over for home. Personally we think that a speedy development after a view is taken will give the best picture. It may often happen that an undeveloped sensitive plate or film will suffer by its travels. There will or may be scratches and what not, which would be absent if the negative is finished at the time. The outfit for development which need only be taken is as follows: four developing dishes, bottles or cartridges of the dry developer, ammonia diluted to half its strength in a glass stoppered bottle (if in a wooden case, as for medicine bottles, it will be a further protection), a couple of tins of hyposulphite *pounded up* before the journey, carried in small tins (such tins as the half-plate platinum paper comes in are very convenient), two or three empty six ounce medicine bottles with good corks, a two or four

HOMEWARDS.
KARL GREGER.

ounce measure, a washing rack with a trough (there is a folding rack in the market which answers admirably; it has v shaped grooves which never damage the edges of the film, and one rack will take twenty-two glasses back to back). A zinc trough can be made to cover the plates with water when in the rack, a lantern (by preference a paper folding one), a dusting brush, a couple of dusters, and blotting paper cut into squares the size of the plates, with which to pack them—it is useful also to have spare pieces of blotting paper to place beneath the plates when drying, also a piece of mackintosh to place on the wash stand during developing operations—an empty pint wine bottle will be got at any hotel and in this the hyposulphite can be dissolved. The list looks formidable but the whole can be readily packed in the hamper of the size given. It will be seen that no intensifying solutions are enumerated amongst the requisites. A negative is better strengthened in the quiet of one's dark-room at home.

Now we must give a hint or two as to the exposures required. We will suppose that on the plates to be used a satisfactory negative of an open English landscape, on a bright June day with fleecy clouds in the sky, can be secured with an aperture of $f/11$ in $\frac{1}{25}$th of a second. If that be so, then on an equally fine day in July or August, at an altitude of about 6000 feet, the same kind of view should theoretically be secured in $\frac{1}{50}$th second, and a stop of $f/16$—that is, the photographic light is about four times as strong. It must, however, be recollected that at this altitude, and particularly near mid-day, the shadows are not illuminated to the same degree from the sky. The darker blue sky shows that the light which at a low altitude goes to make a pale blue sky is to be found in the direct rays of the sun, and not scattered to give a luminous sky. As the shadows are principally illuminated by the light from the sky, it follows that the shadows will be darker at a high than at a low altitude, for this reason amongst others, the exposure should not be curtailed to the amount given above. If the aperture be reduced to $f/16$ it is probable that the exposure of $\frac{1}{25}$th second will be not more than sufficient to give. For our own part we prefer to give longer and to expose well for the deep shadows, trusting to development to give us properly "gradated" pictures. As the sun goes down toward the horizon, the shadows get more illumined from local reflection, and it is scarcely necessary to alter the exposure until considerably nearer sunset than at home, when the exposure must be considerably prolonged. For views in which there is little but ice and snow, the exposure should be very much curtailed. There is so little contrast that if the exposure be at all prolonged the picture will be inevitably flat. The shadows are illumined by an immense quantity of light reflected from the white surface, and the difficulty is to get sufficient contrast. The writer well remembers one set of beautiful views, taken from the top of a mountain some 10,000 feet high, where the eye could see nothing but snow-fields and ice and swirling masses of clouds. The day was not bright, but to get a satisfactory picture a stop of $f/32$ was necessary with only an exposure of $\frac{1}{70}$th of a second. Plates given an exposure of $\frac{1}{25}$th second with a stop $f/16$ showed little besides a plain white mass. It would be difficult to give hints for every kind of view. The judgment of the operator must be brought into play and no actinometer will be of much use under the varied conditions which are the rule, not the exception.

Now as to development. The "one-solution" given by the metol and amidol cartridges are the most readily prepared, and in five times out of six will scarcely be bettered, but for the sixth time may fail, because of their "rigidity." For these exceptional negatives, solutions of an oxidizing agent such as pyrogallol, of a restrainer (bromide), and of an accelerator are to be recommended. For the latter, the carbonate (not the bicarbonate) of potash is much to be recommended, though some prefer ammonia. Two formulæ are given, either of which will be found extremely useful. When the exposure has been prolonged enough for details in deep shadows to be brought out, it will generally happen that over-exposure has been given to the high-lights, and it is to keep these in the printing state that care is required. In the old collodion dry plate days, it was very usual to bring out a complete phantom image of a subject before any density was given to it. When this was properly out, the intensifier of silver nitrate and pyrogallol was applied, and the picture gradually brought up to printing density. It was usually full of detail in the high-lights and shadows, all of which would be found in the finished print. Such is the same procedure which we recommend, strive to get out an image of feeble density but full of detail, and then give the density.

The plate should first of all be thoroughly soaked in a solution of the alkali which can be used, and then a few drops of the pyrogallol solution be dropped into the developing cup with an equal number of drops of the restrainer. The alkaline solution is then returned to the cup and again poured into the dish and over the plate. By degrees the required phantom image will make its appearance, and now bromide and pyrogallol are added until it is evidently complete. The plate is then washed in water, a final wash being given in a very weak solution of acetic acid or citric and water. After a final rinse with water the plate is treated with the pyrogallol solution and restrainer in the proportion recommended for the ordinary development of the plate, omitting the alkali. The density will begin to appear, and when it flags, a little alkali is added (a few drops at a time) to the solution. Keep the image fairly feeble at above half the proper printing density, and fix. The plate should then be kept for intensification, preferably by Mr. Chapman Jones's, when a mercury solution is applied, and then a ferrous oxalate to reduce the latter to the metallic state. It will be found if this procedure is adopted, that the negative is built up with a greater range of light gradation than by bringing it out by a one-solution method of development. If one wishes to exercise artistic treatment, then in the preliminary stage more importance can be given to any desired part by applying a camel's hair brush soaked in normal pyrogallol solution with its restrainer. The prominence thus gained will be kept in the subsequent operations. When applying the brush care must be taken that the image blends as it were with the rest of the picture. No abrupt increase of density must be permitted, as if it be, the result will be anything but satisfactory.

The following is an ammonia-pyro developer, with which the writer usually works.

A
Ammonia .... 1 part.
Water .... 9 parts.

(Of course, should the ammonia be taken half strength allowance must be made for the dilution.)

B
Potassium bromide................. 20 grains.
Water .... 1 ounce.

(When travelling it is very convenient to have the bromide weighed out into 20 grain packets.)

P
Pyrogallol .... dry.

S
Saturated solution of sulphite of soda.

When the view has strong contrasts and the plate has been exposed for the shadows take of A 30 minims and 2 ounces of water and soak the plate in it as given above. Then add to the cup, of B 2 drams, of S 1 dram, and about quarter grain of P. Pour back the solution of ammonia from the dish, and then apply the mixture till all detail appears, and proceed as indicated above. A saturated solution of potassium carbonate may be substituted for the ammonia solution.

Before closing this chapter it may be of use to the reader to tabulate the number of thicknesses of atmospheres through which light has to travel at different altitudes of the sun at sea level.

Altitude.	Atmosphere.
90°	1·000
80°	1·015
70°	1·064
60°	1·155
50°	1·305
40°	1·555
30°	1·995
20°	2·904
15°	3·809
10°	5·571
5°	10·216
4°	12·151
2°	18·882
0°	35·503

If sunlight outside the atmosphere be represented by 1 and say $\frac{1}{10}$th be cut off by 1 atmosphere, then after transmission through 2 atmospheres only ·81 will reach the spectator, and if through 3 only ·729. For any atmosphere the diminution will be $\frac{1}{10}$th, that is, it will be ·9^x where x is the number of atmospheres.

If we ascend the factor varies, there are less thicknesses of atmosphere to go through and we get the following table.

Barometer in Inches.	Visual Transmission (Sunlight outside the Atmospheric being 1).	Photographically Actinic Light Transmitted (Sunlight outside the Atmospheric being 1).
30	·853	·639
29	·866	·654
28	·875	·672
27	·884	·689
26	·891	·708
25	·899	·730
24	·908	·746
23	·915	·763
22	·922	·787
21	·928	·800
20	·934	·819
19	·940	·833

This table and the preceding one will enable a calculation to be made as to the exposure to be given. Thus at sea level with a photographic brightness of sun of 639,000 candles when nearly overhead, it will at 5° above the horizon only have a photographic brightness of about 1000. At about 9000 feet high the photographic brightness would when the sun is overhead be about 800,000 candles, and at 5° it would have a value of 350,000, showing the greater penetration through the thinner atmosphere.

W. de W. Abney, C.B., F.R.S., etc., etc.

Negative Making.

DEVELOPMENT, INTENSIFICATION, REDUCING, Etc.

WHEN a sensitive plate has been properly exposed under ordinary conditions, there is no visible change. The action of light produces what is known as a *latent image* or *developable image*, and in order to convert this into a visible image with sufficient opacity to be useful for printing purposes, it must be *developed*. In the operation of development, the plate is treated with some solution that will act on the exposed parts of the sensitive film and reduce the silver salts contained therein to metallic silver, in quantity proportional to the amount of light-action, whilst at the same time it produces no appreciable change in those parts of the film on which light has acted the least or not at all, and which correspond to the darkest shadows of the object that has been photographed. The solution used for this purpose is called the *developer*.

DEVELOPERS—GENERAL.

The substances that can be employed as photographic developers are now somewhat numerous, but the most useful for negative making are pyrogallic acid (also known as pyrogallol, or for brevity as pyro.), ortol, metol, and hydroquinone (also known as quinol). Ferrous oxalate is likewise used in special circumstances, but not for general work. An ordinary developer as mixed for use contains—

1.—One of the above-mentioned substances (pyrogallic acid, ortol, metol, quinol) which is the actual developing constituent, and is known as *the reducer*, but requires the addition of the next constituent before it can work.

2.—An alkali, which may be sodium carbonate, potassium carbonate, caustic soda, caustic potash, or, if pyrogallic acid is used, ammonia. The alkali sets the reducer in action and is called *the accelerator*.

3.—A soluble bromide, which must be potassium bromide except when ammonia is used as the alkali, and then it may be ammonium bromide. The chief use of the bromide is to retard the action of the developer, and in particular to prevent its affecting those parts of the film that have not been acted on by light. For this reason the bromide is called *the restrainer* or, sometimes, *the retarder*.

AMONG THE ALPS.
CAPT. W. DE W. ABNEY, C.B., F.R.S. ETC.

4.—A sulphite, the function of which is to prevent the solution from becoming strongly discoloured and consequently staining the film. It also affects the colour of the reduced silver that forms the developed image, this colour being browner, and consequently of higher printing opacity, the lower the proportion of sulphite present. Sodium sulphite and potassium metabisulphite are the most commonly used.

The composition of a developer has to be so arranged that, whilst reasonably rapid in its action, it is not so rapid as to be beyond control, and does not produce "general fog" by acting on those parts of the film that have not been acted on by light.

DEVELOPMENT—GENERAL OPERATIONS AND PHENOMENA.

A developer is usually compounded immediately before use by mixing two or more solutions, and in order to ensure uniform action it is essential that the constituents should be thoroughly mixed before the liquid is applied to the plate. If the measuring or mixing vessel is large enough, this can be done by agitating the liquid; if not, the liquid may be poured once or twice from one vessel to another.

The quantity of developer necessary for a plate of a given size depends in some degree upon the size and character of the dish that is used, and is smallest when the bottom of the dish is quite flat and has no ridges or grooves. It is false economy to use too small a quantity, and it may be taken that for a quarter plate $1\frac{1}{2}$ oz., for a half plate $2\frac{1}{2}$ or 3 oz., and for a whole plate 4 oz. of developer should be used.

Ebonite, xylonite, or papier maché dishes are the best for all operations connected with negative making, since they are not so liable as porcelain or earthenware to break a plate if it is allowed to drop into them.

When applying the developer to the plate it is important to cover the whole surface of the plate rapidly and in such a manner as to avoid the formation of air bubbles, and the best way is to begin to pour on the developer at one corner of the developing dish and whilst pouring somewhat quickly move the vessel rapidly but steadily along the edge of the dish to the other corner. If there should be any froth or air bubbles on the surface of the developer, the last portions should not be poured out of the vessel into the dish, and then the risk of air bubbles forming on the surface of the plate will be lessened.

Sometimes after the developer has been poured on and the plate seems to be uniformly wetted, the liquid will recede from one corner or one edge of the plate and the part thus left uncovered will appear as a patch of lower opacity when the negative is finished. This happens either because the dish is not standing level on the table or because the bottom of the dish is not flat; sometimes it happens because too small a quantity of developer has been used.

After the plate has been covered by the developer the dish should be carefully rocked from time to time, and, for reasons that will be explained presently, the time required for the first appearance of the image and the manner in which the different parts of the image follow one another, should be carefully observed.

If the plate has been correctly exposed, the brightest parts of the image will appear (as black, of course,) in about a minute, more or less, according to the temperature, composition of the developer, and character of the plate, and the other parts will follow steadily in the order of their brightness, after which the image as a whole will continue to gain vigour or opacity up to a certain limit. The essential point is that the principal details in the deepest shadows of the subject shall appear and acquire a distinct printable opacity, before the highest lights become so opaque that the details in them are no longer distinguishable. Whether this condition is realisable or not depends very largely on the exposure that the plate has received.

If the image appears in considerably less than a minute and the different parts follow one another very quickly, the plate has been *over-exposed*, and the degree of over-exposure is indicated by the rapidity with which the image appears. In this connection it ought, however, to be stated that with metol and certain other developers, even when the plate has been correctly exposed, the different parts of the image appear almost simultaneously, though the first appearance may not begin until about a minute after the developer has been applied to the plate. It follows that with these developers it is difficult to recognise over-exposure, but it so happens that they are not suitable developers to use when there is any probability that the plates have been over-exposed. On the other hand, if the image is slow in appearing and the brightest parts of the subject are not followed in due course by the middle tones, the plate has been *under-exposed*, and there is considerable danger that the high-lights may become quite opaque before any details have appeared in the shadows, or even, in extreme cases, in the lower middle tones, that is to say, in those parts that are next in darkness to the shadows.

When it is desired, as it frequently is, to alter the composition of the developer during development, the substance or substances to be added should be put into the measuring or mixing glass, the developer poured out of the dish into the glass, and the well-mixed liquid poured over the plate as before. Any attempt to add substances to the developer whilst it is in contact with the plate will probably result in uneven action.

It should be borne in mind that temperature has an important influence on development, the time required for the first appearance of the image and for the completion of development being, as a rule, less the higher the temperature. Further, if the developing solutions are very cold, it is often almost impossible to obtain sufficient opacity.

Perhaps the most difficult thing in connection with development is to know when to stop the process, that is to say, when the image has acquired sufficient opacity, or "density," as it is often called. After all the required detail has become visible, the plate from time to time is lifted carefully out of the developer, allowed to drain for a moment or two, and then held between the developing lamp and the eye; the opacity of the image, especially in the highest lights and deepest shadows, being carefully scrutinised. The appearance of the image as seen when looking at the back of the plate, is also carefully observed.

For this purpose it is very much better that the light of the developing lamp should pass through transparent glass (ruby or deep orange) so that the flame itself is distinctly visible, instead of through ground glass or a coloured translucent fabric. Further, the flame of the lamp, whether gas or oil, should always be turned up to the same height, for it is clear that if the brightness of the flame used for making the examination is not fairly constant, all sorts of variable results will be obtained. For this reason it is much better to judge the opacity of negatives by artificial light than by daylight, the intensity of the latter being so variable.

A paraffin lamp with a circular wick and a deep ruby chimney with a metal cap at the top, answers admirably.

No general rules can be laid down ; the appearance of the properly developed image depends on the thickness of the film, the granularity of the silver salt, the presence or absence of silver iodide, and the composition of the emulsion used. Experience only is of value, and the best way to secure uniformly satisfactory results, is to keep as far as possible to one brand of plates. With some plates, for example, very little of the image should appear at the back of the plate, with others the greater part of the image must be distinctly visible there.

Sometimes, especially when using small sizes of plates, it is not easy to tell whether all the necessary detail in the shadows has been brought out, and this is an important matter, for if the small negatives are to be used for making enlarged negatives or prints, or lantern slides, there should be very little clear glass indeed even in the deepest shadows of the subject. As a rule it may be said that when every part of the image is at least gray the maximum possible amount of detail has been brought out. If the greyness begins to spread to the margins of the plate where it has been protected by the rebate of the dark slide, general fog is being produced, and, as a rule, little will be gained, but much may be lost, by continuing the development for any considerable time after this is observed. When development is completed the developer is poured off, the plate is well rinsed under the tap or in two or three changes of water, and is then ready for fixing.

DEVELOPMENT WITH PYRO-AMMONIA.

This method of development has the advantage that the constituents can be kept in concentrated solutions, considerable modifications in the composition of the developer can be made very readily and the negatives obtained are of excellent printing quality. On the other hand it cannot be satisfactorily employed with certain brands of rapid plates, because with them it has a tendency to produce general fog, and with some other plates, especially when they are old, it has a tendency to produce what is known as green fog.

Three solutions are prepared :—

Reducer.

Pyrogallic acid .... 1 oz. or 10 parts
Potassium metabisulphite*.. 1 oz. or 10 parts
Water, to make up to ...... 10 oz. or 100 parts

Accelerator.

Ammonia .... 1 oz. or 10 parts
Water, to make up to...... 10 oz. or 100 parts

Restrainer.

Ammonium bromide ...... 1 oz. or 10 parts
Water, to make up to ...... 10 oz. or 100 parts

For each ounce of developer, take 20 minims of reducer, 20 minims of restrainer and 40 minims of accelerator, and make up to 1 oz. with water. With some plates 60 minims of accelerator and 30 minims of restrainer may be used, but any greater proportion of accelerator has considerable tendency to produce general fog. On the other hand the proportion of restrainer can often be increased with advantage since, unless the amount added is very large, its chief effect is to prevent general fog; 30 minims of restrainer to 40 minims of accelerator, or 40 minims of accelerator to 60 minims of restrainer are proportions that can be recommended. Too low a proportion of bromide should be carefully avoided.

* The metabisulphite is dissolved in about 8 oz. (80 parts) of water with the aid of heat, and the pyrogallic acid is then added. When the liquid has cooled it is made up to 10 oz. (100 parts) by addition of water, the whole being well mixed by shaking.

It is very important to ascertain, by careful trial with each brand of plates that is to be used, what is the maximum proportion of ammonia that can safely be added, and what proportion of bromide to ammonia is necessary in order to prevent general fog. As a rule, the more rapid the plates the smaller is the quantity of ammonia that can be used with safety.

By far the best plan is to keep development well under control by adding only part of the accelerator at the beginning of development and adding the rest as circumstances require.

For each ounce of developer take 20 minims of pyro. solution and make up to the required bulk with water. In another measure mix for each ounce of developer 40 minims of bromide solution and 60 minims of ammonia solution, and regard this as the maximum quantity that can be added with that bulk of developer. Now to the diluted pyro solution add about a quarter or one-third of the ammonia and bromide solution, pour this mixture on the plate and observe what happens.

If the mode of appearance of the image indicates that the plate has been correctly exposed, about half the remaining ammonia and bromide mixture may be added to the developer at once, and the action allowed to continue, with occasional rocking of the dish. If development proceeds satisfactorily and, in particular, if the chief details in the shadows begin to appear before the highest lights have become too opaque, it is not necessary nor advisable to add the last portion of the ammonia and bromide mixture, since the tendency to general fog and green fog is reduced when the proportion of ammonia is kept as low as possible. On the other hand, if the development flags and the appearance of shadow detail is a little tardy, the rest of the ammonia and bromide mixture must be added.

If the plate seems to be over-exposed, no more of the ammonia and bromide mixture should be added for some time, until it is seen whether the quantity already in the developer will suffice to complete development. If it seems that the over-exposure has been considerable, a further quantity of pyro solution (10 to 20 minims per oz.) and also of bromide solution (10, 20, or 30 minims per oz.) may be added with advantage. Development is then allowed to continue and the negative is examined from time to time; if it is seen that the opacity does not increase, or if sufficient detail in the deep shadows does not appear, further small quantities of the ammonia and bromide mixture may be added *cautiously* until the required result is obtained, waiting a little while to see the result of each small addition before adding more.

When the plate behaves as if under-exposed, dilute the developer at once with half the quantity or an equal quantity of water, according to the degree of under-exposure indicated, and add the whole of the ammonia and bromide mixture. These modifications should check the rate at which the high-lights of the subject gain opacity, whilst accelerating the appearance of the middle tones and shadows. Should this effect not be produced, further quantities of ammonia and bromide mixture may be added or, in extreme cases, ammonia alone, and the developer may be still more diluted with water.

If any considerable parts of the image still show no detail, local development with a brush may be tried as a last resource. A soft camel's hair brush, preferably mounted in quill, is used. Some of the ammonia and bromide mixture is placed in a vessel and diluted with two or three times its volume of water. One corner or edge of the plate is raised so that the part to be treated is lifted out of the developer, the diluted ammonia and bromide mixture is applied rapidly with the brush, and the plate is allowed to drop gently back into the developer. The treatment may be repeated if necessary.

Should all these devices fail, the plate is hopelessly under-exposed.

Sometimes, when working with a diluted developer as just described, it happens that although all the necessary detail has been brought out, the image gains in opacity very slowly. Provided that all the required detail is visible, small quantities of pyro solution may be added in order to gain opacity more quickly.

PYRO-SODA DEVELOPMENT.

When sodium carbonate is used as the alkali in place of ammonia the developer acts somewhat more slowly and is less liable to produce fog, especially with very rapid plates, and there is very little tendency to produce green fog. On the other hand, variations are not so easily made in the composition of the developer. Some people find the absence of the smell of ammonia a decided advantage.

Teasels
By
Carine Cadby.

Stock Pyro Solution.
The same as for Pyro-Ammonia.

Dilute Pyro Solution. *
Stock pyro-solution .... 1 oz. or 10 parts
Water .... 10 oz. or 100 parts

Soda Solution.
Sodium carbonate, crystallised. 1 oz. or 10 parts
Sodium Sulphite .... 1 oz. or 10 parts
Potassium bromide ...... 10 grains or 0·23 part
Water to make up to † .... 10 oz. or 100 parts

For use mix equal parts of dilute pyro solution and soda solution and pour over the plate.

If the exposure has been correct the image will begin to appear in about a minute, and development is then allowed to go on with occasional rocking of the dish, until the negative is sufficiently opaque.

If the plate behaves as if it were under-exposed, *at once* dilute the developer with an equal bulk of water and pour it back over the plate. If the high-lights continue to increase in opacity, but the rest of the image does not appear, add some more of the soda solution with or without some more water. Should parts of the plate still remain blank, apply some of the soda solution to them with the aid of a brush as described under pyro-ammonia (page 32).

If the rapid appearance of the image indicates that the plate is over-exposed, at once pour off the developer into a measure or mixing glass and rinse the plate well with water. Add to the developer a small quantity of potassium bromide solution (1 in 10 of water) which should be kept at hand for this purpose. A small quantity of pyro stock solution may also be added. The

---

* No more of the dilute pyro solution should be made up than is likely to be used during the same day, but it will keep well enough for a day or two.

† The sodium sulphite and carbonate are dissolved, with the aid of heat, in about 8 oz. (80 parts) of water, the bromide added, and the liquid when cold made up to 10 oz. by adding water.

developer is then poured over the plate again. When the over-exposure seems to have been considerable, the amount of potassium bromide added may amount to 4 grains (or 40 minims of the 1 in 10 solution) per ounce of the developer, but this proportion should not be exceeded; even small quantities of bromide in the pyro-soda developer have a marked influence in retarding development.

When there is reason to suspect over-exposure, not more than half the soda solution should be added at the beginning of development, and the rest may be added or not, as the case may require.

DEVELOPMENT WITH ORTOL.

ORTOL SOLUTION.
Ortol .... 130 grains or 1·5 parts
Potassium metabisulphite* 65 grains or 0·75 part
Water to make up to .... 20 ounces or 100 parts

SODA SOLUTION.
The same as for pyro-soda.

Mix equal parts of ortol solution and soda solution.

This developer behaves in much the same way as pyro-soda and gives very similar results. It has the advantage, however, that it does not stain the fingers, and has practically no tendency to produce either fog or stain on the plates. Moreover the same quantity of solution can be used for several plates; when the action becomes perceptibly slower or weaker, part of the old solution is poured away and an equal quantity of freshly mixed ortol and soda solutions is added.

The chief differences to be observed are (1) that the different parts of the image follow one another more rapidly than with pyro-soda, even though the plate may have been correctly exposed, and (2) the colour of the reduced silver is somewhat bluer than with pyro-soda,

* See foot-note to page 30.

and therefore in order to obtain the same degree of *printing* opacity, as distinct from visual opacity, development must be carried a little further.

Apart from these differences, what has been said of pyro-soda holds good for ortol soda and need not be repeated.

DEVELOPMENT WITH HYDROQUINONE (QUINOL).

QUINOL SOLUTION.

Hydroquinone	90 grains	or	2 parts
Sodium sulphite	1 oz.	or	10 parts
Water to make up to....	10 oz.	or	100 parts

ALKALI SOLUTION.

Potassium carbonate (dry)	1 oz.	or	10 parts
Potassium bromide	20 grains	or	0·46 parts
Water to make up to....	10 oz.	or	100 parts

Mix two parts of hydroquinone solution with one part of alkali solution and one part of water, or, if a more energetic developer is wanted, mix equal volumes of the hydroquinone and alkali solutions. Hydroquinone is not an advantageous developer for general purposes, but it is useful when negatives are required showing strong contrast between the highest lights and the deepest shadows, and especially when it is important that there should be no deposit at all in the deepest shadows. This is the case, for example, when copying line engravings, pen and ink drawings and similar subjects.

DEVELOPMENT WITH FERROUS OXALATE.

This method of development also is not well adapted for general work, but it is invaluable for certain purposes. The reduced silver has a pure grey-black colour and there is exceedingly little tendency to produce fog of any kind. On the other hand, the developer admits of little modification in its composition and therefore the exposure must be fairly correct. It is also important to avoid contamination with even minute quantities of hypo, since this substance very readily causes stains.

FERROUS SULPHATE SOLUTION.

Ferrous sulphate	2½ oz.	or 25 parts
Sulphuric acid	Small quantity	
Water to make up to	10 oz.	or 100 parts

About three-quarters of the total quantity of water is mixed with a small quantity (not more than 50 minims per 10 ozs., or one part per 100) of sulphuric acid, and the ferrous sulphate (protosulphate of iron) which must be in clear pale green crystals without any yellowish incrustation, is dissolved in it with the aid of a gentle heat. After the solution has cooled, it is made up to the specified volume with water. This solution alters when exposed to air, and should, therefore, be kept in small (2 oz.) bottles, filled up to the neck and tightly corked.

OXALATE SOLUTION.

Potassium oxalate	10 oz.	or 25 parts
Potassium bromide	40 grains	or 0·23 part
Water to make up to	40 oz.	or 100 parts

For use take four parts of oxalate solution and one part of ferrous sulphate solution, pouring the latter into the former and *not vice versa*. In order to obtain slower action with a rather softer image and a slightly browner deposit, the developer may be diluted with an equal vo'ume of water. Slower action, with slightly increased printing contrasts, and clearer shadows, results from an increase in the proportion of bromide.

FIXING.

After development is finished, the dark-coloured reduced silver that forms the image remains mixed with a considerable quantity of semi-opaque, yellowish unaltered silver bromide, which would not only interfere with the printing, but would also gradually darken when exposed to light. The negative must therefore be "fixed" by dissolving out the unaltered silver bromide, and this is accomplished by immersing the plate in a fairly strong solution of sodium thiosulphate (formerly called sodium hyposulphite) commonly known as "hypo." The usual strength of the fixing is as follows:

FIXING BATH.
Hypo (sodium thiosulphate)　10 oz. or　25 parts
Water to make up to ......　40 oz. or 100 parts

A solution of double this strength is, however, not unfrequently used, and acts more rapidly, especially in cold weather.

The developed plate, after being well rinsed with water, is placed in the fixing bath and allowed to remain in it with frequent rocking until the silver bromide has all been dissolved out of the film. This is ascertained by lifting the plate out of the dish and looking at the back by reflected light, the plate being held in front of something dark. It is not difficult to see whether the silver bromide has all disappeared or not, but in order to ensure complete fixing the plate must not be taken out of the bath as soon as this has happened, but should be left in for a few minutes longer, the dish being rocked so that the dissolved silver salt may diffuse out of the film into the fixing bath.

When removed from the fixing bath the plate should be allowed to drain into the bath for a few moments and should then be washed for five or ten minutes in running water under the tap. It is best to put the plate in a dish standing on the sink and have a piece of flexible indiarubber tubing reaching from the tap to within a couple of inches or so of the top of the dish, so that the water may not splash too much.

After washing in this way, the plate is placed in a grooved zinc rack, which is immersed in a tank (preferably of zinc), containing sufficient water to completely cover the plates, and here it remains until the whole batch of plates in hand has been developed and they can all receive their final washing together. The plates stand upright in the rack, and the entrance and exit of the water must be so arranged that the water enters at the bottom and overflows at the top, or, what is perhaps better, enters at the top and is drawn off from the bottom, the waste pipe opening at the bottom of the tank and being bent and carried upwards until its mouth is at the level at which the water is to stand in the tank.

When running water is not available the plates may be washed in dishes. After being well rinsed to remove the adhering hypo solution, the plate is covered with water (about $3\frac{1}{2}$ oz. for a half plate or 5 oz. for a whole plate) and allowed to remain with frequent rocking for five or six minutes. The water is then well drained off, a second quantity added and allowed to remain for the same time as before, with frequent rocking, when it is poured off in its turn. Treatment in this way with six successive quantities of water will remove all the hypo, provided that the film has not been treated with alum.

Another plan, rather less troublesome, but also less expeditious, is to place the rack containing the plates in a tank not much more than big enough to hold it, taking care that there is not less than two inches between the lower edges of the plates and the bottom of the tank. After standing for some time the rack and the plates are slowly and carefully lifted out and allowed to drain, the tank emptied and filled with fresh water, and the rack and plates then replaced. Eight or ten successive quantities of water applied in this way should remove all the hypo, but if there is any doubt on this point the plates, after they are supposed to be washed and have been removed from the tank, should be allowed to drain into a measuring glass or into a dish, the contents of which are afterwards transferred to a measuring glass and mixed with a small quantity of a solution of silver nitrate. If the plates are really completely washed nothing will happen, or at most a white precipitate will be produced which *will remain white* if not exposed to daylight. If, on the other hand, the plates still retain hypo, the silver nitrate will produce a

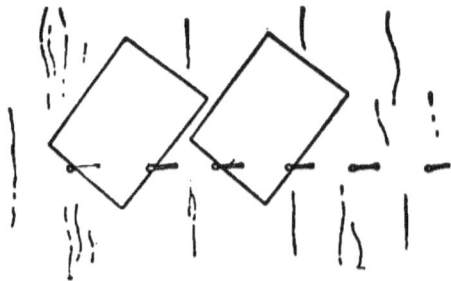

precipitate which will gradually become orange and eventually dark brown. Should this happen, the washing must be continued.

DRYING.—If the negatives are allowed to dry in the rack in which they were washed, the process is slow, and sometimes if the washing has not been complete, the middle portions of the negatives, which dry last, are less opaque than the rest. An excellent method of drying negatives rapidly and in such a way that no dust can fall on the film, is to drive nails (preferably of copper) into a wall or a board fixed against the wall, at distances apart depending on the size of the plates Each plate

WINTER TIME ON THE ALPS.
CAPT. W. DE W. ABNEY, C.B., F.R.S., Etc.

then rests, with the film downwards, between a pair of nails, the lower corner of the plate resting against the wall, as shown on previous page.

ALUM BATH.—It is frequently recommended that all plates should be immersed in a strong solution of alum, for the purpose of preventing "frilling" by hardening the film. Its use is, however, attended with the great disadvantage that liquids diffuse into and out of a film so treated with much greater difficulty than in the case of an ordinary film, and consequently if the film is alumed between development and fixing, the fixing is not only much slower, but the washing after fixing requires a very much longer time. If, therefore, the alum bath is used at all, it should not be applied until after the film has been well washed after fixing. The following solution may be used:—

ALUM BATH.
Alum .... 1 oz. or 5 parts
Water .... 20 oz. or 100 parts

If a strong solution of alum is applied to the plate for a long time, the film may become so thoroughly hardened that it partially loses its adhesiveness, and there is a possibility that it will begin to peel from the glass after the negatives have been stored for some time in a dry place. The solution given above is quite strong enough and plates need not be immersed in it for more than five minutes, after which they must, of course, be again well washed. The hardening of the film, if not carried too far, no doubt makes it less liable to be injured by abrasion and the like.

FRILLING.—It sometimes happens that during the various operations of development, fixing and washing, the film begins to leave the plate and rise in puckers along the edges. This is known as "frilling," and in bad cases it may spread until a large part of the film has detached itself from the glass. It is due to excessive or irregular absorption of water by the gelatine, and at one time was commonly met with, but it rarely occurs with the dry plates of the present day. It is most likely to arise if there is any considerable difference of temperature between the various liquids and the wash-water, or during very hot weather when all the liquids are much warmer than usual.

When frilling does occur, the plate must be treated carefully, so as to avoid tearing the film, but unless it is very bad and shows a tendency to spread, all the operations, including washing after fixing, should be completed before any special measures are taken to remedy the defect. On the other hand, if the frilling spreads rapidly, the plate should be carefully rinsed two or three times with water and placed for five minutes in the alum bath, with occasional gentle rocking, after which it is again well washed to remove the alum, and the various operations are completed. There is one exception to the procedure just indicated; if the frilling becomes bad while the plate is being fixed or during washing after fixing, the alum must not be applied until the fixing and the washing after fixing are completed. If something must be done in these circumstances, the plate, after draining, but without any previous washing, may be placed for about ten minutes in a saturated solution of common salt. It can afterwards be put back into the fixing bath, also without any intermediate washing, and the remainder of the process carried through.

Although the methods just described will check the frilling, they will not remove its effects. For this purpose the plate after its final washing is allowed to drain thoroughly and is then immersed in methylated alcohol, preferably of the old kind, though the new kind can be made to do. The alcohol abstracts water from the film, which consequently shrinks to its original size and can be pressed back with the fingers into its proper position on the plate. Should the film be opalescent it should be removed from the first quantity of alcohol and placed in a second quantity, after which it should be set up to dry. The plates should not remain too long in the alcohol or the gelatine will contract too much.

DEFECTS IN NEGATIVES.

A perfect negative presupposes a perfect plate, correct exposure, and correct development stopped at exactly the right time. It is almost unnecessary to say that all these conditions are rarely satisfied, and consequently most negatives fall more or less short of perfection. The defects may be broadly grouped under two heads, namely, those due to imperfections existing in the film before exposure, and those due to defects or errors in the way in which the plate has been treated. It will be more convenient to deal with the latter, and larger, group first, but there is really no hard and fast division between them.

THE NEGATIVE IS THIN, or in other words, whilst showing good gradation, and sufficient relative contrast between the different parts, is as a whole lacking in opacity or printing strength, and gives prints that are deficient in vigour and contrasts. The plate has been removed from the developer too soon, and the remedy is to intensify the image (see p. 51). Sometimes the want of opacity is due to the fact that the developer was too cold.

THE NEGATIVE IS TOO DENSE OR OPAQUE and consequently although showing good contrasts and gradations, takes a long time to print, especially on dull days. The developer has been too energetic, or development has been continued too long; the remedy is to reduce the image (see p. 50).

The Image is "Flat," or shows comparatively little contrast between the highest lights and the deepest shadows. This may, of course, be due to the absence of contrasts in the subject photographed; it is commonly due to over-exposure; it may be caused by using a developer containing too little reducer, or restrainer, or both, and too much alkali; sometimes it arises from a defect in the quality of the emulsion, or from the fact that the plate has been coated with an abnormally thin film of emulsion.

The Image is "Hard," or shows excessive contrasts between lights and shadows, and is defective in the range of its half-tones. This is probably due to under-exposure, but may have been aggravated by the use of a developer containing too much bromide or too little alkali. Local reduction (see p. 50) may partially remedy the defect.

Fog.—A more or less marked grey deposit of reduced silver extends over the whole surface of the image. It may be due to over-exposure, in which case the edges of the plate that have been protected by the rebate of the dark slide usually remain clear. It may also be caused by using a developer containing too much alkali, or too little restrainer, or both, or by the plate having been exposed to actinic light outside the camera, including the light from the dark-room lamp if the glass or coloured fabric used as the screening material is not efficient. In any of these cases the defect would be observable up to the extreme edges of the film.

The character of the dark-room light should be tested by exposing one half of a plate to it at a distance of say nine or twelve inches for five or ten minutes, the other half of the plate being protected by some opaque substance. The best plan is to put the plate into a dark slide and draw out the shutter half-way. After exposure the plate is treated with a developer in the usual manner, and it can then be seen whether or no the light has exerted any action on the plate.

Slight general fog may as a rule be neglected, but if the amount of fog is at all considerable the plate should be treated with a reducer, and afterwards the image can, if necessary, be intensified.

GREEN FOG.—The surface of the film shows a peculiar brilliant green or yellowish-green lustrous appearance, generally in patches, when examined by reflected light, but is more or less distinctly pink when the plate is looked through. This effect is rarely observed except when pyro-ammonia has been used as the developer, and it most frequently occurs with old plates, especially if development has been long continued or has been forced by the addition of comparatively large quantities of ammonia.

If the green fog is only slight it does not affect the prints made from the negative, but in bad cases the prints have a patchy appearance and are less deeply printed at those points where the green fog is worst. Two methods are available for the removal of green fog.

In one of these the plate, after being fixed and washed, is placed in a hypo solution of half the strength of the ordinary fixing bath, and to this hypo solution is added a very small quantity of a solution of potassium ferricyanide, and the mixture is allowed to act on the plate for some time, the dish being rocked occasionally. The green fog will gradually disappear and some more of the ferricyanide may be added, if necessary, to secure this end, but it is important to keep the proportion of ferricyanide as low as possible, otherwise the image itself will be reduced. For this reason, if it is seen or suspected that the green fog is likely to be bad, development should be carried a little farther than usual in order to allow for the slight reduction that accompanies the removal of the green fog.

The other plan is to immerse the plate in a dilute solution of ferric chloride (perchloride of iron) until the green fog has been completely bleached, then wash, first in a dilute solution of oxalic acid and afterwards in water, and finally treat with a developer, preferably ferrous oxalate. The green fog is converted into a very fine grey deposit which is almost invisible and has no appreciable effect on the printing qualities of the negative.

BLACK SPOTS may be due to particles of dirt that have been allowed to lodge on the film during one or other of the operations, or during drying. They may also be due to particles in the emulsion, and in the latter case are generally round and sharply defined.

BLACK MARKS of the nature of irregular streaks, looking, so to speak, like black scratches, are generally due to mechanical abrasion of the film. Pressure produces a developable image similar to that produced by the action of light.

BLACK BANDS, indistinct or nebulous at the edges, are sometimes caused during the coating of the plate with the emulsion, in which case they, as a rule, extend all the way along or across the plate. More commonly they are due to defects in the hinges of the dark slides, which may produce the bands either by allowing light to pass through, or by giving off exhalations that affect the plates if they are allowed to remain in the dark slide for a long time. If the bands are due to the hinges, they will, of course, correspond with them in position, and if the hinge is double, in the distance between them.

TRANSPARENT BANDS, or bands showing less opacity than the rest of the image, are sometimes caused by exhalations from the material forming the hinges of the dark slides.

TRANSPARENT SPOTS if small ("pinholes"), are generally due to the presence of particles of dust on the surface of the plate when it was exposed. Prevention lies, of course, in carefully dusting the plate and the dark slide with a soft, clean, dry camel's hair brush, before putting the former into the latter. If the spots are larger and circular, they are due either to the formation of air bubbles on the surface of the plate during development, or to the presence in the film of insensitive particles.

UNEVEN OPACITY OR DENSITY, varying gradually from one end or side of the plate to the opposite end or side, is due to uneven coating of the plate. If there is a distinctly defined patch, less opaque than the rest, the plate was not properly covered by the developing solution.

STAINS.—A uniform stain, of a yellowish or brown colour, is produced when the pyro developer contains too small a proportion of sulphite or is allowed to act for a very long time. Such a stain is rarely observed with the other developers mentioned above. The pyro stain can be more or less completely removed by immersing the plate for some time, with repeated rocking, in the alum solution given above, 1 drachm of sulphuric acid being added to every 10 ounces. The plate must afterwards be well washed in soft water. Similar stains in patches may be caused by using dirty dishes or a developer that has become turbid by being frequently used.

DEEP YELLOW-ORANGE OR BROWN STAINS, appearing gradually in patches or all over the negative, some time after it has been fixed, and washed, and dried, are due either to imperfect fixing or to incomplete washing after fixing. There is no practicable remedy.

HALATION.—When the subject photographed includes some part much more brightly lighted than the rest, such as a window in an interior subject, the details of the bright part are not only lost, but the image of it seems to spread in all directions, obliterating the details of the surrounding portions. The effect is especially noticeable when the subject includes dark parts which necessitate a somewhat long exposure. A window at the end of a long dimly lighted interior, or dark trees against a bright sky are cases in point. The effect is really due to the fact that the sensitive film is not perfectly opaque, and some of the incident light passes through the film and is reflected from the back surface of the glass on to the under side of the film, producing a blurred image superposed, as it were, on the normal image formed at the surface of the film by the action of the direct light. The effect is known as "halation." It is prevented by having a perfectly opaque film, which is a condition difficult to realize in practice, and which, moreover, introduces certain other disadvantages. It is also prevented by coating the back of the plate with some substance that will absorb the rays that have

Dock
By
Carine Cadby.

passed through the film, and so prevent their being reflected back against the under side of the film. The substance used must either be opaque or must have a deep orange, brown, or red colour, and it must have the same refractive index as the glass, otherwise the reflection will not be prevented. For practical convenience it must also be easily applied and easily removed. Many substances have been recommended but nothing is so good as caramel, prepared by the action of heat on sugar. In order to get the mixture to dry completely after it has been applied, a somewhat troublesome process of purification is necessary, but caramel specially prepared for the purpose can now be obtained from dealers in photographic materials. The caramel (which is a solid substance) is dissolved in just enough water to make a thick syrup, which is carefully applied to the back of the plates in a thin layer by means of a flat brush.

If the caramel does not dry properly the solution may be thoroughly mixed with about one quarter (or more) of its weight of very finely powdered burnt sienna or burnt umber, "ground in water."

After being coated, the plates require some time to dry, and must, of course, be carefully protected from light. If the dark-room is thoroughly dark, the plates may be put up to dry in the same manner as negatives (see page 40), but if the dark-room is not suitable, some sort of drying box must be used.

After exposure and before development the backing is removed with a damp sponge; if caramel only is used in a form completely soluble in water, it need not be removed unless a developer is being used that is to be applied to several plates in succession.

REDUCTION.

When a negative is too opaque or dense it must be reduced by dissolving away part of the silver that forms the image. The same process is also applied for the removal of general fog, sometimes with a view to subsequent intensification.

The simplest solution to use for this purpose is known as the Howard Farmer reducer and is a solution of hypo mixed with a small quantity of potassium ferricyanide (red prussiate of potash).

FERRICYANIDE SOLUTION.

Potassium ferricyanide...... 1 oz. or 10 parts
Water to make up .... 10 oz. or 100 parts

This solution must be protected from light if it is to be kept for any length of time.

The negative which, if it has been previously dried, must be soaked in water for some time until it is thoroughly and uniformly wetted, is placed in some fresh hypo solution (the ordinary fixing-bath solution diluted with an equal volume of water) to which a small quantity of the ferricyanide solution has been added, and the dish is rocked repeatedly to ensure uniform action. The rapidity of the reducing action depends on the proportion of ferricyanide solution added, and it is very important not to add too much, otherwise the process gets out of control and reduction goes too far. The image should be carefully watched and the plate removed from the solution and rapidly washed before the apparent reduction is quite as great as it is intended to be. It is much better to stop too soon than too late, because if it is found that a little further reduction is necessary, the plate can be again immersed in the hypo and ferricyanide.

The ferricyanide reducer can be applied locally for reducing high-lights, halated windows, etc., and this is often very valuable, especially in the case of under-exposed negatives. A small quantity of hypo and ferricyanide solution is mixed in a measuring glass or some other suitable vessel. The plate is immersed in plain hypo solution in a white dish for a short time and is then raised by one corner or one edge until the part to be reduced is above the solution. The mixture of hypo and ferricyanide is carefully applied with a camel's hair brush to the parts that are too opaque, and after a few moments the plate is allowed to slip back into the hypo solution and the dish is rocked. If the reduction is not sufficient, the same proceeding is gone through as often as necessary. The reducer should not be allowed to act too long before putting the plate back into the hypo, otherwise the reduction may spread further than is desired. Further, the reducer must not be too strong (*i.e.*, contain too much ferricyanide), otherwise it will produce brownish stains and the action may be too energetic.

The other reducer is known as Belitzski's reducer, and is made up as follows:—

Ferric potassium oxalate	1 oz. or	5 parts*
Sodium sulphite	1 oz. or	4 parts
Oxalic acid	¼ oz. or	1 part
Hypo solution (25 in 100) ...	5 oz. or	25 parts
Water	20 oz. or	100 parts

The constituents must be dissolved in water in the order given. The solution can be used at once and it keeps fairly well if protected from light, in well corked bottles filled up to the neck.

INTENSIFICATION.

Intensification is a process in which the opacity of the image is increased by adding some fresh matter, metallic or otherwise, to the reduced silver that constitutes the developed image.

The usual plan is to bleach the image by means of a solution of mercuric chloride (mercury perchloride or

* The formula in "parts" does not strictly correspond with that in ounces, but the difference is immaterial.

corrosive sublimate), which converts the dark-coloured silver into a white mixture of silver chloride and mercurous chloride, and this is subsequently treated with some re-agent which will reconvert the image into a dark product of greater opacity than the original.

It is absolutely essential to successful intensification that the negative be completely fixed and completely washed after fixing, for any trace of hypo left in the film will give rise to brown stains. It is also important, in order to prevent stains of another sort and to secure uniform action, that the mercuric chloride solution be mixed with a small quantity of hydrochloric acid. Too much acid will cause frilling. If the negative has been dried it must be immersed in water for, as a rule, not less than half-an-hour, in order that it may be thoroughly and uniformly wetted.

MERCURIC CHLORIDE SOLUTION.

Mercuric chloride	1 oz.	or	5 parts
Hydrochloric acid	1½ drachms	or	1 part
Water to make up to..	20 oz.	or	100 parts

When uniform intensification is required the negative is allowed to remain in this solution until it is completely bleached. If, however, it is desired to intensify the shadows more than the high-lights, the plate should be removed from the solution as soon as the shadows have bleached, and should be rapidly washed in order to stop the action on the more opaque parts of the image.

In either case the negative must be thoroughly washed after bleaching, and the water used must be soft water. Hard water tends to produce a precipitate of the mercury salt in the film, which may subsequently lead to stain or fog.

Perhaps the best plan of all, when constant results are desired, is to treat the bleached negative with the ferrous oxalate developer, which will gradually convert the white image into a black one, after which the plate is thoroughly washed and dried. It is recommended that the first water used for washing should be slightly acidified with oxalic acid.

Instead of using ferrous oxalate the bleached plate may be treated with a weak solution of ortol or metol to which some sodium carbonate (soda crystals) solution has been added, but *no sulphite*. After the image has blackened completely the plate is washed.

With any of these methods if the first intensification is not sufficient, the plate may be again bleached with the mercury solution and the process repeated.

An old method, frequently used, is to treat the bleached plate with dilute ammonia, which converts the white image into a dark brown one of very considerable printing opacity. The results are often very good, but are somewhat uncertain, since the precise effect obtained depends on the strength of the ammonia solution and the time during which it is allowed to act. With somewhat strong ammonia, allowed to act for a fairly long time, part of the intensification first produced is removed. This affects the shadows more strongly than the lights and the result is to increase the contrast of the negative, which is very useful for certain purposes.

The negatives intensified with mercury solution followed by ammonia are more liable to spontaneous change and deterioration than those intensified with mercury solution followed by one of the developers. The latter, in fact, if properly washed, may safely be regarded as permanent.

URANIUM INTENSIFIER. — A very considerable degree of intensification can be obtained by the use of the uranium intensifier, which is very different in its mode of action, and is a little uncertain in its results. A solution containing potassium ferricyanide and a uranium salt, generally the nitrate, is applied to the negative, and a deposit of a deep orange-red colour is formed upon the silver image and very greatly increases its printing opacity. The great difficulty is to prevent this deposit forming on the whole of the film, and it is absolutely necessary that every trace of hypo should be washed out of the film. The addition of acetic acid to the solution not only promotes uniformity of action, but also helps to keep the shadows of the image clear.

FERRICYANIDE SOLUTION.
The same as for the ferricyanide reducer.

URANIUM SOLUTION.

Uranium nitrate .... 1 oz. or 10 parts
Water to make up to .... 10 oz. or 100 parts

THE INTENSIFIER.

Uranium solution (1 : 10)   1 drachm or   5 parts
Ferricyanide   solution
  (1 : 10) . ...   1 drachm or   5 parts
Acetic acid (glacial) ....   2 drachms or 10 parts
Water to make up to ..   2½ oz.   or 100 parts

The negative is placed in this solution and allowed to remain with occasional rocking until the degree of intensification is sufficient, which can only be learnt by experience. If it is seen that the deposit is beginning to form on the clear parts of the negative, the plate should be at once removed. After intensification the plates are well washed. If the water is "hard" the intensification will be slightly reduced during washing, and this is often useful in removing a slight stain over the whole of the plate. Treatment with water containing a small quantity of ammonia or sodium carbonate removes the whole of the deposit, but leaves the original image slightly reduced and also partially altered in composition.

VARNISHING.

A negative after been thoroughly dried may be used for printing without any further treatment, especially if only a few prints are required and the ordinary ready sensitized papers or emulsion papers are used. It is, however, better to protect the negative from mechanical as well as chemical injury by means of a film of hard varnish or collodion.

Many excellent negative varnishes can now be purchased, and the general mode of application is the same. The negative must be thoroughly dry, and in order to secure this and to make the varnish flow more easily, the negative is very carefully heated in front of a fire or over a small stove until it is just warm, but not hot. The negative is best supported by means of a pneumatic holder held in the left hand, and a fairly large pool of varnish (the exact amount can only be learnt by experience) is poured on the plate somewhat towards the right-hand top corner, and by carefully tilting the plate it is made to run first to the nearest corner, then along the edge to the further left-hand corner down to the nearer left-hand corner, and back to the right-hand bottom corner, from which it is poured into a bottle. The plate is gently rocked whilst it drains into the bottle, and as soon as the varnish ceases to drop the plate is again carefully warmed until the back of it is just too hot for the back of the hand to bear, after which it is placed in a rack to cool.

It is necessary that the varnish should be quite clear and free from any solid particles, and if necessary it must be filtered through a plug of cotton wool moistened with alcohol and placed in the apex of a glass funnel which is resting in the neck of a clean and dry bottle. Since dust may fall into the varnish whilst it is on the negative, it is the best plan to pour the excess of varnish off the negative into a second bottle instead of back into the first, out of which it was poured. To put it in another way, one bottle should be kept for the clear varnish, and a second bottle for the varnish poured off the plate. When the second bottle is full, its contents are filtered into the first bottle for use again.

Instead of varnish, a film of collodion, toughened by the addition of a few drops of castor oil, and known as "leather" collodion, may be used. The collodion is applied to the plate in the same way as varnish except that the plate is not warmed.

C. H. Bothamley.

Lenses.

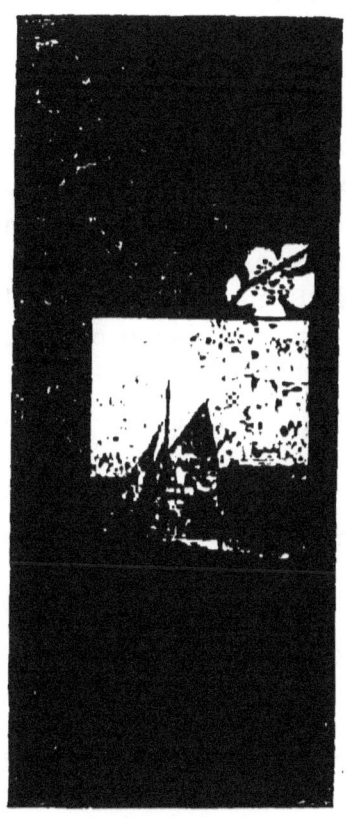

PHOTOGRAPHS of flat objects such as leaves, lace, drawings, etc., can be made by simply putting the object on the sensitive surface and exposing the arrangement to light. But this method will not serve if the photograph is wanted of any other size than the original, nor with solid objects of any size, except perhaps in the production of full-size profiles of faces. It is therefore quite the exception in photography to "print" directly from the object itself, and the only alternative is to produce an image on the sensitive surface.

All illuminated objects reflect light and so become for practical purposes sources of light, just as the moon shines, as we say, although it only shines because it is shone upon by the sun. The simplest source of light to consider is a point of light, and if we can get a dot of light on a white surface from a point of light we have at once an image of that point of light. The smaller the dot the sharper or more perfect is the image, the larger the dot the more diffused or fuzzy is the image. It is impossible by any known means to get the dot so small that it is an actual point, that would be absolute perfection, and on the other hand there is no size of the dot at which it can be definitely said that it ceases to be an image. Every point of an illuminated object is a point of light, and fine definition consists in keeping these points separate in the image. So far as the dots overlap they are confused. Confusion, or diffusion, or fuzziness is sometimes desirable, as for example in a portrait, which may be excellent although it is impossible to distinguish in the picture the individual hairs on the person's head.

The simplest means for getting an image is a small hole in an opaque screen. In fig. 1, two points of light, A and B, shine through the hole in the screen S and

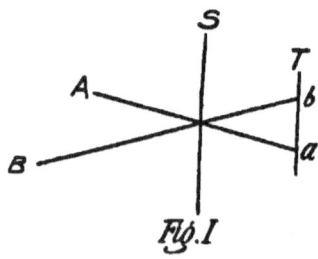

Fig. I

produce two dots of light, *a* and *b*, on the surface T. The two pencils of light do not practically interfere with each other although they pass through the same small hole, nor would any greater number; so that an illuminated object, which may be regarded as consisting of an infinite number of points of light, would give an image on the surface T. The disadvantages of a small hole, or "pinhole," for the production of images are (1) it must be so small that it lets very little light through and therefore gives a very feeble image, (2) that it can never give a sharp image. The first disadvantage is obvious. With regard to the second, a little consideration will show that the image of a point must be larger than the hole itself, it is always larger though it may have a central brighter part that is smaller. If the hole is reduced in size beyond a certain limit, it gives an increased spreading of light on the surface, so that a sharp image can never be produced.

Now the function of a lens is to obviate these drawbacks as far as possible; namely, to let more light through and form a brighter image, and to give sharper definition. In figure 2, the lens L collects all the light that falls upon it from the point B, and condenses it to

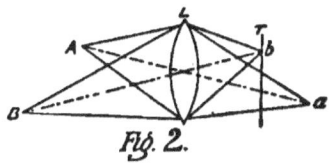

Fig. 2.

the point *b* on the surface T. The light from the point A that falls on the lens is also condensed and would be brought to a point or "focus" at *a* beyond the surface T, but on the surface the light forms a patch of considerable size. Suppose that the lens is thirty times the diameter of the pinhole its area is 900 times as large, and the light that falls upon it is 900 times as much as the light that passes through the hole. Such an enormous gain of light is worth so much that photographers willingly put up with the very many imperfections of lenses for the sake of it, and if to this gain there is added the superior definition that is possible, it will be seen that lenses are indispensable to the photographer. To take a Daguerreotype portrait with a pinhole might have required several days if not weeks exposure of the plate and therefore would have been impossible, so that the gain in brightness of image is a great deal more than a mere convenience.

It will be observed in figure 1 that both points of light, A and B produce images on the surface T, although they are at different distances from it, but in fig. 2, although the effect of the lens is to concentrate the light from both points to two other points, one of these is beyond the surface T. This is a disadvantage inherent in lenses. They have so many other imperfections or "aberrations" that it is desirable to consider these separately. The reader should bear in mind that the one aim of opticians in perfecting lenses is to concentrate as much light as possible from each point in the object to a corresponding point, or as small as possible a dot, in the image, and the image should be flat because the plates used in photography are flat.

Spherical Aberration.—The surfaces of lenses are always ground to spherical curves, and this fact makes it impossible for a single lens, such as that shown in figure 2, to bring to a point all the light that falls upon it from a point. If a pencil of light passes through a piece of glass with sloping sides it is bent or "refracted"

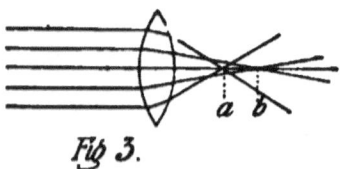

Fig 3.

towards the thicker part of the glass, and the greater the angle of inclination of the two sides the more is it refracted from its original path. In figure 3 it is clear that the two sides of the lens shown in section are inclined to each other at a continually increasing angle as they approach each other at the edges of the lens. The refracting effect of the lens increases from the centre outwards, and it increases to a greater extent than is necessary to bring the incident light to a point. The focus of the pencils of light that pass through the edges of the lens is nearer to the lens than the focus of the pencils that pass through its central part. In the figure two foci are shown, *a* and *b*, but of course, in fact, intermediate parts of the lens produce intermediate foci, and what should be a point in the image, is spread out into a line on the axis of the lens, and all along this line is surrounded with the light that either is coming to a focus or that has come to a focus and has spread out again. On a screen placed at *b* there would be a point of light surrounded by a halo, while at *a*, nearer the lens, the central focus or point is surrounded by a brighter or more condensed light, and the appearance is of a circular patch of light with a brighter boundary. This is positive spherical aberration. Negative spherical aberration is due to over correction, the focus of the light passing through the margins being furthest from the lens, and the appearances on a screen are of course reversed.

Chromatic Aberration.—When light is refracted, that is bent out of its original path by a single piece of glass, it is not refracted as a whole, but each constituent behaves as if none other were present. Ordinary white light or daylight is a mixture of many coloured lights as seen in the rainbow, and when refracted, the blue is bent more than the green, the green more than the yellow, and the yellow more than the red. So that using a single lens the focus of the blue light is nearer the lens than the focus of the red light and the others come in between. In figure 4 this is represented in an exaggerated degree to make it more distinct. It will be observed that a screen placed at the focus of the blue light will show a reddish margin and if removed further from the lens the margin or halo will be bluish.

These two aberrations, spherical and chromatic *were* the principal faults that opticians had to deal with, because they affect the whole of the image, even the very central parts. But in photography it is necessary to get an image of a very large size as compared with the focal length of the lens, and there are some faults that only begin to show themselves at a little distance from the centre of the image and increase as the distance

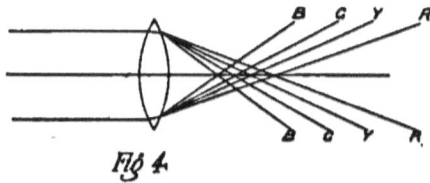

Fig 4.

from the centre is greater. These aberrations were, practically speaking, incurable until a few years ago, but as recent optical advances have provided kinds of glass by the use of which they may be eliminated, or nearly so, they have become of practical importance. They are astigmatism and curvature of field.

Astigmatism and Curvature of Field.—If a diagram of suitable size is made with a series of concentric circles and radial lines upon it, and the centre of it is arranged exactly opposite the centre of the lens, and in a line with the centre of the focussing screen, the screen and diagram being parallel, then if the lens suffers from astigmatism it will be found impossible to get the outer circles and the radial lines where they cross them simultaneouly focussed. Where this difficulty begins the astigmatism begins, and the greater the difference there is between the focal planes of the radial lines and the circles, the greater is the astigmatism. It will probably be found with any of the older types of lenses that neither is in focus at the same time that the centre of the diagram is, but that the screen must be racked in; this is due to curvature of field, and the difference between the curvature of field for the circles and the radial lines is due to astigmatism. In the older lenses a flatter field could only be obtained by the introduction of astigmatism, but now by the employment of the new glasses made at Jena, it is possible to practically eliminate astigmatism, and still keep the field flat.

The Development of Photographic Lenses.—When photography was first practised the best lenses available were those made for use as telescope objectives, and they had to be used with a small diaphragm to get good defi-

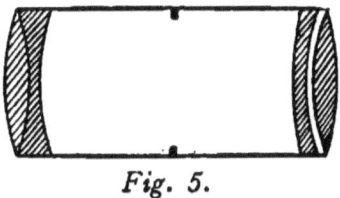

Fig. 5.

nition over a sufficient field. With the slow processes then in vogue a more rapid lens was much desired, and Voigtlander introduced a "portrait" lens constructed according to the results of the calculations of Professor Petzval. This portrait lens is still very largely used, and figure 5 will serve to show its general character and will be a guide to the putting of one together correctly if it has been taken to pieces for cleaning. A rapid lens such as this could not cover a sufficiently large field for landscape work, so that single lenses were still used for work in which rapidity was not of very great importance. Single lenses were improved, and other kinds of lenses were introduced from time to time, but it was not till 1866 that the "rapid rectilinears" or "rapid aplanats," called later "rapid symmetricals," and by innumerable other names according to the fancies of the makers, were introduced. Probably no lens has been made in such large numbers as this.

At about the same time, Dallmeyer introduced his portrait lens in which the position of the convex and concave elements of the back combination is reversed, the concave lens being outside, and this gives the photographer the opportunity of screwing it back a little, and so introducing a measurable amount of spherical aberration which has the effect of modifying the otherwise exceedingly fine definition at the centre of the field, and giving a greater depth of definition.

In 1881, Messrs. Abbe & Schott began a series of experiments in the manufacture of optical glasses, and they were so successful in making new and useful varieties, that an optical glass factory was eventually established at Jena, by Schott & Co. By the use of these newer glasses the limitations that had previously restricted opticians were removed, and it became possible to correct astigmatism and secure a flat field at the same time. Zeiss of Jena, towards the end of 1890, introduced his first series of "anastigmats." The "concentric" lens of Ross was introduced in 1892, a lens which probably remains unsurpassed for flatness of field and freedom from astigmatism; but as spherical aberration is present to a notable degree, an aperture of about $f/22$ is the largest that gives sharp definition. The "double anastigmat" of Goerz of Berlin was put on the market in 1893. It is a symmetrical lens, and in this different from the Zeiss anastigmats that preceded it. It consists of two similar combinations, each of three lenses cemented together. The unsurpassed qualities of this lens stimulated other opticians to seek to rival it, and there appeared similar lenses with four and even five lenses in each combination, besides other lenses that are more or less a copy of the double anastigmat. One of the most notable of these is the "satz-anastigmat" of Zeiss, each combination consisting of four lenses cemented together and forming an excellent single lens. These combinations are interchangeable in the same mount so that with, for example, one mount and three lenses, six different focal lengths can be obtained, as the lenses may be used singly or any two together as a doublet.

The "Cooke" lens is remarkable for the simple means by which the various corrections are made, consisting as it does of only three single lenses separated from each other. Obviously it must be used entire. These lenses do not cover so large a plate in proportion to their focal lengths as most of the other anastigmats, but perform excellently over the plates for which they are constructed.

The "stigmatic" of Dallmeyer is the latest lens of general utility. It gives good definition to the margin of the circle of light that it transmits, reduction of aperture being necessary, when its full field is employed, to get equality of illumination rather than to improve the marginal definition. Its two combinations are different, and either may be used alone as a single lens, giving focal lengths of approximately one-and-a-half and twice the focal length of the whole lens.

The "planar" of Zeiss introduced just as we write, is a symmetrical doublet characterized by a very large aperture, from $f/3·6$ to $f/4$ up to 10 inches in focal length, and a little smaller above that. It is therefore comparable with portrait lenses. Although it is symmetrical, a single combination cannot with advantage be used alone as a single lens. Telephotographic lenses are subsequently referred to.

The one aim of opticians in improving photographic lenses has been to get good definition all over a comparatively large flat surface without having to use small apertures. A defining power on the axis of the lens, that is, at the centre of the field, far exceeding what can be taken practical advantage of in ordinary photography, has long been possible. But until recently, the defining power always rapidly deteriorated as the distance from the centre was increased. But to judge of the quality of a lens, or to compare one lens with another, there are other matters that must be understood, and these we shall proceed to consider. Focal length, aperture and image angle are the chief details concerning lenses, granting that the aberrations referred to above are satisfactorily corrected.

Focal length.—The focal length or focal distance of a thin lens is the distance between it and the point to which it converges parallel rays. The rays of light are parallel when they issue from an object at an infinite distance. For ordinary practical purposes, any object that is not nearer than a thousand focal lengths of the lens may be regarded as at an infinite distance, that is the image of an object so far off, and the image of the sun or stars (which are situated at the nearest approach to an infinitely great distance that we know of) would if separately focussed give an inappreciably small difference of position of the focussing screen. But no photographic lens is very thin. The measurement from the back surface of the lens to the screen, when focussed on a distant object, is called the "back focus," but this is of no use whatever except as to the determining of the camera length necessary. The "equivalent focal length" is the focal length (or focal distance) of a thin lens that would give the same effect, so far as focal length is concerned, as the lens in question. When the simple expression "focal length" is used, it always refers to the equivalent focal length. The single word "focus" is sometimes used erroneously instead of "focal length."

The focal length of all lenses (except to a very small extent, with single or so-called "landscape" lenses) is proportional to the linear dimension of the image that it gives under similar conditions. For example, a lens of 6 inches focal length will give just the same amount of subject on a quarter plate that a lens of 12 inches focal length will give on a whole plate, because the linear measurement of the whole plate is exactly double that of the quarter plate. The easiest way to compare the focal lengths of two lenses, is to focus both on a fairly distant object or view, and to measure in the image the distance between two fixed points in both cases. The proportion between these measurements is the proportion between the focal lengths of the lenses. By this method the focal length of any lens can easily be determined if one has a lens of known focal length.

If a lens is first focussed on a distant object, and the focussing screen is then moved back until the image of any object is of the same size as the object, the distance travelled by the focussing screen is exactly the focal length of the lens. It is however exceedingly difficult to get at the same time an image of an exactly predetermined size, and to secure the very best definition, so that it is more convenient to get the image as near as it happens to come to the size of the object and then to allow for the difference, as then nothing interferes with the operation of focussing. The best near object to use is an accurately divided scale, and the details wanted in addition to those mentioned above are the comparative lengths of the image and the object. To get these, two fine marks are made on the focussing screen, and the distance between these is the length of the image. The scale is focussed with critical exactness and so that it falls over these marks, then the amount of the scale represented between the marks can be measured, and the divisions counted for the length of the object. The distance over which the focussing screen was moved between the two focussings is to be multiplied by the length of the object and divided by the length of the image, and the result is the focal length of the lens.

Aperture.—The "aperture" of a lens is the diameter of the cylinder of light that it can receive and transmit. If the diaphragm is in front of the lens, the hole in the diaphragm is the aperture, but if the diaphragm is behind a part of the lens, so that the incident light passes through a lens first, the hole in the diaphragm is not the "aperture," the "aperture" is larger because the lens condenses the light before it gets to the diaphragm. The aperture of any lens can be measured by focussing a distant object, then replacing the focussing screen by a sheet of cardboard with a pinhole in the middle of it. In a dark-room a light must be placed behind the pinhole, and a bit of ground glass held in front of the lens. A disc of light will be seen on the ground glass and the diameter of this is the diameter of the aperture, or simply, the "aperture," with the diaphragm employed.

Rapidity.—The rapidity of a lens depends almost wholly on its focal length and aperture. The thickness of the glass makes a little difference, and at every surface in contact with air there is loss by reflection, but these and analogous matters are of comparatively little importance, and as they are uncertain and cannot be determined it is customary to refer rapidity to the focal length and aperture only. The aperture found, that is, the diameter of the effective incident cylinder of parallel rays, should be divided into the focal length, and the diaphragm corresponding to the aperture should then be marked with a fractional expression indicating the proportion of aperture to focal length. Thus if the aperture is one eighth the focal length, it is marked $f/8$, if a sixteenth $f/16$, and so on. All lenses with the same aperture as so marked may be regarded as of equal rapidity whatever their focal lengths may be. Now the more rapid a lens is the shorter the exposure that it is necessary to give for any subject, and the exposure required is proportional to the square of the figure in the expressions as given above. Namely 8 and 16 squared give 64 and 256 which are as one to four, the proportional exposures required. Or we may say that 8 to 16 are as 1 to 2 and square these and get 1 to 4 the proportional exposures.

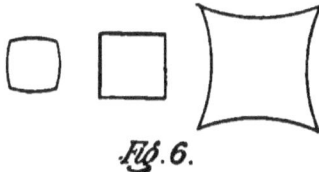

Fig. 6.

The best way to mark stops is, for example, $f/8$ and $f/16$, as these expressions are universally understood, but some persons think that the relative rapidities or intensities are better, others prefer to express the relative exposure necessary, and every system of numbering on these plans has a unit which is merely empirical, not one of them adopting the only true or scientific unit of $f/1$.

Zeiss has recently changed his unit from $f/100$ to $f/50$. Dallmeyer marks some of his lenses now with the practical expression. The following table may be of service to those who happen to have lenses with their diaphragms marked on any of these empirical systems.

f/	Royal Photographic Society	Dallmeyer	Paris Congress	Zeiss (old)	Zeiss (new)	f/	Royal Photographic Society	Dallmeyer	Paris Congress	Zeiss (old)	Zeiss (new)
3.16		1	1/10			18				32	8
3.2				1024	256	20			40		
4	1					22.36			50	4	
5		2.5	1/4			22.6	32			5	
4.5				512	128	25				16	4
5.66	2					27.36			75	7.5	
6.3		4	1/2	256	64	31.62			100	10	
7.07		5				32	64				
8	4					36				8	2
8.66		7.5	3/4			38.7			150	15	
9				128	32	44.72			200	20	
10		10	1			45.2	128				
11.3	8					50			250	25	4	1
12.25		15	1.5			54.77			300	30	
12.5				64	16	63.25			400	40	
14.14		20	2			64	256				
15.81		25	2.5			70.71			500	50	
16	16					71				2	
17.32		30	3			100				1	

Image Angle.—The image angle represents what is called covering power. It may be expressed in terms of the focal length, and doubtless this is the best method, but it is not customary. It may be expressed as an angle, the angle formed when a line is drawn from each extremity of a line equal to the diameter of the circle covered, and caused to meet at a point distant from the base line equal to the focal length of the lens. The angle where the two lines meet is the image angle. But generally the covering power is expressed more roughly, as the ordinary size of the plate that sufficiently good definition can be obtained on.

Tele-Photographic Lenses.—If a negative (or dispersing or concave) lens is introduced between the ordinary lens and the plate, the equivalent focal length of the arrangement is greater than that of the ordinary lens alone, but the length of camera necessary is not proportionately great. It is possible therefore to obtain an image of a size that would otherwise require a lens of long focal length and a corresponding and perhaps impossible length of camera. But this is not the only advantage, for if the ordinary lens and the negative lens are separable to a variable extent, the amount of magnification of the image, or increase in the equivalent focal length of the optical system, is adjustable at will. For further details concerning tele-photographic lenses and their use, reference should be made to Mr. Dallmeyer's pamphlet on the subject.

There are two other subjects connected with the production of images by photographic lenses that must be referred to, though neither of them is of great importance if we exclude the use of hand cameras (which are separately treated of) and bear in mind the ordinary practice of to-day. These are depth of definition and the distortion due to the use of single lenses.

Depth of Definition.—It has already been shown that the action of the lens is to bring to a point in the image all the light that falls upon it from the corresponding point of the object. Now it is clear from fig. 2 that, if different parts of the object are at different distances from the lens, and this must be the case with solid objects, these different parts cannot be in focus at the same time. Still it is possible to get them so nearly in focus that the result is serviceable, and the ordinary method of doing this is to examine the image on the ground glass, and if the whole subject is not sharp enough, to reduce the size of the aperture. Depth of definition is increased by using a lens of shorter focal length or by reducing the aperture. If a large aperture has to be used, the focal length must be short if much depth of definition is wanted, or conversely, if the focal length must be long the aperture must be small. It follows that very rapid lenses that have a very long focus are of no use, for in portraiture, for example, this combination of properties would lead to the ear in the image being fuzzy if the eye was sharp.

If a lens were perfect and had a flat field, the depth of definition would depend only on the aperture and focal length. But if the lens gives inferior definition towards the edges of the field, it is quite obvious that there must be less depth of definition there, if a minimum of defining power is accepted. The definition at its best may be inferior to the minimum accepted and then obviously there is no depth. Depth of definition therefore at the centre of the plate depends entirely on the focal length and aperture, but away from the centre it depends also on the quality of the lens, and is much greater in a flat field anastigmat than in a lens of an older type. But depth of definition is not a quality apart, it depends entirely upon other factors, and it is better in examining a lens to determine these factors separately rather than to lump them together as depth.

Distortion produced by single lenses is due to the fact that the diaphragm is either in front of or behind them. If the diaphragm is in front, the image is drawn towards the centre of the plate to an extent that increases as the margin of the field is approached. A line along one side of the plate has its ends drawn in to a greater amount than its centre, because they are further from the middle of the plate, and therefore it becomes curved like the side of a barrel, and this effect is called barrel-shaped distortion. If the diaphragm is behind the lens, the displacement is outwards, also increasing towards the edges of the field, and a straight line at the edge of the plate becomes curved so that it is convex towards the centre of the plate. This is known as hour-glass distortion. Both these effects are illustrated (and exaggerated

MELTON MEADOWS.
A. HORSLEY HINTON.

for clearness' sake) in fig. 6, the central square representing the true figure. This "curvilinear distortion" is absent in all cases in the middle of the plate and generally for a considerable area, and if single lenses of only long focal length are used, say of a focal length equal to at least one and a half times the length of the largest side of the plate, it may be neglected. Wide-angle single lenses should never be used except on a suitably small plate, so that the above conditions hold. The nearer the diaphragm is to the lens the less is the distortion, and some of the most modern single lenses have the diaphragm so near that the photographer is even more safe in the use of them.

The Comparison and Use of Lenses.—The optician when he tests lenses looks for each fault individually, but this the ordinary photographer is hardly able to do, nor is it particularly desirable for him, because if a lens is inferior it matters little to him why it is so. On the other hand occasion may arise when he wants to identify a fault, then the information already given will probably be sufficient to enable him to do so, if to it is added that a small pinhole with a flame behind it is a convenient point of light, and that if the image of this luminous point is examined with a good eyepiece, without the focussing screen, at various parts of the field, the character of the defect may be discovered.

The main things that the photographer needs to look to in judging of a lens or comparing it with another, are (1) that it works to focus, (2) the quality of its defining power especially towards the edges of the plate. There must also be taken into account the focal length and aperture, and if both these are not the same in the lenses to be compared they should be nearly the same, and the proportion that the aperture bears to the focal length should be exactly the same. A special diaphragm may have to be cut out of card for one of them. The best test object that is always at hand is a newspaper pinned flat against a flat wall. The camera must not be moved during the work. Each lens is very carefully focussed and a negative made, using the same aperture, time of development, and in all ways similar treatment for both. If the focal lengths are different, the images will be of correspondingly different sizes, and then the same detail must be compared, not the definition at the same distance from the centre.

All good lenses work to focus, but some of the cheaper ones do not. To test this, any series of small objects arranged side by side, but at distances varying by intervals of say two inches from the camera, is photographed after carefully focussing on the middle one. If any other than the middle one is the best defined, the lens is at fault. But in this, as in all similar tests, it must be remembered that ordinary dry plates are not quite flat, and the error of the plate may make an appreciable difference.

The use of lenses comprises the whole art of working with the camera, it is therefore not our province to say much about it. But so far as lenses themselves are concerned it may be remarked that, if a lens has a round field, it may be advantageous to tip up the lens with regard to the plate when only a part of the plate is being used, as for example sometimes in taking a landscape. But in using the modern flat field lenses special care should be taken to keep the lens and plate exactly true to each other, the plate exactly at right angles to the lens axis. The image and plate must coincide or definition will suffer. If the image is rounded and the plate flat, then in any case the result is only a compromise, but to take full advantage of the larger apertures when the field is flat, much more care than has been usual must be devoted to this matter.

Simple uncorrected lenses such as *spectacle lenses* or "*monocles*," suffer from the defects that have already been described, and are valued on this account by some workers because they give blurred or "soft" images. With a small enough diaphragm they will give good definition, and generally it may be stated that reducing the aperture lessens the effect of any fault that a lens may possess. To get the best definition that a simple lens will give, the plate must be brought nearer the lens after focussing by about one-fiftieth of the focal length of the lens, so that it may be brought from the best focus of visual light into the best focus of the photographically active light. If the object photographed is nearer to the lens than about one hundred times its focal length, the amount of movement after focussing must be increased. If four focal lengths distant, the correction is nearly one-thirtieth of the focal length, at three focal lengths distant, nearly one-twentieth, and at two focal lengths, about a thirteenth.

Pinholes give an image that for all practical purposes may be said to be equally blurred or "soft" over the whole plate. Much has been written about pinholes and their use, but it is not definitely known yet whether the exposure should be longer or shorter than the exposure required when a lens is used, allowing, of course, for the smallness of the aperture. The following short table and exposure rules from the writer's "Science and Practice of Photography," will probably prove useful:—

Pinholes—diameters	$\frac{1}{18}$	$\frac{1}{27}$	$\frac{1}{37}$	$\frac{1}{45}$	$\frac{1}{54}$
Distance from plate for sharpest image	64	32	16	8	4

All the above figures are in inches. Whatever pinhole and at whatever distance, estimate the exposure for a lens at $f/16$, $f/22$, $f/32$, $f/45$, or $f/64$, as the case may be, and multiply it by the *square* of the number of inches that the plate is distant from the pinhole. But if the distance is as given above for any hole, it is sufficient to expose for as many minutes as the plate is inches distant from the hole, for a subject that would require one second with an aperture of $f/16$.

Chapman Jones.

Portraiture.

THE photographer who may be expert at landscape or architectural work, will find himself at a loss when he essays portraiture. For apart from the art of managing the sitter (a most important element in producing a successful result), he will soon find that the kind of plate that is suitable for outdoor work does not answer well for portraits, unless the developer is greatly modified, for quite a different kind of negative is required. As a general rule it is advisable to use very rapid plates for portrait work; and in this respect, at the present day we are much better supplied than even five or six years ago, and with an extra-rapid plate it is possible to secure a fully exposed negative in half a second, in weather and under lighting that was quite impossible ten years ago.

The best expression and pose are generally secured when the sitter is unaware of the actual moment of exposure; and for this purpose a silent shutter working inside the camera is best. The sitter should never be *asked* to keep still unless, in groups, and when circumstances necessitate a long exposure; and nowadays an exposure of five or six seconds is a long one. Every effort should be made to put the sitter quite at ease.

A head-rest should not be used unless absolutely necessary, and few photographers are aware how easily it can be dispensed with, and fail to realize how strong an objection nearly every sitter has to it. It is far better to have an occasional plate spoilt by working without the rest than to make every sitter uncomfortable by its use. In fact some portrait negatives are actually improved by a slight movement. In a special kind of lighting when the face is in *shadow* relieved against a light background, a slight movement which produces the effect of diffusion of focus greatly improves the result.

Great care must be exercised in choosing the background even when it is only plain or graduated, and it is well worth exposing three or four plates on the same sitter, in the same position and lighting, and with the same exposure, but with different backgrounds, and then carefully comparing the resulting prints. Even if only one background is at hand its depth can be varied by placing it nearer or farther from the source of light. The background must also be selected to suit the lighting of the sitter, as a background of medium tint suitable for what is called "ordinary lighting" would be quite unsuitable for "Rembrandt" effects, or where strong contrasts of light and shade are used, when part of the face is in dark shadow. For such effects a dark background is usually best, as it gives luminosity to the shadow side of the face. But such dark grounds are not suitable for "ordinary lighting" where the face should be full of delicate half-tone, all of which would be killed by the strength of the dark background.

For the Rembrandt effects a much longer exposure is necessary as less light is reflected from the face on to the sensitive plate; they will often need twice or three times as much as for ordinary portraits.

When pictorial backgrounds or accessories are used it must be remembered that the object of the photograph is to secure a portrait of the *sitter*, not to show what a large stock of accessories the photographer possesses. It is best to use as few accessories as possible; I have heard a lady complain bitterly of a well-known photographer, who having posed her in a very difficult position, kept her waiting for five minutes while he arranged a screen, a palm, a footstool, a tiger-skin, etc., so that she felt positively ill before the exposure was made. The sitter should not be kept waiting in the pose to be photographed any longer than is absolutely necessary. If accessories must be used they should be simple and suitable.

When portraits have to be taken in ordinary rooms it is advisable to get a friend or assistant to experiment upon, if possible beforehand. Even a few minutes spent in studying the possibilities of light and arrangement of furniture will save a great deal of worry when making the actual exposures, and nothing upsets nervous sitters more than having all kinds of experiments and arrangements made with them. But it is sometimes well worth wasting a few plates on exposures which the photographer thinks will be useless, in order to give the sitter time to get accustomed to the room; it must not be done in a fussy, irritating way, but rather to show that it is not such a very dreadful operation and really "doesn't hurt." This plan often works well with nervous children, who soon become accustomed to the room and the photographer. There is a great deal to be said in favour of the maxim "leave your sitters alone." The photographer must cultivate quick observation so that he sees at once a good pose, and secures it; and here again quick plates are essential, as many of the most charming poses are caught unexpectedly. It has been well said that the best poses the photographer secures are those he *observes*, not those he *creates*. But a spontaneous pose may not be quite perfect and a slight alteration may be easily made without disturbing the rest of the figure. It will generally be found that a pose that takes a great deal of arranging is not a success.

When taking portraits in an ordinary room it is usual to place the sitter near the window, so that one side of the face is strongly lighted and the other in deep shadow, and then use a white reflector to light up the shadow side. It is often better, when the window is a large one, to place the sitter farther back in the room almost facing the window, and put the camera near the middle of the window looking into the room; a softer lighting will then be secured. For outdoor portraits a shady corner is best, and if possible, one where the side light is much subdued on one side; a light head-shade may be used with advantage. A large grey rug out of focus makes a good background; a blanket is too light.

A portrait lens is best for the work; but if the photographer does not possess one, he need not despair of producing good work. A rapid rectilinear lens used at a large aperture will answer the purpose well; it should always be used at full aperture, partly for the sake of quickness in exposure, and partly to prevent accessories and parts of the dress appearing too sharp and competing in importance with the face. Subordination of parts is one of the essentials of a picture; and if we examine a *good* portrait we shall find that probably no part of the photograph is quite sharp except the eyes and face. Otherwise the less important details are apt to obtrude themselves on our notice. A stop will generally be necessary, however, with a portrait lens if a full or three-quarter length is to be taken, and it will be found that heads only (as a rule) can be taken at full aperture. Just as good work, however, can be done with a rapid rectilinear as with a lens specially made for portraits, except where rapid exposures are to be made; but it is necessary to use one of fairly long focus. A rapid rectilinear lens used for landscape work on a half plate would be much too short in focus for giving good portraits on the same sized plate, for in order to get the figure large enough it is necessary to place the camera so near the sitter as to produce distortion. For portraits on a half plate a lens of at least nine inches focus should be used and for a whole plate not less than sixteen or eighteen inches, and longer if possible.

The swing back of the camera will be found useful in portrait work for getting parts of the figures into focus that are either too far behind or two far in front of the plane of the face. For instance, a full-length figure leaning back in a chair will have the feet out of focus when the face is sharp if the back of the camera is vertical, and this applies with even greater force to groups. A side swing too is useful, but is not absolutely necessary. Even in bust portraits the swing back is useful in getting the shoulders in focus when using a large aperture, for although it is well not to have the whole of the figure in *perfect* focus all over, it is not advisable to have the face sharp and the rest so out of focus as to be blurred.

The development of a portrait plate should be different from that of a landscape, because a different kind of negative is required. A rapid plate developed so as to give a soft delicate image is best; and a developer containing more alkali and less density giver is good, and it may be considerably diluted with advantage. The image should appear within ten seconds of pouring on the developer, and the negative will generally be developed to sufficient density in from two to three minutes. With a good average rapid plate the image should show fairly well on the back of the plate, but this and the time of development will vary so much with different developers, and with the taste of each photographer that no hard and fast rule can be laid down.

Developers that give a brown deposit, or that stain the film will require shorter development than those of the newer developing agents that give a cold black colour to the negative; another fact to be borne in mind is that the image formed by these latter appears to lose more density in fixing than when pyrogallic acid is used.

A perfect portrait negative should have no clear glass shadows, and no part should be so dense as to give white in the finished print, and some negatives which give the best results may have a decided veiled appearance in the shadows.

The temperature of the developer is another important point, in very cold weather the developer should be kept warm, or if in concentrated solutions may be diluted with warm water. In cases of known underexposure the developer may be used quite hot with advantage. A convincing experiment can be made by cutting an exposed plate in two and developing one half with icy cold developer and the other half with warm. The difference is really remarkable. If the developer has been used hot enough to make the gelatine of the plate feel "slimy" an alum bath is necessary, unless the fixing bath contains chrome alum.

METOL.

1.

Water	100 parts or	10 ozs.
Metol	1 part or	50 grains
Sodium sulphite	10 parts or	1 oz.

2.

Water	100 parts or	10 ozs.
Potassium carbonate	10 parts or	1 oz.

3.

Potassium bromide	1 part or	1 oz.
Water	10 parts or	10 ozs.

For normal exposures take 3 parts No. 1 and 1 part No. 2; to each ounce of mixed developer add 40 minims of No. 3.

PYRO AND SODA.

1.

Pyro	1 oz.
Water	70 ozs.
Nitric acid	12 drops

2.

Sodium sulphite	10 ozs.
Sodium carbonate (pure)	8 ozs.
Water	70 ozs.

Equal parts of each, for soft negatives dilute with water. To restrain for over-exposure use potassium, not ammonium bromide. Unless an acid fixing bath is used the negatives are rather green in colour.

RODINAL AND HYDROKINONE.

A.

Sodium sulphite	1 oz.
Water	20 ozs.
Citric acid	1 crystal
Potassium bromide	1 dram
Hydrokinone	2 drams

B.

Potassium carbonate	2 ozs.
Water	20 ozs.
Rodinal	1 fluid oz.

Use 1 part A, 1 part B, and 1 part of water.

The question of retouching is a difficult one. There is no doubt that a certain amount of it is necessary on nearly all portrait negatives and even on those of children. But it is equally certain that the great majority of portrait negatives are over-retouched, so much so that their value both as portraits and pictures is nearly destroyed. Yet a certain amount is necessary even for pictorial effect, and perhaps still more when the question of likeness is considered. For as a rule the untouched negative is no more a true likeness than the over-retouched one. The truth lies somewhere between the two. Even if isochromatic plates are used the little differences of colour in the face, and the incipient wrinkles are exaggerated in an unpleasant way. Under-exposed negatives will show these defects in a very marked manner, full exposure will greatly reduce them. Large heavy patches of shadow may be lightened by coating the back of the negative with matt varnish, and when it is quite hard "hatching" upon it with a soft lead. Harsh lights may be reduced by scraping away the matt varnish with the point of a knife. In some cases the matt varnish may be stained with a little aurine or uranine. Exaggerated lines and small shadows must be worked upon from the front and a retouching desk is necessary. The film of the negative will not take the pencil without some preparation. The best surface is obtained by spreading a little retouching medium with the tip of the finger on the part to be touched. A thin film of soft resin is left upon the plate which takes pencil marks readily. A hard lead, No. 4 Faber or Hardtmuth, should be used. The loose leads used in what are called the "ever-pointed holders" are most convenient. The point must be very long and fine, like a large darning needle, and is best made by rubbing the lead on a piece of fine glass-paper. The pencil must be held very lightly and the lines touched away with short *light* strokes, a heavy stroke only rubs the medium up.

The little shadow at the end of the mouth often has to be reduced, often at the risk of spoiling the shape of the lips, but sitters *will* insist upon it being done, and say " You have made my mouth much too large." Freckled faces are perhaps the most difficult to retouch, as it is well nigh impossible to remove the black patches caused by the freckles without at the same time destroying the modelling of the face. Yet it must be done, for probably the most severe stickler for truth would not insist on the black blotches that freckles produce in a photograph.

A great deal can be done to improve a hard negative as soon as it leaves the fixing bath, by applying a mixture of hypo solution and a solution of ferricyanide (not ferro) of potash with a piece of cotton wool to the dense parts. The proportions for this reducing bath are as follows:— To each ounce of the ordinary hyposulphite of soda fixing bath add a few drops of a 10% solution of ferricyanide of potassium or red prussiate of potash, making the whole about the colour of pale brandy. By adding more of the ferricyanide solution the reducing action is quicker, but there is a greater liability to stain the film. The work should be done over a sink with a tap of running water at hand. The solution should be of a deep lemon colour (it is almost impossible to give exact quantities), and after a short application must be washed off under the tap, and the negative may then be examined, and the reducer applied again and again till the desired reduction is obtained. It is advisable to make a few trials on spoilt plates. For if any really good work is to be done there will be plenty of rejected negatives. Probably, of all the plates exposed on portraits by first-rate professional photographers, not more than one-fourth ever get as far as the printing-frame.

Moral: Do not be chary of exposing plates, they are cheap enough now. Don't feel, "Oh! this will be good enough. I won't do another." On the other hand don't expose carelessly and recklessly and say, "It will all come right in developing." Good work is not done that way. Use every opportunity of seeing good work. Study the work of great portrait painters, but don't neglect the photographers. Go to all the exhibitions of pictures and photographs within reach.

Don't be satisfied with what you have done, but make a resolve to do something better next time. Remember, what is worth doing at all is worth doing well.

Harold Baker.

Off Boulogne.   By A. Horsley Hinton.

Pictorial Photography.

UNLIKE the subjects of the other articles in this book, in pictorial photography we are not brought to consider one of the many processes which go to make up the photographic craft, but merely a special and exceptional application of any and all means known to the photographer.

The particular end to which this application is made will be explained as far as the limits of space will permit, and some of the methods of such application will be described. Beyond this I have no intention of going. I do not present pictorial photography as a branch of photography especially worthy of study—I am not concerned in making converts. It is for the photographer who has already formed a desire to give his attention to the pictorial side of photography and who is seeking help, that this chapter is designed.

First let us come to a mutual understanding as to the term Pictorial Photography. Picture-making by photography would perhaps be a simpler phrase, but that to my mind the word " picture-making " is too similar in idea to boot-making, lace-making, etc., all of which imply a mechanical manufacturing, whereas a picture—a real picture—like a musical composition, a poem or a beautiful thought, grows or is evolved rather than made to order.

Art photography would be a better term, but that in photography the word "art" has been so often coupled with things the very antithesis of artistic and might hence be misleading, moreover the photographer will show discretion rather than weakness if he be not too hasty to claim for photography a position among the arts, and whilst its claims to that dignity remain as yet in dispute, we may be content with "Pictorial Photography" as a less assuming title, yet one which will sufficiently differentiate between what we may call the ordinary photographic production and—— Well, what?

That is the first thing I have to try and explain.

Look at the illustrations in this book on pages 72, 136, and 120, and, making due allowance for some loss of quality due to reproduction by a "half-tone" block, try to imagine what the originals were like. Then say if they please you. If you say no, you do not care for them, they do not appeal to you, you do not mind if you never saw anything of the kind again from this day henceforth; very well, doubtless there are other things in the world in which you can find pleasure, but so far as my present subject is concerned, here you and I part company. These illustrations are more or less successful reproductions of pictorial work, and if you do not like

MISS LILY HANBURY—A PORTRAIT.
HAROLD BAKER.

them, making as I have said due allowance for their being reproduced and reduced, then it is certain you do not want to hear anything about them, and it is not my intention to persuade you, so please pass on and make room for those who do care for these things and wish to learn all they can concerning them, or at most stand aside and peradventure some stray word dropped unintentionally may quicken your interest and discover in you a sympathy of which you were previously unconscious.

Referring now again to the illustrations which in the absence of anything else we take as fairly typical of pictorial photographs and assuming that one or the other, if not all, do please some of my readers, I will ask them to endeavour to analyse their feelings when confronting such productions.

Take now an ordinary commercial photographic view such as one may purchase from any seaside stationer, and compare the sensations awakened by each. In the case of the topographical view we feel some satisfaction at being able to recognise a familiar spot, or the view reminds us of some other place, or it may be quaint buildings, or rugged mountains, or miles of foliage, or what not inspire curiosity or interest because we know the photograph to be a true record of facts, that is to say we accept the photograph in lieu of the actual presence of the objects represented, and experience nearly the same feelings as we should were we to visit the spot represented. We know that the wonderful, curious, or unusual things portrayed have an existence, otherwise we could not have a photograph of them.

In all such cases our interest and value of the photograph would vastly diminish, were it possible for a photograph of this kind to be made simply by the photographer's hand and imagination without any original at all.

G

You look at a photograph of this or that sea-side place and remark, "Ah, yes, that's dear old Yarmouth, many a time, etc., etc.," or else, "Dear me, I wonder what place that is, it's so like —— " such and such a town, or it may be you enquire "Where's that?" and you express or think to yourself you would like to go and visit the spot. These and kindred sensations are those kindled by the average photograph, but there is yet another, for you may be impelled to exclaim, "How wonderfully clear and bright that photograph is," "What a good photograph." In this case you are interested purely in the execution as an example of clever manipulation and skilful craftsmanship.

Now, compare such feelings as these with those stirred by an example of good pictorial work. In the first place your esteem for it, if you value it at all, is quite as great whether you know the place where it was made or not. If it pleases you, that pleasure is not dependent upon the fact that it does represent some place. In the case of paintings and drawings as often as not they do not pretend to represent any place at all, but are pure fiction, yet we do not value them the less. To what then is the pleasure we feel when looking at a good picture due? Is it not that a picture stirs up, that is, *creates* pleasant or beautiful thoughts and ideas—by pleasant I do not mean necessarily merry or joyous ones, for some hearts feel profounder pleasure in the grandeur of storm or the majesty of the mountain than in the sweet wilderness of flowery wastes, but notice that such beautiful ideas are *created* by the picture. You were thinking of something totally different before you came upon the landscape picture which instantly made you feel the glowing light, the stirring breeze, and hear the rustling corn and noisy brook, and yet it cannot be said it is because we *recognise* these things in the picture that we receive these impressions, at least it is not the kind of recognition which takes place when we see a photograph of Brighton Pier or Haddon Hall.

Notice, it is not the exact and faithful portrayal of objects that creates the emotions instanced, for if you closely observe the manner in which a good painting is done you will find that rude splashes of paint, broad brush strokes, and the like stand for foliage or water, or corn stalks as the case may be, when we know that had the painter desired he *could* have produced his likeness of nature with a good deal more of the precise detail and fidelity to outlines which photography excels in, *had he wished*. But if the painter or other pictorial artist needs not to trouble about accuracy to details to secure the effect aimed at he must be faithful to general facts. There is a great difference between not recognising things or having no particular wish to do so, and feeling conscious that a portrayal is so utterly unlike anything in our past experience of nature that we should not recognise the objects even if we *were* acquainted with them. To take an extreme case—our enjoyment of the effect and sentiment of a beautiful landscape picture is not enhanced by our being able to recognise whether the trees are oaks or elms, but it would be distinctly disturbed if the palm trees were represented as growing on the slopes of a Welsh mountain. Innumerable examples and instances might be given to show that the artist, whatsoever his medium, be it colour or monochrome, may depart from truth, or may be indifferent to precise details, *only so far as he avoids palpable untruth*.

Why is this?

When we look at a powerful and impressive picture we feel at once the sentiment, our emotions are at once stirred, subsequently we recognise objects and facts portrayed, but only when we begin to look for them or think about them; but a gross exaggeration or a very obvious error strikes us at once before we begin to receive sentiments and ideas, and that error or exaggeration once seen is never lost sight of, and whole enjoyment of the picture is hopelessly marred.

Now, from the foregoing (for want of space I am aware that the argument is incomplete, and must therefore ask the student to think the matter out and grasp the side issues by reading between the lines) we may formulate the broad definition that a picture does not depend for its excellence on the faithful representation of objects, and is not chiefly valuable on account of our immediate recognition of things portrayed, yet on the other hand it must not let us feel that there is obvious inaccuracy.

Here then we have two opposite positions in both of which the mere objects employed to build up the picture are subordinated to the effect or impression of the picture. In one case the spectator must not be allowed to feel that the representation is *wrong*, in the other success will not directly depend on the representation being very *right*, neither startling rightness or truth nor the obvious wrongness or untruth should thrust the objects composing the picture upon the beholder's attention, he should be left free to receive the expression or sentiment of it.

I hope the reader is following me in this line of thought closely. I am aware that it may seem dry and uninteresting, but I see no other way of placing the student in a proper position at the outset than by explaining the essential elements of pictorial work, and I will make this introductory part as brief as possible.

Reverting now to our argument, I have in other words suggested that obvious violation of truth will prevent the sentiment or effect of the picture from being paramount, and now I will submit that an excess of accuracy to detail is equally detrimental to the success of a picture as a picture.

If by now the reader is prepared to admit that the chief purpose of a picture is the feelings, emotions, ideas which it suggests or creates, and not the facts it portrays, he will be able to go further and perceive that in a landscape, for instance, cottages, trees, or what not are introduced, not for their own intrinsic interest but as vehicles of light and shade, which go to express the picture's sentiments.

If we stand before a good picture with closed eyes and suddenly open them, our first impression (precluding any question of colour) is that of masses of light and shade pleasingly and harmoniously arranged; if we retreat to such a distance that the objects constituting those lights and shades are unrecognisable the balance and pleasing arrangement should still be felt, and our æsthetic sense is satisfied, although we do not see fully of what the picture is composed. This is the quality which is termed breadth and which is admittedly of very great value.

If on the other hand the shadow masses are filled with innumerable details, and are thus broken up into tiny lights and shadows they no longer exist as broad masses of dark, but if before retreating as proposed from the picture, the lights or shadows appear so blank as to prompt particular investigation, and upon examination we find detail absent which we know must have been present, then we encounter an instance of untruth and exaggeration which is obvious and which disturbs our appreciation of other fine qualities. Thus we require *sufficient detail to avoid giving the idea that detail is left out.*

The delineation of sharp outlines and redundance of detail is not wrong in itself, but it is usually inexpedient when considered with respect to the effect to be produced, similarly the suppression of sharp focus both as regards outlines and details has no artistic merit of itself except as it assists the picture to impress the beholder first with the general effect.

The painter and photographer start from two opposite standpoints. The painter, or draughtsman, starts with nothing but blank paper, and having built up his picture and produced his desired effect he elaborates no further; the photographer with his more or less mechanically produced *facsimile* starts from the opposite extreme with a transcendentally elaborate image, from which he will require to eliminate all such excess of truth as is likely to force the mere facts of the view upon the beholder's attention.

Photography, so faultlessly complete in its delineation, gives us *more than the pictorial worker needs for the expression of an idea*, and this is why I would remind the student that pictorial photography is not photography in the full sense of the word, but the application of some of its powers, just as much as we need and no more, to a definite end.

As just hinted the purpose of a picture is to express ideas, hence I will fall back on a kind of definition which I have used on a previous occasion that a picture is the portrayal of visible concrete things for the expression of abstract ideas.

To give an example by way of exposition we may look upon a picture and be made to feel by it the calm and luminous atmosphere of evening; we feel at once the restfulness, and almost feel the warmth of the humid air, giving place to the chill gathering mists of night; but the same objects, the same tangible materials, paper, pigment, metallic salts, etc., in another picture give us the sense of angry turbulent storm or perhaps bright joyous sunshine frolicing with the fresh breezes on the hill-tops. These are abstract ideas expressed or created by the manner in which concrete things, commonplace facts, are portrayed and rendered.

Finally, let me enunciate that a very excellent photograph may not necessarily be a good picture, because it may contain more than is required for the expression of its idea, and the surplus will overwhelm it; again, a good pictorial photograph may be but a poor photograph, because if we claim the right to apply photographic means to pictorial ends, we may find it convenient to leave out the very qualities which the scientific or technical expert considers most precious.

And now I think we may proceed to more practical matters.

COMPOSITION AND SELECTION.

In all matters from which the eye expects to derive pleasure, symmetry of design seems essential. In the formation of the letters that we write, in personal attire, in the decoration of our homes, in buildings, and practically in everything which is not of a purely utilitarian character, a sense of proportion and a symmetrical disposition of parts is observed. Hence it is no source of surprise that in a picture which as much as anything should aim at pleasing the eye, design, otherwise Composition, is with Expression a co-essential.

In a purely decorative production this natural desire of design is the only thing to be observed, but in a picture which *may* be decorative, but *must* be something more, we have expression as well to consider If decoration alone were to be regarded, something like fixed rules might perhaps be tyrannically laid down, but in a picture the implicit observance of rules of composition would be certain to make itself seen in the result, and the undue obtrusiveness of a code of rules would be as inimical to the supremacy of ideas and feelings, as the excessive prominence of fact would be, which has already been described.

Hence the difficulty in prescribing any definite course for the beginner, because whilst to most instinctive artistic temperaments a certain knowledge of or feeling for composition is natural, so soon as this is reduced to definite rule and given to another, the, as it were, secondhand use, is nearly certain to betray itself by its misapplication. I would ask therefore that any suggestions given here on the subject of composition should be taken as one takes lessons in the rudiments of a language, which rudiments we violate and forget so soon as we have become proficient enough to speak it. *Such rules in composition should be observed only so far as to avoid the appearance of having infringed or ignored them.*

The rules of composition which may be found to apply in one of the pictorial arts must necessarily apply equally in the others, and so therefore to pictorial photography which at least aspires to be considered an art. If on a sheet of paper a rectangular space is given us wherein to draw the likeness of anything, the most natural course to pursue would be to draw that figure in the centre or thereabouts, and if then we are asked to add the likeness of two or three more objects we should naturally place these near the first object. Thus should we compose a group of objects which draw the attention to the middle of the picture or space.

Suppose we are asked to draw the picture of a church tower we should probably comply with the request somewhat as shown in fig. 1. Next we will suppose we are asked to add a cottage, some trees, and a path to the church, we should, if possessed of some sense of symmetry and order, coupled with average intelligence, make the additions somewhat as in fig. 2. It would surely be an unusual thing to follow instead the course suggested by figs. 3 and 4.

In figs. 1 and 2 we have instinctively placed the primary object in or near the centre, and the others near

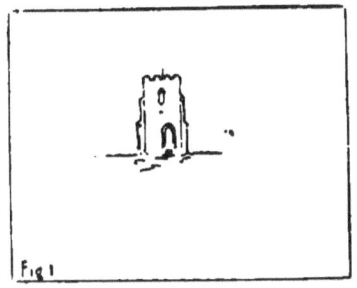

and around it, and the result strikes one at once as being better composed, that is, more symmetrical, than in fig. 4, in which amongst other things one is not sure which object to regard as the principal one, and one also feels that but for the boundaries of the picture left and right we might have seen a good deal more beyond, which would have added to the interest of the picture.

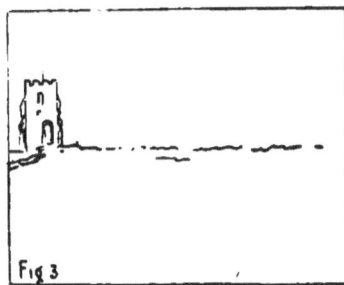

In this we have one of the first rules in composition, namely, that the principal object should be near the centre, and the next important near to, and as it were supporting it, and no object likely to attract the eye should be so near the edge of the picture as to make us instantly conscious of the boundaries and wish to see more beyond.

But now if in compliance with the supposed request we had made our drawing as in fig. 5, might it not at once be felt by the observer that we had put the objects in a central position *intentionally*, which is equivalent to saying that we had allowed our endeavour to observe the rule just laid down to betray itself. Fig. 2 is preferable as being only just sufficiently symmetrical to avoid being unsymmetrical, which is an example of what has already

Fig. 5. Fig. 6.

been said about the necessity of observing rules of composition just so far as to escape the appearance of having broken them.

If this rule is right as regards voluntarily drawing a picture, it is equally so in the case of a photograph, but instead of deliberately placing things in such and such positions, we attain the same end by moving the camera and selecting our point of view so that the objects come into the positions desired.

Now suppose then, we have done this, but in doing it we are quite unable to prevent other objects coming into the field of view and occupying undesirable places near the margins of the picture, as for instance in fig. 6. Here we are brought to consider another rule or principle in composition, namely, that there must be one and only one chief object in the picture, whereas in fig. 6, apart from the gate and tree on the one side and the windmill on the other attracting attention to the margins of the picture, these same objects arrest the attention quite as much as the church, and we feel the eye wandering about from one to the other and missing the sensation of centralization and rest which fig. 2 gives.

If we were drawing or painting we should put in what we want and then stop, we should omit or ignore what we did not require, but in photography our powers in this direction are limited, and hence we must as far as possible select those views, and only accept such, as comply with what we feel to be right.

The angle of view included by different lenses is an auxiliary not to be neglected, for by substituting a narrower angle lens, that is, one of longer focus, we may cut off or leave out undesirable objects which the shorter focus lens might include. Then again, when the print is finished we can after careful consideration cut off what would have been better left out, for it will be better to have a picture half the size well composed, than double the number of inches with a distracting and unsatisfactory arrangement of objects, hence with many most successful workers it is no uncommon thing to take quite a small portion of a negative, and either print it as it is or else enlarge it up to the desired size, but mere size will reckon as nothing as compared with pleasing composition.

If it is inexpedient to let the principal object or group of objects occupy the exact centre of the picture, measured from left to right, it is equally so if the centre be measured from top to bottom, and hence we may formulate the rule (to be broken perhaps later when we are strong enough to be independent of guiding) that the horizon should not be allowed to come midway between the top and the base of the picture.

Fig. 7.

Remembering now that, as set forth in the earlier part of this article, a picture should appeal to our feelings

Fig 8.

and stir our emotions, it may be pointed out that in most ordinary things, and certainly in the arts, the most powerful things are those which possess *one* dominant idea or feature, as in a piece of music the refrain keeps recurring, a preacher takes a text, in a story there is *one* hero, and so forth, and in point of composition fig. 7 is better than fig. 8, although the view is less comprehensive.

Fig. 9.

It may not, however, always be easy for the beginner to determine what is the chief object which should occupy the central position, or which object or group to choose in a landscape.

This brings us to speak of another important matter, and that is the right disposition of lines which form the

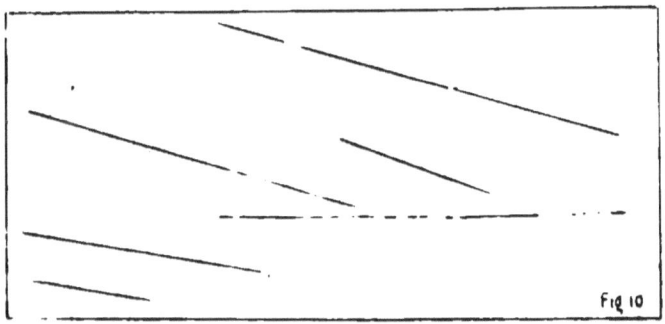

Fig. 10.

view or the selection of view so that the lines formed by the component parts shall fall in a desirable manner. The various objects in any view tend to form or suggest lines, thus in fig. 9 the outline of the trees, the bank along the shore, the clouds, and the boats suggest the lines shown in the diagram, fig. 10, which lines all run the same way, but in fig. 11 we have a similar view in which the lines suggested counterbalance each other, and not only so, but by their convergence they carry the

Fig. 11.

eye to a spot near the centre, and so make the boat, although not very large nor conspicuous, the one and principal object (see diagram fig. 12).

For the sake of training one's perceptions look at

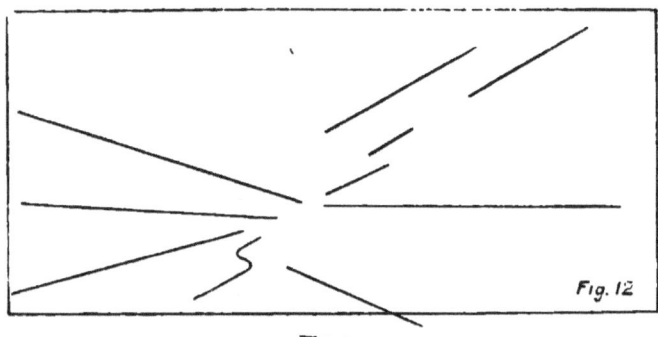

Fig. 12.

any good pictures, and in your mind resolve them into line diagrams and see how these lines fall, and in considering any landscape or other subject to be photographed make up your mind as to what lines are suggested, and then select your point of view so that these lines balance or are symmetrical in arrangement, and also that they converge towards some point well within the picture, and near the centre of it.

Fig. 13.

But in fig. 13 we have a subject in part well composed, but the composition is spoilt because of the line formed by the road and fence, which seem to cut the picture in two, whereas could we have chosen the same

Fig. 14.

subject from a point of view giving such an arrangement as fig. 14, a difference is at once felt and a more pleasing effect gained.

Lines which seem to separate us from the picture and cut off one part from another must be carefully avoided, and an endeavour to find something which will, as it were, lead the eye into the picture, should be

Fig. 15.

diligently sought for, and indeed a subject, however it may interest us, must often be abandoned if it lacks those things which go to make pleasing composition, remember-

Fig. 16.

ing as we should always do that in pictorial work the fact that objects are curious, or interesting, or pretty, has nothing to do with the case, but that they are only to be valued according as they act as media for expressing pleasing ideas, beautiful thoughts and sentiments, which they will not do if some part creates a feeling of unpleasing arrangement or design. If a scene does not compose well, we should as pictorial workers feel no desire to reproduce it. But you may say "Cannot we often by changing our point of view get an otherwise ill-composed subject to compose well?" Most decidedly, that is precisely what we should do, but it is no longer the same subject or view.

And now let me say that it is often surprising how much alteration may be made by changing our position. Figs. 15 and 16 are together an instance of this, the outline here given being made from a pencil sketch made on the spot, whilst figs. 17 and 18 are examples of

Fig. 17.

Fig. 18.

the desirable change brought about by watching and waiting for a change in the position of light and the condition of the river's tide.

Where the beginner most often fails is in taking things as they are without pausing to consider whether

H

they might not be improved, and if so in what way, and then patiently searching to see if such better way can be found.

Pictorial success will as often as not depend on the exercise of fastidious taste, which is satisfied with nothing but the very best, and not quite content even then.

A great deal more might usefully be said with reference to the composition of lines if space would permit, but this general reference may be given as a sort of summing up.

If the disposition of the lines constitutes such a perfectly symmetrical design that it is at once recognised as symmetrical, then it is wrong, because the artifice by which pleasing composition is attained is betrayed, and we feel the thing to be artificial. If, on the other hand, the lines fall so as to make the beholder conscious of their presence, as, for instance, cutting off a portion of the subject or presenting a one-sided appearance, again it is wrong. *In neither case should the lines or the objects suggesting them be felt at all until sought for, neither as being very right or very wrong.*

In art it is a maxim that the means by which the thing is done should not proclaim itself, and hence it must apply to pictorial photography, which is an effort after the artistic. A composition should please without our quite knowing why, and without our being able to see the machinery, as it were, by which our pleasurable sensations are set in motion.

But whilst it is convenient to speak of *lines* in the landscape, it is only a manner of speaking, for, as we know very well, photography, unlike pen drawing, has to do with "tones," that is, *masses* of light and shade. Now the general rules suggested as regards the arrangement of lines, apply in much the same way if we regard a picture (as we should do) as consisting of masses of light and shade.

If when standing before a picture we close the eyes and then suddenly open them, our attention is certain to be drawn to the highest light or the deepest shadow, and hence, as a general rule, whichever of these is the strongest to attract attention, that should be in or near the principal object (indeed it will make of itself the principal object), and should therefore be well removed from the margins of the picture.

Refer back to fig. 8, in which the light patch of sky, the light in the water and the two clusters of light rushes, all form competing points of attraction, and if these are too near the margins, they remind us of those margins, hence the improvement in effect when these are cut away or left out.

But disposing of the highest light and deepest dark does not finish the matter. There is a certain relative degree of lightness and darkness between everything in nature. Moreover, colours have to be interpreted by certain degrees of light and shade according to the distance objects are away from us, and according to the amount of light falling on them.

Such relative lightness and darkness is called "*tone*." The word used in this sense has nothing to do with "tone" as applied to the colour of a print, which colour we change by a process we call "toning," and upon the correct rendering of relative tones so much of the effect of a picture depends, and so much of its emotional qualities.

Generally speaking, although there are often exceptions, the further an object is from us the grayer it seems. White becomes less white, and dark objects grow less dark, until in the distance both, under ordinary circumstances, come almost to the same "tone," and we see the distance only as a gray hazy mass.

If for a subject we have a figure of a woman by a stream of water and we make an under-exposed negative of it, or develop the negative to too great a density, we shall very likely have a print in which the water and the woman's apron and cap come very much whiter with regard to the rest of the subject than ever they appear in nature, whilst the distance will very likely come too dark. Here we show a disregard for the correct rendering of relative tones and the effect is hard and harsh, unlike nature. We must therefore endeavour, both in exposure and development and printing, to preserve relative tones exactly as they are in nature, and constant study and observation of nature should be carried on in order that the eye may be trained to know how things come relatively in nature, and so be able to decide at a glance if the photograph is good.

Ultimate success, by the way, often depends less on knowing what to take and how to take it than on a well-trained judgment which knows what is good or bad when we have taken it.

Whilst the mere lines or forms of objects may impart some amount of feeling and sentiment to a scene, inasmuch as there is restfulness and repose in the long horizontal lines of the river-side pastures, something rythmical in the sinuous curves of the winding stream, or vigour and variety in the irregular forms of the rugged cliffs and so on, yet the ideas and feelings which the picture will promote depend more on the lights and shades, and the masses contrasting or merging each with each.

But Nature does not always present herself in pleasingly arranged masses, and is consequently at such times commonplace and unpicturesque in the literal sense of the word. At such times she will not attract the pictorial worker any more than she will when perchance the lines and groupings are unsuitable.

The landscape which basks under the full blaze of sun, glittering throughout every inch with a myriad twinkling lights and sharp details, awakens no feeling akin to those which probably everyone feels when in the twilight of evening plane after plane recedes as one broad flat tint behind the other. Under the bright light of day we may wonder at the richness and plenty upon the earth, we may rejoice in that there are so many curious and pretty things to look at, but these are like the

Fig. 19.

feelings inspired by reading a book on natural history, rather than the emotions created by the perusal of a poem, or listening to sweet music.

Compare for a moment the two photographs, fig. 19 and fig. 20.

The first is by no means an extreme case of the ordinary photograph, and notice that although the composition is fairly good as far as grouping goes, there is an absence of any quality which might make one feel anything outside the bare recognition of the facts depicted, but the second, if it be good at all, must depend for admiration on a certain amount of sentiment which it suggests or creates. You will notice that in the first there is no sense of distance, and although a church tower, behind the masts of the boats, is half a mile or so away it does not possess the "tone" and veiling of atmosphere which would make it appear distant. Every part of the view seems equally near, or

Fig. 20.

nearly so; the eye wanders over the whole, alighting on details here and there which interest and amuse, yet there is an absence of just that breadth which is noticeably present in the second example.

Now let it be distinctly understood that detail, its omission or suppression, and its introduction or sharp delineation, is not a question of lens focus only, or even chiefly, but it is largely a question of light. Imagine the photograph, fig. 19, with the greater part of the detail taken out so that the quay, the houses, the shore, etc. were just broad masses of lighter or darker tone, should we not then get a composition which would be less disturbing, more compact, more concentrated in interest? Is not this the case in fig. 20, in which detail is almost entirely absent? And yet detail could not have been truthfully introduced in this photograph, because with the light in the position it is, and in the misty evening air, *no detail was there to reproduce*; it was the fact that objects ranged themselves in masses one against the other, leaving room for imagination and creating ideas that determined its selection and its consequent portrayal.

In many cases a clear and sharp delineation of details will perhaps be desirable, not, however, for the sake of showing detail, but just so far as the production of the effect may require; on the other hand, just the full amount of detail that a lens will give is by no means always wanted.

Lenses were not invented for pictorial purposes, and therefore there is no reason for concluding that what the lens gives is necessarily right, for remember that we started with the distinct understanding that we were merely *applying* to a certain purpose just so much of the photographic process as we considered we needed; because I have the means of travelling at sixty miles an hour there is no reason why I should not apply the same means of locomotion to coaching a pedestrian at a tenth of that speed if I choose. It may be said that in the two photographs referred to the comparison is not a fair one, because so much depends on the sky. Granted that much in the second example does depend on the sky, which is an essential part of the picture, and indeed one cause of its very existence, but in the other (fig. 19) the presence of clouds would not improve the pictorial faults to which reference has been made. As a mere record or portrayal of Old Woodbridge Quay, the absence of clouds is as much a characteristic of its particular species, as the clouds in the second one are inseparable from its existence.

So, but little more than half hinting at the principles involved in the due suppression of unnecessary details, and the elimination of undesirable objects in order to obtain breadth, and having said but little as to the preservation of correct relative values or tones, I must pass on.

Every corner of nature's broad expanse is, as it were, enveloped in atmosphere, and invisible as we are commonly in the habit of considering it to be, it affects to a greater or less degree everything we see, and the visible atmosphere is often responsible for some of nature's most beautiful and most appealing aspects. Obviously then we cannot afford to leave out so important a contributory to picturesque effect, and it is on this account rather than on account of sharp or unsharp detail that the question of stops and lens apertures comes in.

Look at the image of a landscape on a moderately hazy day, as it appears on the ground-glass focussing screen of your camera, using the lens at full aperture—then quickly insert $f/32$, and notice the difference. Not alone have objects near at hand and more remote become more sharply or more equally defined, but you may also notice that objects are *more brilliant*, and that a sense of atmosphere has been cut out.

Compare if you will two photographs, the one made respectively with full aperture of $f/6$ or $f/8$ and the other made with $f/32$ or $f/45$, and provided that in the first case we have not actual blurring to the extent of destroying form and structure, does not the first remind you more of nature? I do not say it is so instructive, so surprising, so dainty, or of such exquisite finish, but is it not more reminiscent of the *effects* we remember to have seen and *felt* in nature. It is not the function of this article to say to what optical laws this difference is due, and yet the student may expect to receive something by way of practical working instructions.

My recommendation is then to use a single landscape lens or the single combination of a doublet, and in starting to use the full aperture.

With this it may be that when the foreground is moderately sharp, trees more remote are so ill defined as to appear as a collection of little blots and irregular patches. Whilst sharp detail in all places may not be productive of pictorial effect, yet the extreme opposite will be displeasing in another way, and it will be best to secure just *so much definition and no more* as shall save the representation from appearing to have been wilfully put out of focus—once let the destruction of detail be obvious and we betray the artifice by which we are working, which is just what we should avoid.

In the case just supposed then, we may now introduce the first stop, simultaneously racking the lens in a little until we get middle distance without unpleasantly obvious blurring. The foreground may be a little out of focus, and in practice I find it is rather helpful to general effect if detail is sacrificed more in the foreground than in the middle distance.

This I believe is contrary to the teaching of many, but my feeling is that with a sharply defined foreground the eye is attracted and the interest so far arrested, that it is difficult to travel further and enter into the poetry and sentiment of the scene beyond.

Wide-angle lenses have a double disadvantage, shared in part by so-called rapid rectilinear doublet lenses. In the first place they flatten the view, bringing distant planes to appear as near as the nearer ones, and by including a comparatively wide angle they bring into the plane of the foreground, objects so near that they appear out of proportion, and hence proportions are false when judged as the observer must judge by the standard of visual perspective.

A long-focus, narrow-angle lens necessitates a camera which racks out to a considerable length, and probably a greater extension than any camera in the ordinary way can give, would be an advantage on some occasions.

Passing reference has been made to the interpretation of colours in nature in their true relative value of black and white.

If we have a subject in which brilliant orange-coloured rushes in autumn are seen as glowing bright against a background of dark blue water, and the rushes made still more golden of hue by the ruddy rays of a sinking sun, a difficult case is before us.

Such a case I remember very well in the south of Devonshire, close to what is known as Slapton Ley. It was late afternoon in November, and from over the rounded hills behind me to the westward, the declining sun sent warm red rays on to the belt of faded reeds which stretched out into the expanse of the still land-locked water of the Ley—a great sheet of fresh water which placidly lay under the shelter of the bank of shingle which alone separated it from the ever-restless sea—placidly listening to the ceaseless voices of sea music, and at this particular hour reflecting the sky deep blue and of almost leaden hue—just above the bank rose the full moon, orange in tint, on a background of blue-green sky—the yellow reeds, kindled into glowing amber tints by the sun's rays, flamed out from the deep blue water—yellow the shingle bank against the blue water and green-blue sky, deeper yellow the moon as it rose from out the sea. So grand a scheme of colour that by its side the essays of the most daring painter might well seem feeble, so exquisite a poem that the intrusion of the photographer, analysing the values and tones and calculating his powers of reproduction seemed like sacrilege. In the main it was yellow, orange-yellow, and red standing out as luminous against the deep blue of water and only a little less blue sky. It was gorgeous non-actinic colour appearing as *light* against a highly actinic but *darker* colour. The consequence of an indiscreet exposure with an ordinary plate might be anticipated to produce *dark* rushes against a *pale grey* background of water, and so probably the very effect we were minded to secure, reversed and dissipated.

This is an extreme case, perhaps, but throughout the whole range of nature the contrasting and blending of adjacent colours is so subtle a thing that I should feel one were throwing away at least a possible advantage by not using colour-corrected or isochromatic plates on nearly every occasion, and in order to get the full advantage of isochromatic plates, I should consider the addition of a yellow screen an essential.

The rapidity of one's plates, isochromatic or otherwise, must be governed entirely by the nature of the subject, as also to some degree must be development and subsequent printing.

In every case I would endeavour to get a comparatively thin negative, with even the portions representing deepest shadows slightly veiled. "Clear glass shadows" is an enormity and an outrage both of science and art; equally are solid high-lights to be shunned. With modern printing methods it needs much less than actual opacity in the negative to produce white paper, and if the picture requires any part of it at all to appear as quite white, no subject will need more than the very smallest region to be so. A general softness and very subtle gradation, with a total absence of "sparkle" and brilliancy in the negative, will yield by at least most processes the most suggestive print, bearing in mind that delicate gradations suggest atmosphere, and atmosphere is one of nature's most precious qualities.

Whilst plain salted papers sensitized with silver present possibilities not yet sufficiently exploited, yet until such time that something more entirely satisfactory in all respects is given us in silver papers, platinotype and carbon, and perhaps also gum bichromate will be the processes most suitable for our purpose. Personally, platinotype has been the favoured medium, being, as I believe, more ductile and more amenable to various methods of control than is generally recognised.

And leaving much more of importance unsaid than space limits admit of my saying, I must leave it.

A. Horsley Hinton.

Architectural Photography.

TO the majority of amateurs, the photographing of architectural subjects presents considerable, and in many cases apparently insurmountable difficulties. Undoubtedly there are difficulties to be grappled with, but they are neither so formidable nor so numerous, but that any ordinary photographer with the average amount of common sense can master them be he so minded.

Unfortunately there are a great many who take up photography as an amusement to whom the slightest departure from the ordinary routine presents a difficulty. It is however to the amateur photographer who desires to be able to portray architecture, be it either of our cathedrals, churches, historic mansions, or places of personal interest, and at the same time wishes to be able to do the subjects fair justice, that it is hoped the following particulars may be of some service.

To the beginner taking up this or indeed any branch of photography, size is of course a great consideration either from the weight carrying or pecuniary point of view. Another reason is the fact that young photographic workers have an idea that the smaller the plate, the easier the working. Sound though this reasoning may appear, nevertheless it is not entirely correct.

As a matter of fact all things being taken into consideration the larger the plate up to 12 × 10 or 15 × 12 employed the more rapidly will the worker progress.

Large plates, especially in architectural work, tend to make the operator more careful and conscientious when out with the camera; and even more so when in the developing room. So much more can be done with a large plate than with a small one; the use of a large plate moreover checks the common failing so prevalent among amateurs of rushing work and recklessly using plates.

Taking all things into consideration, I would strongly recommend the whole plate or 10 × 8 camera to the student taking up this branch of our art.

In selecting a camera purchase a front extending one with bellows only slightly tapering. See that it has both rising and cross movement to the front, and also that the amount of movement in each case is a not too restricted one. Makers, unfortunately, do not give sufficient attention to this matter, the usual rise allowed being very slight whereas it should be at least equal to one-third of the longest way of the plate; even more than this is advantageous if it can be obtained. By the rise I mean the amount of upward movement that can be obtained, the lens being in the centre before starting.

The cross-front should have a movement of about one-quarter of the length of the plate each way.

It may be useful to know that a little more rise can be obtained by the placing of the lens above the centre of the cross-front; reference to the photograph of camera will explain this matter more fully.

The swing-back should be a practical one, working from the centre, and capable of being swung either to or from the lens.

In many of the cheaper front extension cameras it is not possible to use the swing-back when tilting the camera down, only when tilting upwards. The swing-front, although not an absolute necessity, is undoubtedly a movement possessing great advantages, especially when the front is raised rather high, and one is using a lens of limited covering power This movement should be acquired if possible.

The camera should possess double extension, focussing by rackwork, and having a reversing back so made that it will fit on all ways; it is then possible to draw the slide shutter out in any position.

In selecting a tripod stand purchase one of the kind known as the sliding leg variety, two-fold is better than three, giving greater sliding power. The top of stand should be as large as possible; this is preferable to a turntable, as this piece of workmanship is seldom rigid after a little use, and some difficulty is experienced when trying to spread the legs out rather wide. A two-fold Ashford stand is as good as any on the market.

The blocks herewith illustrate the kind of camera used by myself, and with the exception of the turntable, which is not a great success, it answers all requirements.

In the selecting of suitable lenses a great deal will depend upon the inclination of the purchaser and the depth of his pocket.

There is such a great variety upon the market at the present time, that to the young photographer the buying of the right lenses is somewhat a difficult problem.

The Zeiss series are undoubtedly the finest obtainable and for architectural work are unrivalled, possessing

 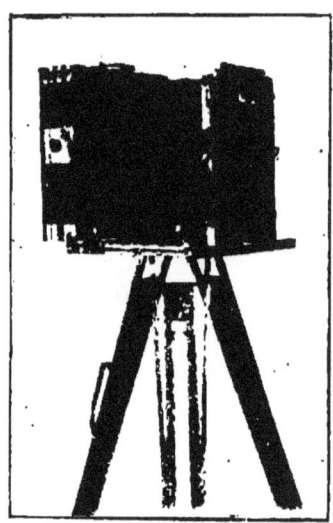

great covering power, good marginal definition, and in fact very fine definition all over the plate. The lenses of this series, although quite new, have met with great favour amongst architectural workers.

They work at an aperture of $f/18$, but I understand that they can be opened to $f/16$ and numbered on the f system. As regards their relative working capabilities they give about the same picture at $f/32$ that the majority of wide-angle lenses give at $f/64$.

The Goerz anastigmats are also another very fine series but do not give anything like the covering power of the last mentioned, and moreover are nearly double the price. Their special merit is that one can work

at $f/8$ or $f/11$, and get a picture sharp up to the edges. Taylor, Taylor & Hobson also make a good wide-angle lens, possessing great covering power and at a moderately low price. With one of their nine inch lenses I have covered a plate 12 × 10 inches.

For a whole-plate camera, a useful battery would be a 5 inches, 7½ inches, 9 inches and 12 inches; for 10 × 8, 7 inches, 9 inches, 10½ inches and 14 inches. The three last in each case are the most useful.

Having selected the lenses, another very important point and one not to be decided hastily is the question of levels. Four are required, two circular and two ordinary. They are placed as follows: Fix the circular levels, one on the baseboard near the front of the camera, the other on the top of the back part of camera. The other two should be placed one on the side of the back part and the other on the back of camera just under the reversing back. Care must be taken to purchase slow moving levels as some work so quickly that it is next to impossible to level the camera with them, and as this is one of the most important points in the whole business, too much care cannot be taken in selecting and fixing the right kind of level.

The focussing screen should be ruled as accompanying diagram. This will divide the screen into inch squares, working from the centre, and will considerably assist the photographer in "sizing his subject up."

One other thing required is a set of clamps for binding the tripod legs together. These are, I believe, made by George Mason, of Glasgow, but any dealer will procure them for you.

The use of the right kind of plate constitutes a very important factor in the production of a satisfactory negative, particularly in this branch.

Owing to the greater difficulty experienced in developing extra rapid plates, one generally sees the slower variety recommended. No hard and fast rule can however be laid down. To gain the best result, the plate must be suited to the subject.

For instance, in a very dark interior in which heavy black shadows predominate, many of them appearing much darker than they really are owing to their close proximity to a strong light, the quicker the plate used the better. This tends to break down the harsh contrasts, and at the same time the shadow detail is considerably better rendered.

On the other hand, working in a light interior or one which is flat owing possibly to the large amount of light present, a slower plate can be used with advantage, and, providing the exposure is sufficient the result will be all that is wished for.

Exteriors, particularly those in sunshine, should be photographed on a fairly quick plate. Slow plates, although good, do not yield nearly such good negatives, and unless very fully exposed give excessive hardness.

Taking this class of work all round, the quick plate is the more useful of the two and is undoubtedly the best for interior work, particularly such interiors as one meets in our English cathedrals.

For all subjects possessing strong high-lights, such as windows, stained or otherwise, rapid plates combined with a suitable backing composition yield the best results, and I would impress upon the reader the fact that no plate should ever be placed in a dark slide without being covered at the back with a suitable composition for the prevention of halation.

The value of this agent is distinctly demonstrated by the accompanying illustrations, and I would point out

the fact that the negatives were both developed with the utmost care. The unbacked plate was so developed as to prevent the appearance of halation as much as possible, and it will be noticed that all portions of the photograph, other than that where halation has occurred, are nearly as good in the unbacked as in the backed one.

Having obtained all the apparatus and materials, a very good subject to begin on and one giving good opportunities for the exercise of the various movements connected with the camera, etc., is a general view of the choir in some cathedral or church near at hand.

Having erected the camera, the next thing is to decide upon the most pleasing point of view.

Speaking from my own experience I would advise the shifting of the camera either to the right or left, so that the centre aisle is thrown slightly in perspective. This tends to give a much better and decidedly more pleasing effect to the resulting photograph. Of the two sides, moving to the right seems to be the best. The next item is the fixing of your ground line, this must be so arranged that it is quite clear, not obstructed by the backs of chairs, etc., which look very badly if left standing. Personally, I have generally found it necessary to move one or two rows of chairs so as to make the ground line myself.

In adjusting the height of the camera from the ground it is well never to exceed six feet. Five feet to five feet six inches is the most useful height. This will give a photograph in which the point of sight is the same as that of the person actually viewing the subject.

The placing of the camera on step ladders, chairs, or other supports, so as to overlook objects in the immediate foreground is a practice to be condemned, giving results very rarely pleasing and always bad from the sightseer's point of view.

Having settled upon the point of view and the lens to be used, the student should then roughly focus the image. Notice the amount of subject on the plate and how much rise is required.

If having a camera such as described, the rise is easily accomplished and the camera can then be truly levelled up. Care should be taken over this as unless you have the camera exactly level you cannot expect a true picture. The bubbles of the levels should be *exactly* in the centre, *a little bit out will not do.*

If it is found that the rising front fails to give the amount of subject required, recourse must be made to the swings, and it is here that the swing front triumphs over the swing back.

To swing the back necessitates the shifting of the camera and tripod stand, and at once throws all the levels out of gear. Then comes re-focussing, etc. Sometimes this will have to be gone through five or six times before the desired amount of swing has been achieved. Owing to the re-focussing required every time the camera is moved it is very difficult, especially for the beginner, to rightly estimate the amount of rise required.

With the swing front the desired amount of rise is attained easily and quickly, and it can be worked with the head still under the focussing cloth, which is a great convenience. At the same time the baseboard and back of camera always remain level.

After gaining the correct amount of rise the sides of the subject should be considered. A golden rule to remember in this class of work is when you show a column, show the base of it, and always start the sides of plate with either half or three-quarters of a column. It looks very queer to see the bend of an arch wandering away out of the side of the picture without any apparent support. In arranging the sides it is usual to have a preponderance of subject on the opposite side to which the camera is, and to start that side with a column. Sometimes the subject fails to fit the plate nicely, in that case it is better to trim the print than to have uninteresting features present.

Of course a great deal depends upon the personal taste of the worker, what one man considers right another will rebel against; so although I advocate the use of columns to fill the sides of the plate it does not follow that that is the one and only method of photographing these subjects.

The student having carefully gone into these matters and arranged the subjects to suit his own satisfaction the question of what point to focus for arises, and indeed in very dark interiors the question of focussing anything at all comes in. A method I use myself is to roughly divide the distance from the camera to the farthest object in half, and then to focus midway between the camera and the middle of the subject. Then stop down the lens until the most distant object is sharp. In practice I have found this rule so good that I can recommend its adoption for all subjects, and if carried out correctly will always result in the production of crisp negatives.

Exposure is not a very difficult thing to overcome. Arrange the focussing cloth well over the head, open the lens out to its largest aperture and remain under the cloth until you can see the image distinctly all over the plate. Then without uncovering the head proceed to slowly stop down until you can only just see the image all over the plate. Now using a plate of the rapidity of Barnet extra rapid, an exposure of ten minutes will yield a satisfactory fully exposed negative.

The varying exposures for other plates and stops are easily obtained. For instance you find the image can just be seen all over at $f/32$ and you wish to use $f/64$. The exposure will be forty minutes.

After having used this method for over seven years, and having invariably found it correct, I can unhesitatingly recommend its adoption, and if used with a little common sense the worker will seldom suffer from his plates being either badly under or over-exposed.

In photographing side aisles, transepts, or long rows of pillars, the worker is often troubled by the unnatural way in which the floor runs up. This is more especially noticeable when there are no prominent objects in the immediate foreground. A considerable amount of this can however be overcome by the lowering of the camera to about three feet from the ground. It is here where the sliding legs of the tripod stand become of service.

I would ask the student always to use the longest focus lens possible, consistent with the effect desired.

The use of extreme wide-angle lenses has had a disastrous effect upon the public taste in respect to architectural photography due principally to the abortions one sees exposed for sale in the shop windows of our cathedral cities.

It should be seldom necessary for the amateur to use very wide-angle lenses. Of course, when it is a question of getting a detailed photograph in a confined situation a wide-angle lens is of great service. But it is when you see the whole length of a cathedral photographed on a whole plate with a five inch lens that the fault is so noticeable.

In photographing exteriors great care should be taken in the placing of the camera in a suitable spot. Try and so arrange it that the short side of the building does not run off too violently, indeed, it is often much better to leave out a portion of the subject rather than to cram the whole subject upon the plate.

General views are much better if photographed when there is a little sunlight. This gives to the subject a sharp, clean-cut appearance.

Details on the other hand are better if photographed in a subdued light and slightly over-exposed.

In focussing very high subjects some difficulty will be found in getting bottom and top in focus at the same time, especially if the lens be strained by either altering the back or front of the camera.

The best place to focus is a little way above the centre of the screen, so that when stopped down the bottom of the building is quite sharp. A slight softness towards the top of the subject is scarcely noticeable in the final print.

The exposure of exteriors varies between three seconds at $f/64$ to ten minutes, and no correct guide can possibly be given. To the beginner a Watkins' exposure meter will here be of some service.

If people are continually passing and repassing stop the lens down to $f/64$ and give as long an exposure as is possible; this will as a rule completely obliterate them. I have found that an exposure of from ten to twenty seconds entirely destroys all trace of moving objects.

Another method of making an exposure where there is much traffic past the building, and perhaps people standing about whom you cannot very well ask to move, is, to break the exposure as many times as possible. Expose for two seconds, then wait until the traffic has somewhat altered; then give another two seconds and so on until finished. By this means I have been able to photograph buildings in the centre of a crowded street or thoroughfare without a trace of anybody showing.

It is often interesting for the student to be able to successfully tackle the photographing of drawing-room, ball-room, or other apartments either of his own or friends' houses.

This work is considerably more difficult than it seems; and it is in such subjects that the taste of the operator becomes manifest. A great deal depends upon the point of view chosen and also upon the arrangement of the furniture.

If a long room, the camera should be placed at one end at about a quarter of the width of room away from one side and from the end wall. Keep the camera parallel with the sides of the room and use the sliding front so as to obtain more of the opposite side of the room. This will give the ceiling a true square appearance and the side of the ceiling will not run off with an unpleasing effect.

In some subjects it is perhaps necessary to include one or more windows. This can of course be accomplished by the aid of backed plates, but it is always better to block those particular windows out. This is usually done by covering the outside with black cloth or brown paper or pulling the sun blinds down. To get the effect of the windows you must remove the paper or cloth at the end of the exposure for a few minutes, three minutes being generally sufficient. By this means it is possible to show the landscape as seen from the window. Do not place your camera too high. Four feet to four feet six inches is quite sufficient. If the camera is higher you look over the immediate foreground objects, touching the ground past them, which is undesirable.

In arranging the furniture be careful that round or oval objects are not placed so that they appear on the edges of the plate which gives them an exaggerated appearance.

In exposing on all such interiors I would strongly recommend a very full exposure, the object being to flatten the subject. A great thing to study in this branch of work is the careful lighting of your subject. This can be largely varied by the use of the inside blinds, also by the sun blinds found outside many windows. It is *not* advisable to draw the blinds up to their fullest extent. By so doing you accentuate your cast shadows thrown by tables, chairs, etc. In fact, the softer the light in the room coupled with a corresponding exposure, the better the result. Another point to notice is that a comparatively dull day is often the best for interior work, the light being much softer and subdued. As a slight guide to exposure I would suggest that an additional twenty-five per cent. be added to that recommended for church work.

John H. Avery.

The Hand Camera and its use.

WHAT is the best form of hand camera? How often this question is asked, and yet how impossible to give any definite reply, the conditions of use, and requirements of each worker being so widely different. One, desires a form of apparatus, capable of being closed up into the smallest space, weighing but the least possible number of ounces, the necessary movements, confined to touching a spring, or pressing a button, and the total cost not to exceed two or three pounds, while others do not care so much as to its possessing these qualities, if by a little increase in bulk, weight, and cost, it is capable of use in a less restricted manner, on subjects of wide variety, and under such conditions of light, and atmospheric effects, as, when shutter exposures are being given, call for the *maximum light passage* to the plate.

Assuming the camera to be intended exclusively for use without a tripod, then it becomes not a difficult matter to point out its essential features. First and foremost, it should be characterized by simplicity in construction, and every part be easily accessible, complicated movements being rarely found necessary, except perhaps, to raise the price of the instrument. When being employed in the field, the camera and its working parts ought not to need the slightest consideration, each movement, whether they be few, or many, being made, without requiring troublesome attention at the moment when every thought should be devoted to the subject.

The component parts of an instrument, complete and effective for this class of work, may be taken to be a good lens capable of covering at $f/8$, a shutter, some simple means of focussing, adequate finders, and the means of carrying plates either in some form of magazine, or ordinary dark slides.

Each system of holder for plates possesses its own distinctive advantages, which are preferable, depending entirely on individual needs, or tastes. Some admire one method, and some the other.

When plates are carried in one of the many forms of magazine which cameras are nowadays fitted with, it is *important when re-charging it*, that care be taken to see *each sheath and plate is laid true* in its place, as the slightest irregularity at this point, means certain trouble when changing a plate after exposure, indeed, perhaps fifty per cent. of the misfortunes which occur when out at work, from failure to act of the changing arrangements, *are directly caused by carelessness when laying the plates in the magazine*. Given reasonable care in this matter, almost any of the modern automatic changing methods, may be relied on to answer satisfactorily. When however the slight additional bulk, weight, and it may be increase of cost is not objected to, then there can be no denying separate dark slides possess many and important advantages.

No need to fear a wasted day, caused by some plate sticking, and rendering further work impossible, without having recourse to a dark-room, which probably is miles away; and again, one must not overlook the opportunity they give of carrying plates of different degrees of sensitiveness, a matter of service, when subjects to be dealt with are varied, such as, say, clouds and water, landscapes and figures. In the first case, when light is fairly good, the ordinary speed plate will be found amply quick enough during the daytime, and fifty per cent cheaper in price. When open landscapes are being taken, during summer time, medium rapid plates generally will be quick enough, but many opportunities, for pictorial work, arise under conditions of atmosphere and light, in which to obtain fully exposed negatives with a shutter, demands a plate of extreme sensitiveness, and if for no other reason than that they offer this opportunity of carrying a varied assortment of plates, many workers prefer dark slides, to any form of magazine.

There are advantages, and disadvantages, with both systems, and it becomes simply a question for each worker to consider which fulfills his requirements best.

The Lens.—Good work can be, and is done, with cheap single lenses, but the opportunities offered are considerably restricted, what is needed, being such a lens as may be used at full aperture of $f/8$ or $f/6$, and will then cover the plate from corner to corner, sharply. This is necessary not only because the actinic quality of light is not always over good, but that moving subjects demand the shutter should be working with rapidity, sometimes indeed with considerable speed; under which conditions two factors are absolutely essential, a large working lens aperture, and a rapid plate. It is well, therefore, to *buy the best lens you can afford*, it more than pays in every way. For ¼-plate work, a *rectilinear* of 5, or 5½ in. focus, working say at $f/5\cdot6$, and with iris diaphragm, by one of the best makers, will allow work being done under any condition of weather, or other circumstances, when shutter work is possible.

Finders.—Years ago, the question of whether finders were necessary, or not, in a camera of this kind, was a matter on which some at least expressed very different opinions, from those now held by most workers. Further experience has shown that when certainty in working is desired, some kind of finder is an absolute necessity as part of the working mechanism. It usually takes the form of a small camera obscura, what is required being, that it should not be too small, should give a perfectly discernible image, and be so adjusted, that only so much of it is shown, as will be projected on to the sensitive plate, when the exposure is made. The reason of its importance is that it *enables the subject being arranged* tastefully, as well as ensuring that the whole of it is on the plate.

Where no attempt at pictorial work is intended, and the important matter is simply that the object being photographed should be in the *centre of the plate*, then it is only necessary that the finder should show as wide an angle of vision, or a little wider than the lens being employed inside the camera. But when something more is aimed at, *viz.*: *Tasteful composition over the whole plate*, then it is necessary to block out on the finder all excess of view, beyond what will be received on the sensitive plate.

The Shutter.—What particular form may be best is a matter of doubt, but whatever it be, exposure must be possible without vibration, it should give greater exposure to the foreground than the sky, and ought to allow of being regulated for exposures ranging from $\frac{1}{4}$th of a second up to perhaps $\frac{1}{100}$th, for ordinary work.

Where shutter work has to be done, which demands anything less than $\frac{1}{100}$th of a second, then special shutters for the purpose are needed, but after having used hand cameras of one form or another for the last nine or ten years on such classes of subjects as are ordinarily dealt with, the occasions on which any greater speed than $\frac{1}{30}$th of a second has been called for have been extremely rare. It may be said this would not allow of taking subjects such as a close finish of a cycle race and such like, which is quite true; did occasion arise for so doing, then a shutter such as the focal plane would be employed as a matter of course. But by far the greater amount of work done with hand cameras would be the better for receiving a longer exposure, better because light action on the sensitive plate would be more thorough, and far better because when slowly moving objects, such as waves rolling shoreward, are given $\frac{1}{10}$th instead of $\frac{1}{100}$th of a second, we get less of "*petrified naturo*," and a more natural appearance in the resulting photographs. As a general rule it is well to give the *slowest exposure possible*.

The Focussing Arrangements.—These need be only very simple, and generally are done by scale to distances. As a rule with the lens working at $f/11$, and the scale set at 15 feet, it will be found that the depth of focus is sufficient for most ordinary work, and any alteration in the focussing seldom necessary, when dealing with subjects where figures are included, that are not required to be approached much closer than the distance mentioned.

So far as may be necessary for *hand-camera work* simply, the instrument should be without complications, is better for having a *good rectilinear lens*, needs a shutter easily adjusted for exposures ranging if possible, from a $\frac{1}{4}$th of a second, up to say $\frac{1}{100}$th, properly adjusted finders, some means of quickly altering the focus of lens, one or other method of carrying the plates or films, and for *purely hand-camera* work, there is *no need* for any other addition to it.

Passing away from the camera to its use, one is faced immediately with the fact, that in spite of the multitude of such instruments now in use, the *general average of results* produced by its means are, in quality, unmistakably below those done with a camera and tripod, nor is the reason for this far to seek. In the latter case, a plate of medium rapidity is generally employed, such an exposure given, as makes no serious *strain* on the developer used to bring the latent image fully out; the action of light having been ample, and the plate not so easily spoiled, as one of higher sensitiveness, there is not that call for such skilful treatment, as where light action on a highly delicate emulsion, has been but brief, and needs to receive careful handling, before good, well-graded negatives may be produced.

To use a hand camera is the simplest matter imaginable, to properly employ it the most difficult—simple, because of the facility with which plates may be exposed, difficult, because to succeed, demands careful practice, and a thorough understanding of photographic manipulation. We must have *learnt to see*, and that quickly, must have gained coolness and self-restraint, and perhaps not the *least qualification necessary is that of being a good photographer.* Whether content to produce good straightforward representations of such scenes as come before you, or more ambitious attempts at pictorial work be made, they can both be done with the hand camera quite as well, nay indeed, given sufficient technical skill, and trained perception to see the beauty

BIRCH AND BRACKEN,
W. THOMAS.

presented in line and mass, it is by no means clear this form of implement does not offer greater facilities for successful working, than the more complicated form used with a tripod.

The choice of subject is only bounded by the limits of exposure, speed of plate and actinic action of light available. The first has already been touched upon, when the lens, and shutter, were dealt with.

Plates have recently been so increased in speed, that it becomes necessary to somewhat modify advice, which a year or two ago, might have been perfectly correct, *viz.*, to work with the fastest plate procurable. But there is this advantage now, as then, that if some convenient form of actinometer be used to test the light, we are able to judge at once, what speed of plate will be necessary to deal with each subject as it arises. There are several forms available, amongst which, the one introduced by Watkins, made so that it becomes a permanent part of the camera, answers remarkably well, especially as it cannot be left at home, without being noticed. In developing shutter-exposed plates, if full exposure has been obtained, then the ordinary modes of procedure suffice, so also when over-exposure occurs, but by far the greater proportion of failures one sees in this class of work, arise simply *from under-exposure.* There seems so much charm in driving a shutter at its highest speed, and at the same time using the lens stopped down, to secure sharp definition, the wonder is, not that failures flourish, but that any good work is done at all.

With regard to particular developers there is only this to be said. Whatever agent be employed, so arrange that before density is obtained, *all the detail you require* is first brought out; this simply means, if pyro is being used, it is kept low, until the plate is ready to be treated for density, then a further addition of pyro and bromide will generally suffice to rapidly finish off the work.

When a batch of exposed plates is being dealt with, a most certain method of negative making, will be found in employing in one dish, either one or other of the following one-solution developers:—

No. 1 Formula.

Amidol	20 grains
Sodium sulphite	½ oz.
Water	7 ,,

No. 2 Formula.

Dissolve in water	20 oz.
Metol	75 grains
then add	
Sodium sulphite	1¾ oz.
Carbonate of soda (crystals)	1¾ ,,
Bromide of potassium	6 grains

No. 3 Formula.

Sodium sulphite	1¼ oz.
Carbonate of potassium	½ ,,
Eikonogen	¼ ,,
Boiling water	12 ,,

Any of the above developers will be found to rapidly bring out all there is in the plate, and if over-exposure is feared, they may all with advantage be diluted, with an equal quantity of water, in order to slow down their action.

In another dish, it is advisable to have the following *re-developer*, to impart density to the plates, as they become ready for that operation, or to successfully deal with any, which are found to have been considerably over-exposed, and upon which, the first developer is acting too vigorously.

RE-DEVELOPER.
No. 1.

Hydroquinone	¾ ounce
Sodium sulphite	2 ,,
Potassium bromide	¼ ,,
Boiling water	12 ,,

No. 2.

Washing soda	2 ounces
Sodium sulphite	2 ,,
Water to make	12 ,,

For use mix equal quantities.

By employing two different developers in the manner suggested, it becomes a simple matter to produce good negatives, from plates having had all kinds of exposures, some under, some over, and it may be some which have had about the right exposure; in this way one of the most fruitful causes of failure in the production of hand-camera pictures, *error in exposure and development*, is minimized, if not altogether done away with.

There are sometimes occasions when out with a hand camera, when subjects present themselves, offering exceedingly good opportunities for securing pleasing little pictures, but which require one, or two seconds' exposure, to render them successfully. At such times it may generally be arranged to rest the camera on a stone, wall, or gate, or to hold it pressed against a tree, or some other rigid support. As an example, the illustration of a woodside with birch trees, facing page 136, may be pointed to. In this instance, when out cycling, the place and lighting on the tree trunks, struck us as pleasing, and worth trying to secure a record of, even though but a hand camera was being carried at the time.

Having dismounted, and found a point from where it might be attempted, and where conveniently grew a single tree, the lens was opened to (if recollection does not deceive) $f/11$. Then the camera jammed close to the tree trunk, and two seconds' exposure given, taking especial care that no movement took place.

The plate being in due time carefully developed, and as far as possible contrasts kept down, the result proved satisfactory enough.

It could more conveniently have been photographed, of course, if a camera and tripod had been available, but it is one of many such instances, where, when shutter exposures only had been prepared for, occasions arose, demanding longer exposures than were possible, unless, some such temporary support be pressed into use, as in this instance.

For successful work, see that the camera is simple, its parts, of the best your pocket can afford. Give the slowest exposures your subject will allow. Develop for softly modelled negatives first, getting what density is required afterwards. See that the camera is held perfectly steady, during exposure, and don't forget it is simply a camera, and lens, and will require *you behind it*, just the same as any other employed with a tripod, and in conclusion bear always in mind, *it is the simplest form of camera work and the most difficult,* making the utmost demands on your skill, if high-class results are to be the outcome of its use.

W. Thomas.

Lantern Slides.

A LANTERN Slide is a transparent positive on glass or other transparent support, usually $3\frac{1}{4}$ inches square, and is placed in the lantern in such a way that by suitable illumination and optical arrangements the image on the slide is made to intercept some of the light given off by the illuminant from a screen, which without the screen would be wholly and evenly illuminated by the light.

In viewing a paper print we are really observing the paper by reflected light, part of our view being intercepted by the image formed of pigment or reduced metal; the amount of light not being very great a very thin layer of pigment is required to produce the appearance of a sufficiently robust image. If the image alone or with its vehicle be stripped from a good print on paper this image viewed by transmitted light will be found to be extremely faint, far too faint to be of any use as a "transparency," and also too thin to be of any use as a lantern slide. On the other hand, what we know as a "transparency," such as is often used for window decoration, backed, perhaps, with ground glass, would be found much too dense or robust for use as a lantern slide. In density, then, a "slide," as it shall hereafter be called, comes between the image on a paper print and that on a "transparency." In "gradation," or gamut of tones, the slide ought to be superior to either the paper print with its almost absolute clearness over large areas, or the transparency with its dense shadows and its comparatively heavy lights. In fact, in a good slide we have every grade of deposit from perfect transparency to nearly complete opacity. But the extremes must be very sparingly present, and the transition from one tone to another must be gradual, all intermediate notes between highest and lowest should be represented.

Other qualities go to make the perfect slide ; the metallic or other deposit forming the image must be in the utmost degree fine, no approach to "grain" must be perceptible even under the highest magnification. The colour, or "tone," must be not only pleasant but appropriate.

The loss of light in its journey from the illuminant to our eyes is enormous; the disc on the screen is simply a greatly magnified image of the light, and here is great loss ; add to this the interception of some light by the opacity of the slide, and the fact that much more is lost in reflection from the screen, and absorption by the screen, and it is easy to realize that the image from the screen reaching our eyes is vastly less bright than that reaching the eye when, for instance, we examine a slide in the hand by transmitted light. And loss of light means increase of contrast, so that a slide which would seem about right in gradation in the hand would be altogether soot-and-chalk as a screen-image. So too if we have in the slide already shut out much light, by making the slide foggy, or over dense, it is easy to see that when the image reaches our eyes from the screen this vicious opacity will be immensely increased in its mischievous properties. The first style of slide gives screen-images sometimes called "midsummer snow-scenes"; the other slide is simply called "foggy." Both must be assiduously avoided.

It need hardly be said that the plates prepared by some processes are more likely to yield good slides, such as are described above, than plates prepared by other processes; no one process can claim to possess in itself superiority in all respects. Collodion, for instance, is less apt to give foggy slides, and it is easier to intensify than gelatine, but it is also more prone to give "hard" images. Collodion is at its finest in the form of collodio-bromide emulsion, which gives slides remarkable for fineness of grain, for clearness, and for richness of tones; but when we have to copy in the camera, the operation with collodion emulsion is protracted, unless we have bright daylight or a condensing arrangement, which with large negatives is often out of the question. On the whole it may be taken that gelatine-bromide emulsion is the process to be recommended, not only on account of its convenience and celerity, but in view of the many inherent points of excellence that it possesses. In any case, want of space will cause us to confine attention here to that process, and any one mastering the use of gelatine-bromide slide-plates will have nothing to fear from competition with other processes in all-round work. The writer has a leaning towards slide-plates as slow as he can procure them, because slowness almost always goes hand in hand with fineness of grain and freedom from fog.

There is one point of importance that should be noted in working with gelatine for this purpose. Distilled water should be used if possible for all solutions. Tap water—especially hard water—is apt to produce with the gelatine a certain amount of scum which, if present in any appreciable degree, cannot fail to affect the quality of the slides; but treatment with an acid alum bath as described later has a very salutory effect in removing any scum that may have formed during the "liquid" operations.

In the mechanics of making a slide from a negative we have only two methods to consider. If the slide-image is to be the same size as the negative, or a part of the negative, we print by *contact*, that is, we put the negative and the slide-plate face to face in contact, and we expose to light, the negative being next to the light; this corresponds with making a print on paper. But when we desire to make a slide including all the subject of a negative larger than a slide-plate, or, in fact, when we desire to alter the size of the image at all, we copy the negative "in the camera." The simplest method of doing this is to fix up the negative so that it is evenly lighted and make a photograph of it in a camera; but the adjustments necessary for such an operation would be found awkward, and so a "reducing camera" of some kind is generally used. Many such cameras are on the market, and consist of devices for holding the negative in a suitable position with regard to a small camera furnished with a lens and a dark slide holding a lantern plate. Either the negative-holder or the camera should have possible movement in all directions vertical to the optical axis of the whole, and in addition it is often desirable to have a certain amount of movement in other planes, in order to correct certain optical defects that are sometimes found in negatives. The writer has for many years used a small camera with its front stuck into the front of a large camera, one or other of these cameras has every necessary movement. The device is figured here.

Whatever arrangement is used the end of the apparatus bearing the negative is directed towards a good and even light; and it is well to place about two inches in front of the negative towards the light a piece of finely ground glass for ordinary negatives; this glass is with advantage omitted with extra dense negatives.

It goes without saying that the exposure, whether we are working by contact or in the camera is of the utmost importance; but it is not possible in an article such as this to give even an approximate idea of the exposure suitable under any concatention of conditions. The best clue to exposure is to be found in development, and in results. It is necessary to know what happens after normal exposure with a given developer, and then if any variation is noticed to alter the exposure. If a plate develops more rapidly than the normal, it may fairly be deduced that the exposure has been too long; but if we are dealing with a specially contrasted negative it is better so. On the other hand, when we are dealing with a thin negative, especially if the scale of gradation is short, we require an exposure less than what would under normal conditions lead to complete development in the normal time. And again some plates require to be developed to a greater point of apparent density than others; this is a matter of experience. Briefly put, there is no royal road to good slide-making, experience is necessary.

In actually making the exposures certain points must be kept in mind. If we are copying in the camera with daylight as illuminant it is very important to use the light from the north; if we use other light we shall be much put out on most occasions by awkward variations of the brightness. A very large number of operations are rendered nugatory by carelessness in this matter. Even the most experienced worker will find it impossible to expose plates with anything like accuracy when he has to deal with direct sunshine at one time, thin white clouds at another, and dark clouds at a third. And in making exposures by contact the beginner must be fairly accurate in judging the time of exposure and the distance from the radiant. A good plan is to tie to the gas jet a piece of cord having knots at convenient intervals, such as at 9, 12, 18 and 24 inches, and in making an exposure to use these knots as guides to the distance; moreover, the law of "squares of distance" must be remembered; the intensity of light varies inversely as the square of distance from radiant to receiver, provided, of course, no optical arrangement is introduced to modify the path of the rays. Consequently, for example, if ten seconds is found to be a proper exposure at nine inches from the light, the corresponding exposure at eighteen inches will not be twenty, but forty seconds ($9^2=81$, $18^2=324$). And as it is sometimes awkward to hold the frame and attend to a watch at the same time, a metronome, ticking seconds, will be found convenient, or a clock with a second hand may be placed where it can be seen during the exposure. A landscape slide without clouds, if the horizon is in the picture, is usually considered a failure, and has been dubbed "bald-headed." Really good workers often put clouds into slides by "combination printing," which in some cases is comparatively easy, in others very difficult. If we are working by reduction from a good-sized negative, with a fairly even horizon, the difficulty is not great. The landscape part of the negative is first exposed, the sky being masked if necessary, and a cloud negative is then substituted for the landscape negative, a part of the former being masked to correspond with the landscape on the latter, and a second exposure is made on the same slide-plate. Admittedly in all cases this requires "some doing," in many cases it is extremely difficult. An easier, if less "sportsmanlike," method is to make the cloud slide on a separate slide-plate, and to use the latter as a "cover-glass" for the slide. The cloud may cover the whole of the second slide, and that part of it not required may be wiped out by means of a reducing solution, used with a brush, such as the ferricyanide and hypo one described later. This method will be found useful even in contact slide making, but it also requires not only good taste in the selection of the cloud, but some deftness in manipulation; but the neat-handed beginner need not fear to make the attempt.

DEVELOPMENT.

It has already been stated that judgment of exposure is a matter of experience, and that results are the best criterion; here follow some more explicit statements on the same matter.

Whatever plate or developer is used, and whatever the time occupied in complete development:

> *1st.*—If by the time the high-lights are sufficiently strong the shadows are too dense or blocked, the plate has been under-exposed.

2nd.—If by the time the high-lights are sufficiently strong the shadows have not attained sufficient density, or are veiled, the plate has been over-exposed.

3rd.—If at the same moment the high-lights show sufficiently and the shadows are transparent but sufficiently plucky, the plate has been properly exposed.

4th.—With a normal negative the normal exposure is the proper exposure; but *(a)* a negative abnormally strong in contrasts will require an abnormally long exposure; and *(b)* a thin negative, or one with a very short scale of gradation from densest to clearest, will require an abnormally short exposure, with probably some after-treatment in the direction of "intensification."

Ambitious slide-makers generally aim at warm-toned slides for pictorial effect, and rightly. But slides intended for scientific purposes are generally better when cold in tone, the definition is usually better. But whatever the aim, a good tone of one kind is preferable to a poor one of another kind, and the beginner should first make sure of getting a really good cold tone, which is comparatively easy, and then try his "'prentice hand" on warm tones.

Warm tones are obtained by using greatly super-normal exposures and greatly restrained developers; and the danger probably lies in the fact that the long exposures are apt to lead to fog, and the great restraint to over-density in the shadows, the latter especially when the exposure has not been quite long enough for the developer used; herein probably lies the whole secret of warm slide-making. If we aim at really warm tones and use developers suited to such design, we must on no account stint the exposure.

COLD TONE DEVELOPING SOLUTIONS.

The classical solution for cold tone slides is a solution of ferrous oxalate in potassic oxalate. Of all developers it is most free from fogging propensities. It is made from so-called "saturated solutions" of proto-sulphate of

iron and potassium oxalate. Thus, into a bottle put a quantity of iron proto-sulphate, and pour on about three times its weight of water containing a dram of sulphuric acid to each pint. Shake well, and keep always at about 60° Fahr.; some of the iron must always be visible in the bottle, if not, more is to be added. The crystals of iron salt must be green and not rusty in colour. This is the "iron solution."

The "oxalate solution" is made by dissolving potassium oxalate in about three times its weight of water. This also must be kept at 60° Fahr., shaken occasionally, and oxalate added if none is visible in the bottle.

To make the ferrous oxalate solution we *pour* one part of the iron solution *into* six parts of the oxalate, and it is advisable to add to each ounce of developer at least half a grain of potassium bromide; 5 minims of a 10% solution, made by dissolving one ounce of the bromide in about 9 ounces of water, and then making up to 10 ounces—all chemical.

In about four minutes or less this ought to fully develop a properly exposed plate. If the development is much shorter the slide is apt to have an unpleasant greenish tone, a result that may also follow the use of an inordinate amount of bromide in the developer. The developing solution may be made in quantity greater than is required for one plate, and may be used several times if a little of the surplus and fresh solution is added when the quantity in use becomes slow in action.

For really fine cold black tones the following formula by Messrs. Elliott & Son will be found admirable:—

<pre>
                    A
     Metol .... 40 grains.
     Soda sulphite .... 1 ounce.
     Water .... 8 ounces.
                    B
     Potassium carbonate .... 120 grains.
     Ammonium bromide 24   ,,
     Potassium bromide 48   ,,
     Water .... 8 ounces.
</pre>

The developing solution consists of equal parts of A and B.

If either of the above developers is to be used, the exposure is to be kept down as compared with the exposure to be followed by developers intended for very warm tones.

The two developers which follow next, require about the same exposure as the two already formulated. "Ortol" is a reducing agent quite lately introduced by Mr. Hauff, of Feuerbach in Germany, and Mr. Hauff's agents in this country are Messrs. Fuerst Bros., of London. "Ortol" gives the finest tones of the warm black type that we have as yet come across, it is singularly free from fogging propensity, and the tones do not easily degenerate into the greens so apt to occur after severe over-exposure with other "black" developers. We suggest a simple formula :—

A

Water	20 ounces.
Metabisulphite of potassium	75 grains.
Ortol	150 grains.

B

Water	20 ounces.
Soda carbonate	3½ ounces.
Soda sulphite	2½ ounces.

To make the developer, take one part of A, one of B, and one of water, and to each ounce of the mixture add one and a half or two grains of potassium bromide. The development of a properly exposed slide will take two or three minutes, and the result will probably be highly appreciated.

The above is worthy to stand alone as representing developers for warm black tones, but the following works well. (Messrs. Elliott & Son.)

A

Hydroquinone	80 grains.
Soda sulphite	1 ounce.
Potassium bromide	15 grains.
Water	10 ounces.

B

Caustic soda	80 grains.
Water	10 ozs.

The developing solution consists of equal parts of A and B, and the plate may be fully developed in about two to three minutes.

It has already been stated that in order to obtain really warm red or reddish tones by development, it is necessary to give very long exposure, and to use a developer very much restrained. It is further found that carbonate of ammonia has a considerable effect in reddening the developed image, and so we now come to procedure based on these lines. Carbonate of ammonia is found in commerce in the shape of " chunks " more or less square. If one of these is pared with a knife—unless the sample is quite fresh—the outside will be found to be a soft amorphous powder, the inside a clear, very hard crystal; the clear crystal is in development an "accelerator," though a very weak one, the outside substance is a restrainer. Probably both the inside—sesquicarbonate—and the outside—bicarbonate—are useful, and the best plan is to make a ten per cent. solution of the substance as obtained from a good chemist—not druggist. Of this solution one grain of the salt is represented by ten minims. If now we take an ounce of A, and one of B of the last formula, and if we add to the ounce of A 3 grains of ammonium bromide, and to the ounce of B 3 grains of ammonium carbonate, and if we have given a proper exposure and develop with equal parts of the A and B modified as above, we shall get a slide of rich chocolate colour; and if we double the proportions of carbonate and bromide, and expose still longer, we shall get a slide still ruddier in tone, even to red. But there is always danger of fog, and of clogged shadows, and this must be reckoned with. There is a more certain and less dangerous way of getting handsome tones, which shall be described presently.

Gelatine slides are always fixed in hyposulphite of soda, about one part by weight to six parts of water ; after this they must be well washed, say five minutes under a good rose tap, or in many changes of water in a dish for an hour, and every slide should be treated with a saturated solution of potash alum, of which each pint should contain a dram of hydrochloric acid.

Very many, if not most, slides are all the better for just a touch of a "reducer" such as follows:—The ordinary "hypo." solution is weakened with about four times its measure of water, and the plate is soaked for a minute in this. A few drops of a ten per cent. solution of potassium ferricyanide are put into the measure, and the hypo. mixed with it, and the whole allowed to work on the plate for a short time, carefully watched. Of course a weak slide must not be thus treated, but it is often a good plan to develop slides to such a point that they will permit of this treatment.

On the other hand it is often advisable to keep a slide thin in development, for instance, when the negative wants pluck, and intensification is indicated; or when we wish a good warm tone after a "black" developer such as our metol formula: a good average treatment is as follows:—

Take half an ounce each of ammonium chloride and mercury bichloride and dissolve in 16 ounces of water, soak the slide in this till it is bleached. Wash well and treat with weak liquid ammonia, or a solution of soda sulphite, or of metabisulphite of potass, or fresh lime water. This will strengthen the slide and give it in most cases a fine rich colour. It is important to let these solutions act thoroughly, and not to stop the action half-way. The writer considers this the best and safest way to obtain warm tones, the reader may find out for himself which of these solutions produces the tones he chiefly affects,

L

Crystal varnish is *not* wasted even on a gelatine slide.

In conclusion, it must be realized that the screen-image is a greatly enlarged edition of the slide-image; any small defect on the slide is a huge one on the screen. Consequently the slide-maker must sedulously cultivate cleanliness and manipulative care.

Andrew Pringle.

Fishing Smacks.   W. Thomas.

How to make Enlargements.

ENLARGEMENTS may be made by daylight, or by artificial light, and there are two methods of producing them, namely, by enlarging direct from the negative on to a sheet of bromide paper; or by first making a small transparency, and from that producing an enlarged negative upon a slow dry plate. The first is the method usually adopted by amateurs, probably because the necessary operations are fewer, and perhaps more simple. The second plan, however, possesses the advantage that the prints may be made by any process, be it carbon, platinum, or silver, and thus a great variety of effect obtained.

The first point however that the reader must decide is whether he will work by artificial light or by daylight. Each may be said to possess certain advantages, and with many the question resolves itself into one of personal convenience. Artificial light is, or should be, fairly constant in intensity, and if adopted there will probably be less waste of material through miscalculation of exposure. But if the source of light employed be other than a mixed jet, or the arc-light, if in fact it be of low intensity, negatives of a somewhat delicate type will be required in order to produce enlargements of the highest excellence. If the negatives are dense and strong, illuminants of low intensity, like oil or gas, do not possess sufficient penetration to duly register the denser portions of the negative, and the enlargements so made are apt to be deficient in half-tone, and hard. With well-graded negatives of suitable quality, however, most excellent enlargements may be produced by artificial light. When artificial light is used work may be carried on at any time of day or night, in winter or summer. Those who adopt the daylight plan will, of course, be subjected to greater restrictions, at any rate, during the winter months, but amateurs who take a real interest in the work will do well to adopt the writer's plan, and provide themselves with apparatus for each method of working.

ENLARGING BY DAYLIGHT.

There are two ways of enlarging by daylight. The first involves the exclusion of all actinic light from a room except that which passes through the negative. The alternative method of working is to employ an ordinary enlarging camera, such as are made by Middlemiss, or Lancaster. It is desirable, but not necessary, if the first plan be adopted, to secure the exclusive use of a room. One with a northerly aspect should be chosen, for if sunlight falls upon the window shadows will at some period of the day fall upon the negative, and produce unevenly lighted enlargements.

An upper room will be most suitable, and, if the light be a northern one, and there are no trees or buildings to obstruct the view, a reflector may be dispensed with. If external objects intervene, however, one must be employed. It should be fixed outside the window-sill, at an angle of 45°, and should be capable of adjustment. Let it be *the full width of the window*, and *securely fixed* for obvious reasons. A plate-glass mirror is effective, but expensive. A large drawing board painted dead white also answers well, but should not be left outside exposed to the weather.

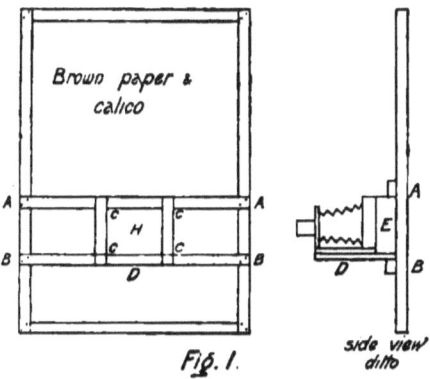

Fig. 1.

Provision for excluding the light from the room is best secured by making a wooden frame large enough to fit closely against the window frame. Upon this a piece of stout calico should be tightly strained and secured with tacks. It should then be sized, and when dry will be as tight as a drum; it must then be covered with two thicknesses of stout brown paper pasted on. The frame is shown complete in Fig. 1. Now at A.A. B.B. screw two strips of wood, the distance apart must be regulated by the size of the negatives to be enlarged. The ordinary camera is intended to be used as the enlarging camera, and the distance from C. to C. should be just equal to the size of the back portion of the camera. On the lower rail BB. screw a piece of 9 in. board to form a shelf or support D. for the enlarging camera. Make a frame E. of ½ in. wood 1 in. deep, the same size as the back of the camera, and screw to the shelf and top rail AA. Now carefully cut away the brown paper and calico from the inside of this frame, at the part marked H. and paste strips of brown paper round it so as to prevent any light passing except through the opening H. A strip of felt should be tacked all round the large frame to prevent any light from

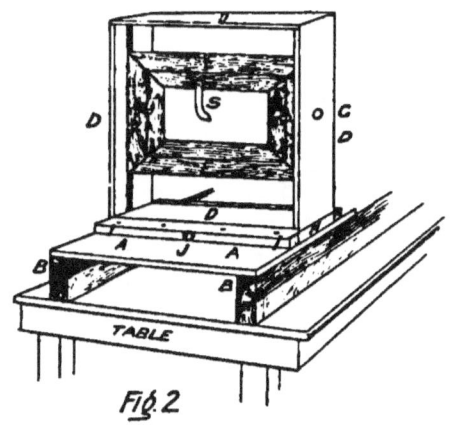

Fig. 2

creeping in between it and the window frame. A couple of turn buttons will keep it in position. A *firm* table should be placed against the window close up to the wall to form a support for the enlarging easel. Now a little care must be taken in fitting up this portion of the apparatus, and it is better to have something more exact than the propped-up drawing board or printing frame, which is sometimes recommended. Get a carpenter to run out two V shaped rails as shown in Fig. 2 at CC. They should be about the length of the table, and screwed down upon it. Procure a cheap drawing board about 15 × 12, and to the under side affix two pieces of wood with V shaped grooves corresponding in angle to the rails. This forms the base of the easel AA. Make a frame 22 × 20, or rather larger than the biggest enlargement that it is desired to produce. It should be constructed of ½ in. wood, and be 2 in. deep. It is shown in Fig. 2 at 1 DDDD. Now make, or get made, a set of carriers EE, the largest of which should just fit into the frame. Narrow fillets of wood screwed each side will afford a rise and fall adjustment, and a thumb screw at G will fix the carrier in any desired position. To obtain the cross-movement screw the frame DDDD to a piece of inch board 5 in. wide HH. Place this exactly in the centre of the base board, and screw fillets II of 1 in. wood to each side. This will afford a cross motion, and a thumb screw at J will fix the carrier frame when the necessary adjustment has been made.

In setting up an enlarging apparatus, whether it be for day or artificial light, it is absolutely essential to preserve the parallelism of its various parts, otherwise it will be impossible to produce sharp or evenly defined enlargements, and for this reason I have described somewhat fully the construction of a suitable easel. I may add that it will serve equally well for either daylight or artificial illumination, and I strongly advise the reader to construct, or have constructed, an easel on the lines I have laid down. With it either direct enlargements on paper can be produced, or plates may be used and enlarged negatives made. The easiest way of holding the paper during exposure is to procure two sheets of clear glass, patent plate is most suitable, sandwich the bromide paper between them, and secure with two strong bands of elastic. The complete apparatus in position for working is shown at Fig. 3.

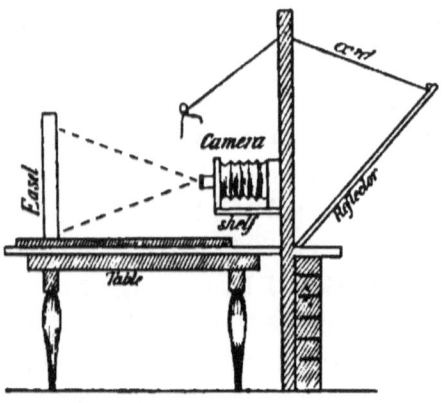

Fig. 3.

The second method of enlarging by daylight is by employing an ordinary enlarging camera. The same conditions as to lighting, etc., should be sought for, and the most convenient way of working will be to tilt the

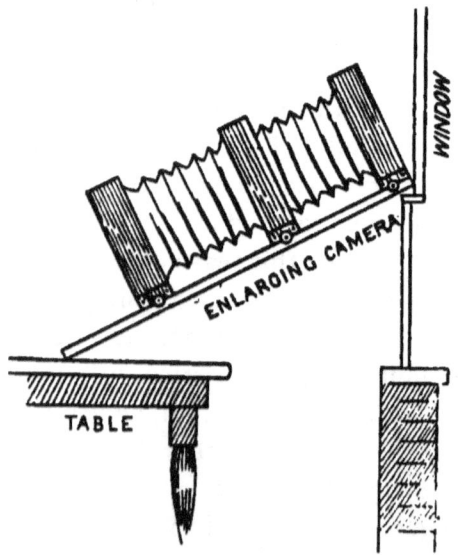

Fig. 4.

camera at such an angle as that the negative receives unobstructed illumination from the sky. A reflector in this case will not be necessary, but a piece of very finely ground glass should be placed about an inch in front of the negative in order to soften and diffuse the light. This method of working is shown in Fig. 4.

ENLARGING BY ARTIFICIAL LIGHT.

Before describing the actual process of making an enlargement it will be well to deal with the alternative method of working, namely, by artificial light, as the manipulations of the sensitive material used are the same in either case. Practically the most satisfactory way of working by the latter method is to use an enlarging lantern properly fitted with a condenser. The general principles of such an apparatus are identical with those which obtain in an ordinary optical lantern. Methods which dispense with the use of a condenser are more or less unsatisfactory, and should be avoided. In the space at the disposal of the writer it is not possible to give directions for the construction of an enlarging lantern, but those

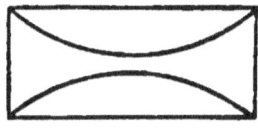

Fig. 5.

who may desire to make their own, will find full instructions and working drawings in " *Practical Enlarging."

Enlarging lanterns of excellent quality are obtainable commercially, but for the guidance of the uninitiated it may be useful to refer a little in detail to one or two important points with regard to their construction. The condenser will first claim attention. The ordinary pattern consists of two plano-convex lenses mounted as shown in section at Fig. 5. This answers fairly well with the smaller sizes, but when the diameter

* Iliffe & Son.

of the condenser is large, a good deal of light may be lost. The interposition of a small meniscus or plano-convex lens, in the manner first suggested by the late J. Traill Taylor, and shown in Fig. 6, will be found a great improvement. Its proper position will be at the point where the divergent cone of rays proceeding from it just covers the large condenser. In our own practice we always place a diffusing screen of very finely ground-glass in front of the condenser at E.E. The diameter of the condenser is governed by the size of the negatives to be enlarged, it must be of sufficient size to include the longer sides of the plate within its circumference without cutting the corners. If it is much larger than this, an unnecessary loss of light will occur, because only that which passes through the negative can be utilized.

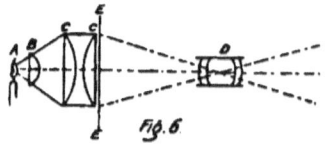

Fig. 6

THE ILLUMINANT.

The smaller and more intense the light, the nearer we approach to the ideal projection illuminant, and the better will be the definition of our enlargements. The arc light most nearly fulfils the desired conditions, and if it be available it should certainly be employed. Next in point of utility comes the limelight, preferably in the form of the mixed jet, and those who understand its manipulation are recommended to adopt it, but the majority of amateurs will probably find it more convenient to use either incandescent gaslight or an oil-lamp. Parallel wick-lamps should be avoided on account of the unequal illumination they produce, and if oil must be used a good circular wick burner will be found more suitable. Where house-gas is available the incandescent gaslight is however much to be preferred. The light is perhaps not so powerful as that given by a really good parallel wick-lamp, but it is far more actinic and penetrating. The writer has used this light with great satisfaction, and therefore has no hesitation in recommending it. Some workers have been troubled by the appearance of an image of the mantle on the screen, but this can usually be got rid of by a suitable adjustment of the lenses and the light, and in any case by the interposition of a piece of ground glass between condenser and negative.

THE CHOICE OF THE LENS.

It is commonly stated that the lens with which the original negative was taken will serve equally well to enlarge it, and in the abstract the statement is perhaps not inaccurate. But assuming that a lens of a focus equal to about $1\frac{1}{4}$ times the base of the plate has been used, it will be found that better results, both in regard to definition and equality of illumination, will be obtained by substituting a lens of rather longer focus, for example a half-plate lens for enlarging from quarter-plate negatives. This, although applying to both methods of working is particularly desirable when enlarging by artificial light, for an objective of small diameter and short focus cannot possibly pick up or receive the whole of the cone of rays proceeding from the condenser. A reference to Figs. 7 and 8 will explain why this is so. In Fig. 7 we see what happens when a lens of too short a focus is used, but when one of longer focus is substituted, the whole of the cone of rays passes through and is utilized (Fig. 8). In selecting a lens one should be chosen which has a sufficiently large diameter to permit the apex of the cone of rays from the condenser to pass through. This point will, of course, vary with the degree of amplification, and in order to obtain the best results optically, the distance of the light from the condenser must be carefully adjusted in every case, and a clear, evenly lighted disc obtained before inserting the negative to be enlarged.

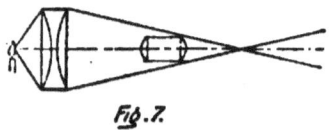

Fig. 7.

With regard to the type of lens, one of the rapid rectilinear form will answer well. A portrait lens is often used on account of the brilliancy of image, but although it answers well for enlarging portraits, the roundness of its field makes it less suitable for landscapes unless it is considerably stopped down. If the very finest results as regards definition are required,

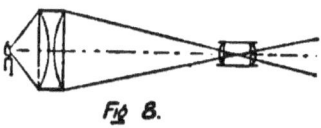

Fig 8.

then one of the now numerous flat-field lenses should be used. The writer can from practical experience speak well of the Ross-Goerz and the Cooke lens. The latter is perhaps preferable for working with artificial light on account of the larger diameter of the back lens. Wide-angle lenses, on account of their small aperture and short focus, are not suitable for use with a condenser, both for the reasons given, and on account of the difficulty in focussing owing to the small amount of light transmitted. When daylight is used, however, there is less objection to their employment.

Before leaving this part of the subject it should be noted that in regard to preserving the parallelism of its parts the same care in erecting and fitting up the enlarging lantern must be observed, as was insisted upon in the description of the apparatus for daylight. It will be found convenient, therefore, to mount the lantern on a

Fig. 9.

base similar to that upon which the easel rests, so that both may move on the same rails. The easel described for daylight enlarging will serve equally well for working by artificial light. The complete apparatus is shown at Fig. 9, which is a reproduction from a photograph of the apparatus constructed and used by the writer.

THE NEGATIVE.

In general practice one may find it necessary at times to enlarge from negatives of very dissimilar types, but there is no reason, when the negatives are to be produced with the special object of subsequently making enlargements from them, why care should not be taken to make them of a suitable character. Thin delicate negatives should be enlarged by artificial light; dense, strong ones by daylight. If the negatives are very strong it will be difficult to produce soft and well-graded enlargements with a weak illuminant, the light not being sufficiently intense to properly penetrate the high-lights. A soft and clear negative, with good gradation, fully exposed, and neither exhibiting patches of clear glass shadow devoid of detail, nor of hard impenetrable high-light, will be found most suitable. Fog should be avoided, as also should the yellow stain produced by pyro when improperly used. Not that the pyro developer is unsuitable, for if sufficient sulphite is used, and the quantity of pyro kept down, negatives of very beautiful quality for enlarging purposes may be produced. Great care should be taken to avoid bubbles, stains, scratches, or any kind of mechanical defects, as such when enlarged become painfully obtrusive, and spoil the effect of the best work. It will be found a good plan to bind the edge of the negative before enlarging it with a strip of lantern slide binding, so as to cover the clear glass rebate mark. If this be omitted the margins of the enlargement may become fogged by the lateral spreading action of the light. No hand-work should be attempted on the original negative, for any such treatment will become painfully apparent in the enlargement. If retouching be deemed necessary, it should in the case of a direct enlargement be executed upon the print itself, or upon the enlarged negative or preferably upon the enlarged transparency, when that method of reproduction has been adopted.

DIRECT ENLARGEMENTS.

The following concise instructions for enlarging upon bromide paper will apply equally to the daylight or artificial light methods of working. In the first case the negative is placed in the dark slide of the camera, both shutters being drawn fully out. The camera is then put upon the shelf close up against the opening in the shutter, as shown in Fig. 3, any light creeping in between shutter and camera being blocked out with the focussing cloth. If the enlarging lantern is used the negative will be placed in the carrier, just in the same way as a lantern slide, with the film side towards the enlarging lens. Now the first difficulty that will be experienced will be to get the enlarged image of the required size. It will be well to content ourselves at the outset with a moderate degree of enlargement, say from $\frac{1}{4}$ plate to 12 × 10, and when proficiency is acquired, larger sizes can be attempted. At first we shall probably not succeed in getting any image at all. In adjusting the various parts of the apparatus we shall find the work easier if we remember that the nearer we place the lens to the negative the further will it be necessary to move the easel from the lens, and the greater will be the enlargement. A useful table of enlargements will be found in the "British Journal Almanac," showing the distance of lens from negative, and negative from paper, for almost any required degree of amplification.

Now it will be found much easier to focus the enlarged image by looking at it through a piece of finely ground glass, than by receiving it on a piece of card or paper, and the adoption of the easel plan of focussing previously described will enable this to be done. The ground surface of the glass (which must be of the same thickness as the piece behind which the paper is to be exposed) should be away from the lens and towards the person focussing, when it is placed in the carrier of the easel, it being retained in position with the spring S., Fig. 2. Focussing must be carefully performed, and is effected by sliding the easel to and fro upon the runners, and which should have been previously rubbed with blacklead.

Bromide paper is made in several varieties, such as smooth, rough, snow-enamel, cream crayon, etc., and is put up either in tubes, or packed flat. The latter is decidedly the more convenient, it being somewhat difficult to take the curl out of paper that has been rolled. The choice of paper is a matter of taste; for landscape work the rough paper or the cream crayon will perhaps be found most suitable. For finer work, and some classes of portraiture the enamel will prove effective. Rough paper is better for strong broad effects, smooth for more delicate work and the rendering of fine detail. The coated side may be distinguished by its tendency to curl inwards. The easiest way of exposing it is to procure two pieces of patent plate glass of the same thickness as the focussing glass, sandwich the sheet of paper between the two, and secure with strong elastic bands. This will hold it quite flat during exposure, and will not disturb the actinism of the lens or impair the definition of the enlargement.

DEVELOPMENT.

This part of the work of producing an enlargement will only be lightly dealt with, as the subject is fully treated elsewhere in this volume. The writer prefers the ferrous-oxalate developer for bromide enlargements to any of the more recently introduced developers, but as it requires more skill and judgment to employ it with complete success, beginners may find it better to use amidol or metol, either of which when

DRIFTING STORM CLOUDS.
W. THOMAS

properly used gives excellent results. Hydrokinone we do not recommend for this purpose owing to its tendency to give rusty blacks in the event of over-exposure, or undue hardness if it has been too short. With amidol a pure delicate black is easily obtainable, and it is moreover a very simple developer to use. Our own plan is to employ a weak solution and give a full exposure, and by these means we find no difficulty in obtaining good gradation and pure blacks. The dish used for development must not be used for other developers or stains will probably occur. Although a quick appearance of the image is usually a characteristic of amidol, no trouble will be experienced when the developer is used in the way we advise, for the picture will be found to develop slowly and regularly, and gradually grow in strength. Quick development by this method would be an indication of over-exposure. A correctly exposed enlargement should take about ten minutes to develop. One stock solution only is necessary. It will keep indefinitely.

Sulphite of soda	1 ounce.
Citric acid	20 grains.
Distilled water	40 ounces.
Potassium bromide	15 grains.

To each ounce of the above add, just before using, three grains of dry amidol. The exposure must be accurately timed. It is, however, impossible to give useful information on this head, unless such varying factors as the rapidity of the paper, the intensity of the light, the aperture of the lens, and the degree of enlargement are known. The best plan is to cut one of the sheets of bromide paper into twelve strips, and on these make several test exposures, carefully noting the duration of each. It is better (at any rate for a beginner) not to vary the constituents or strength of the developer, but to increase or diminish the exposure until a good result in colour and tonality is obtained. By entering full details relating to the production of a successful enlargement in a notebook, great exactitude in working will be obtained, and there need be little or no waste of material when additional enlargements have to be made from the same negatives at a future time.

A glass dish, though expensive, is very suitable for developing, for being flat-bottomed a minimum of solution can be used, and moreover if the dish should be dirty, the fact is at once apparent. The exposed paper should be soaked in water for a few minutes until uniformly wetted, and any air-bells removed with a camel-hair brush. The water is then poured off, and the developer applied in an even wave, so that the whole of the paper is covered uniformly and quickly. The image will appear slowly, and gradually gain in detail. When all the detail has appeared it may still appear lacking in vigour and contrast, but this will come if sufficient time be allowed. *Development should not be stopped until the print is of the full strength required*, but it is not advisable to allow it to become much darker than it is desired to appear when finished, because there is very little loss of strength in the fixing bath.

If the image flashes out immediately upon the application of the developer, the paper has been over-exposed. A strong dose (one or two drams) of ten per cent. bromide added to the developer may help to save it, but the enlargement will probably look poor and flat and of bad colour when finished. If the picture appears very slowly, and refuses to gain in strength, under-exposure is the cause, and two or three drams of a ten per cent. solution of sulphite of soda may improve matters, but as a rule the most satisfactory plan will be to make another exposure. With regard to the strength of the developer, that given is very suitable for negatives of normal density, but some papers may require a little more amidol, the appearance of the finished enlargements will guide the reader in regulating the quantity to suit the particular paper with which he may be working. The enlargement should be washed in plenty of running water from the tap to arrest development, and then fixed in :—

> Hyposulphite of soda .... 4 ounces.
> Water .... 20 ,,

A quarter of an hour should be allowed for fixation, but it is better to use two baths, giving ten minutes in each. After washing in running water for a couple of hours they may be hung up by one corner to dry, or pinned down to a blotting board.

Enlargements produced in the manner described should be of a pure engraving black colour, and if they are mounted upon *pure* boards with *freshly* made Glenfield starch, they should prove permanent. Enlargements are frequently toned to various shades of brown and red, generally by the employment of the uranium-toning bath. Although the colours so obtained are often very artistic and pleasing, no reliance can be placed upon the permanence of an enlargement so treated, and the writer strongly recommends that when warm coloured prints are desired, an enlarged negative should be made and prints made therefrom in carbon, silver, or sepia platinotype.

ENLARGED NEGATIVES.

The production of an enlarged negative presents no difficulty that need deter any careful worker from attempting the work. No additional apparatus to that already described will be required, and either day or artificial light may be employed. In the first place a transparency must be made from the small original negative. It may be made either by contact or in the camera, preferably the latter as then the acme of sharpness will be obtained. If, however, the reader is acquainted with the carbon process he cannot do better than make a carbon transparency, for such are specially adapted for the production of enlarged negatives. Many, however, will prefer to make the transparency on a bromide plate, and as this is the part of the process which requires the greatest amount of care, and as *in fact* the *quality of the enlarged negative will entirely depend upon the character of the small transparency*, it is necessary to deal with the matter somewhat in detail. Preconceived ideas of quality based upon the appearance of a good lantern slide must be put aside, for that is not at all what is required. What is wanted is a transparency in which every possible detail existing in the negative has been reproduced, and which in comparison with a lantern slide would look rather flat and over-exposed. Every possible precaution should be taken to avoid granularity or coarseness of image, therefore a slow plate is almost essential; plates coated with lantern-slide emulsion are now obtainable, and will be found very suitable. A full exposure should be given, and a weak and well-restrained developer employed. These conditions tend to the production of the qualities desired. Warm coloured transparencies so produced generally have a finer grain than those developed to a black or colder colour, but unless the colours produced are fairly uniform, considerable variation in exposure when making the enlarged negatives will be necessary, and for this reason it would perhaps be better for the beginner to aim at the production of good black transparencies possessing the qualities indicated.

The small transparency, having been fixed, washed and dried, should be edged with black paper to prevent any subsequent fogging of the plate, by the lateral spreading action of the light. It is then placed in the enlarging apparatus, just as in the case of a negative, and carefully focussed. This operation must be very carefully performed. The writer uses a thin and very sharp negative of an architectural subject to focus with, afterwards substituting the transparency which is to be enlarged. Landscape subjects, consisting chiefly of foliage, are seldom critically sharp, and it is then difficult to secure a sharply-focussed enlargement. The remainder of the operation is extremely simple. In the place of the ground-glass screen (which in this case should have its rough or ground side nearest to the enlarging lens) a slow dry plate is placed, backed with a piece of cardboard covered with black velvet to avoid reflections and possible fog. The exposure should be full, and a weak developer employed. Trial exposures may be made on quarter-plates, coated from the same batch of emulsion, which the manufacturers will willingly supply, if the purpose for which they are required is made known. Pyro will be found the most suitable developer, but it should contain a full proportion of sulphite, and not be too strong. Exposure and development should be so adjusted that by the time every possible detail has been developed up, the plate will not have become unduly dense. If expense has to be considered, a piece of slow smooth bromide paper may be substituted for the large dry plate in which case the result will be an enlarged paper negative. For large sizes, 15×12 and beyond, the latter is a very economical method of working, and the negatives will be found to yield most artistic prints, and if the operations have been carried out as described, and the prescribed conditions carefully observed, the grain of the paper will not show obtrusively or unpleasantly in the prints.

An alternative method of working, and one which admits of a large amount of control over the ultimate result, is to make in the first place a large transparency of the full size that the enlarged negative is desired to be. All the precautions upon which stress has been laid should be observed in regard to the choice of plate, developer, etc.; but in this case the enlarged transparency may be given a little more vigour and sparkle than would be desirable if the other method of reproduction were adopted, though in this the reader must be guided by the particular effect which he may be seeking to produce in his prints. For this purpose pyro will be found to be the most suitable developer, in that it permits of a large amount of control. From the large transparency a negative is produced by contact printing either upon a plate, or upon a piece of bromide paper.

The great advantages of the latter mode of working are the facilities which are afforded for retouching or working upon the large transparency. Negative retouching is always a difficult operation to an amateur, for he cannot see the effect of his work until he has made a print; whereas, in retouching a transparency the effect produced by each stroke of the pencil or brush is at once apparent. In the space at disposal it is not possible to describe the various ways in which improvements can be effected. First there are the chemical aids of local intensification or reduction. Then much may be done by the judicious use of a pencil, but the part to be retouched must first be lightly rubbed with a little retouching medium in order to make the pencil bite. In extreme cases the back of the negative may be covered with tissue paper upon which a stump and chalk may be used *at discretion*.

The novice must not be disappointed with the appearance of his enlarged negative when it is finished, nor should he form an adverse opinion of its printing qualities until he has made a print from it. Confessedly an enlarged negative generally presents a different appearance to one that has been taken direct, and may even seem to lack some of those qualities that are commonly regarded as essential to perfection, but if the final result, the picture, comes up to our expectations, we may surely dismiss any lingering doubts as to whether the enlarged negative conforms to certain preconceived notions of technique, and it should be enough for us to know (and the fact is incontrovertible) that some of the finest and most artistic photographs ever shown owe their existence to this method of production.

John A. Hodges.

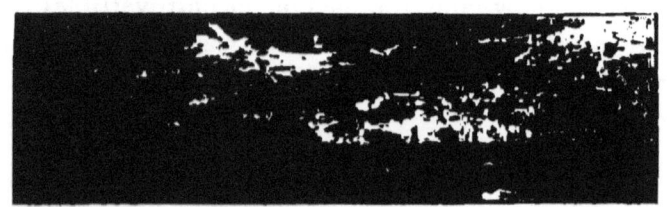

Walberswick. By Rev. A. H. Blake.

P.O.P.

THE three letters "P.O.P." are now so widely understood as referring to the Gelatino-Chloride Printing-Out class of Papers that it may be said that P.O.P. is known to many who are not acquainted with the fully-written name of this class of productions.

Also it should be mentioned that when these papers are spoken of as gelatino-chloride papers it is not to be concluded therefrom that chloride of silver is the only silver salt present. What they do actually contain is probably only known to their respective producers. But generally speaking, it is enough to say that so far as the ordinary consumer is concerned, the family resemblance is so strong and chief characteristics so general that the following directions for using them may be held as generally applicable to the various well-known brands now on the market. At the outset, however, it will be convenient to note that for the purposes of manipulation we may roughly group them into two chief classes—*viz.*, the matt (probably from the German word "matt," *i.e.*, dull) and the glazed, glossy or enamelled. The latter comes to us with a highly glazed, *i.e.*, shiny smooth surface, the former being slightly rough, of a surface and texture somewhat like that of very finely ground glass.

Care of the Paper.—The paper is sent out either in the full-sized sheet, measuring about 24×17 inches, or in smaller cut sizes, suitable for the usual $\frac{1}{4}$, $\frac{1}{2}$, $\frac{1}{1}$ plate and other popular dimensions of plates. Compared with albumenized print-out paper, P.O.P. is more sensitive to light; therefore, some care must be taken to avoid needlessly exposing it to the influence of daylight or strong artificial light. For example, the printing frames should be filled as far away from any window as possible, and the prints examined from time to time either by gaslight or as feeble daylight as possible.

In handling the paper—cutting it up, etc.—care must be taken to avoid touching the sensitive surface with the fingers in any case. The touch of a moist or hot finger is very likely to produce a mark or stain which is usually irremovable. The paper should be protected from damp, excessive heat and impure air. If kept *rolled* in a tin tube or *flat* under pressure in the original packages, it will keep a considerable time—*i.e.*, longer than ordinary albumenized paper.

Printing is done in the usual way. Strong diffused light reflected from the sky or clouds usually gives a better print than direct sunshine. In case, however, of a thin flat negative—*i.e.*, one with insufficient contrast—good results may sometimes be obtained by covering the printing frame with a sheet of green glass and printing in moderately strong sunshine. In hot summer sunshine it is as well to cover the green glass with a sheet of tissue paper or fine-ground glass. Care must be always taken when printing in sunshine or very hot weather to see that the negative itself does not get too warm, or the paper may stick to it. In this case the print is of course lost, and the negative, unless varnished, is also probably seriously damaged by silver stains, which are very difficult to remove. Printing should not be carried quite so far as in the case of ordinary albumenized paper because in the subsequent operations of toning, etc., not so much strength is lost. The same care as regards shielding from light, etc., should be given to the prints after they leave the printing frame. They may be procceded with at once or kept for some days before being toned, etc., but if this is done the prints should be kept under pressure. Some workers have thought that the light action goes on, "continues" in the print after it is removed from the printing frame. This, however, is not the generally received opinion.

Washing.—It is important that the first washing should be done with some care, or the prints may become stained. The points calling for attention are (1) running water and plenty of it, (2) care to see that the prints do not stick together. What is needed is that the soluble salts should be washed out of the paper as quickly as possible, and that the prints be not allowed to remain in the water containing these soluble salts longer than is necessary. Hence the advantage of running water and plenty of it. The washing water must not be too cold or the salts will not pass out of the paper quickly enough; and again, it must not be too warm or the gelatine will melt. The best temperature is about 65°F., and the limits should not go beyond 60° and 70°F., and preferably are kept within 60° and 65°F. As the paper is usually rather stout, it will need washing in running or constantly changed water for about ten to fifteen minutes, and in any case must be continued until all milky appearance of the water ceases. The print at this stage has a red-brown colour. If it is now passed direct into the fixing bath without toning it becomes somewhat more yellow, and when dry is usually a colour somewhat between yellow ochre and sienna.

Toning is usually our next operation, and for this purpose we have a variety of toning baths recommended by different workers. The sulphocyanide and gold is perhaps the chief favourite.

1. Ammonium sulphocyanide .... 10 to 15 grains.
   Gold chloride .... 1 grain.
   Water........................ 8 to 10 ounces.

The proper way to mix this bath is to add the gold to the solution of sulphocyanide a little at a time. The following method will be found convenient. As ammonium sulphocyanide is somewhat deliquescent, it is convenient to keep it in solution. Therefore, one ounce of the salt dissolved in twenty ounces of (distilled or filtered rain) water gives us roughly a strength of twenty-two grains per ounce. Dissolve the contents of a fifteen-grain chloride of gold in fifteen drams of distilled water. To mix a bath, take of the sulphocyanide solution half-an ounce; to this add eight ounces of water. Now take one dram of the gold solution and dilute with one ounce of water. Then add this dilute gold solution a *little* at a time to the eight ounces of sulphocyanide solution, and stir well with a glass rod. It will be noticed that as the gold solution drops into the sulphocyanide solution an orange-red precipitate is formed, which is redissolved on stirring. Hence the gold must be added to the sulphocyanide, and not *vice versa*.

2. Another favourite bath is as follows :—

Ammonium sulphocyanide	22 grains.
Soda sulphite	2 ,,
Gold chloride	2 ,,
Water	20 to 25 ounces.

Instead of weighing out two grains of sulphite it is more convenient to weigh twenty grains and dissolve in two-and-a-half ounces of water—*i.e.*, at the rate of one grain per dram of solution. Thus, to mix this bath, take an ounce of the above-mentioned sulphocyanide solution dilute with twenty ounces water. To this add two drams ($\frac{1}{4}$ oz.) of the sulphite solution. Then take two drams of the gold chloride solution and dilute with an ounce of water, and add slowly with stirring as before.

3. Another favourite bath is :—

Sodium chloride (table salt)....	60 grains.
Ammonium sulphocyanide	15 ,,
Gold chloride	2 ,,
Water	10 to 12 ounces.

Some of the adherents of this bath recommend that the prints be only washed in running water for a few minutes and then put into the toning bath. Others advise the prints to be immersed in the toning bath without any previous washing—*i.e.*, straight from the printing frame.

4. Here, again, is another bath which usually yields excellent results :—

Soda phosphate...................	5 grains.
Sodium chloride (table salt)	20 ,,
Gold chloride.....................	1 grain.
Water	10 ounces.

5. Other workers omit the sodium chloride and increase the phosphate and get good tones.

Soda phosphate...................	20 grains.
Gold chloride.....................	1 grain.
Water	10 ounces.

6. Others, again, combine the phosphate and sulphocyanide baths thus:—

Sodium phosphate	10 grains.
Ammonium sulphocyanide	15 ,,
Gold	1 ,,
Water	10 ounces.

The various toning baths mentioned above have one drawback common to them all in varying degrees—*viz.*, that when once mixed and used they do not keep in good working order longer than a few hours.

7. The following bath claims to have the advantage that it will keep in working order for a short time at any rate, but the disadvantage that it cannot be used until it has been mixed twelve to twenty-four hours.

Soda acetate	60 grains.
Ammonium sulphocyanide	20 ,,
Gold chloride	1 grain.
Water	12 ounces.

Toning should be conducted in very weak daylight, or what is much better, gas or lamplight. The latter, being practically constant, enables the operator to judge the relative colour of the prints from time to time. Care must be taken so that the prints do not stick together in the toning bath, and preferably only a few, say half-a-dozen or so, dealt with at a time, so that each print can be frequently turned over and examined. The change of colours proceeds somewhat slowly at first, but when once it begins it seems to gain in rapidity of rate of change, so that a careful watch must be kept. Let it be remembered that the print, after fixing and drying, will appear a little darker and more blue (less red) than when wet in the toning bath. The temperature of the bath must not be too cold or toning is very slow, nor too warm or the gelatine may melt and toning be uneven. From 60° to 65°F. will be found a convenient range. The prints should not be touched on their printed surface more than can be helped. The fingers must be quite clean, the solutions uncontaminated with other chemicals, and a dish set apart for toning operations only. This dish should always be washed out well with tepid or cold water before and after use, and when put away should rest flat, opening downwards, on a shelf covered with a sheet of clean blotting paper. Many failures in toning are entirely due to lack of care in details and sufficient attention to cleanliness.

When toning is judged to be carried far enough, the prints should be placed in a roomy dish containing a solution of common salt, strength one ounce to twenty or thirty ounces of water, to stop further toning.

Fixing is done with a "one in ten" solution of sodium thiosulphite—*i.e.*, hypo. This should be prepared with tepid water, or some time before use, as the dissolving of hypo in water is accompanied by a fall of temperature. A convenient method is to place a couple of ounces of hypo in a clean pint jug, and add about half a pint of fairly warm water and stir with a glass rod until the salt is dissolved, then fill up the jug from the tap with cold water. It is highly desirable to have plenty of fixing solution, and never attempt to use the same lot twice. Place each print face down in the bath and submerge by pressing on its back. Again see that the prints do not stick to each other, and turn each print two or three times. They should be in the fixing bath not less than twelve or fifteen minutes, and a few minutes longer will do no harm. At the end of, say, fifteen minutes, pour away about one half of the fixing bath and slowly fill up with water. Turn the prints again, and then transfer them one by one to another roomy dish and wash in running water for a couple of hours, or in a dozen changes of water every five or ten minutes. Then hang up to dry, using either clips or pin a corner to the edge of a wooden shelf or long lath suspended in a cool, airy place.

Alum Bath.—Hot weather considerably increases the danger of the gelatine melting. To meet this trouble the following plan has to be resorted to :—

8. Dissolve common (potash) alum, one ounce in a pint of tepid water. Let it stand until cold and pour off gently the clear part should any sediment appear. After washing and before toning, place the prints in this alum bath for about ten minutes and *again* wash before toning for ten or fifteen minutes in running water.

The Combined (Toning and Fixing) Bath.—The general weight of opinion is *not* in favour of combining these two operations at one time when reliable results are desired. Nevertheless, there are times when this method may be found a convenience and yield results which are all that may be desired. The following bath is a favourite with some workers ;—

9. Ammonium sulphocyanide............ 15 grains
   Table salt .... 30 grains
   Hypo .... 2 ounces
   Water .... 10 ounces

To this is *slowly* added one grain of gold chloride in half an ounce of water. The prints first washed for five or ten minutes in running water, and placed in the combined bath and kept moving by being constantly turned over and over for about ten or fifteen minutes. The longer they remain in the bath the more blue and less red will they be when dried.

Here is another bath which finds some stout supporters :—

10. Ammonium sulphocyanide .... 20 grains
    Hypo .... 1 ounce
    Alum .... 30 grains
    Water .... 10 ounces

Shake well, until thoroughly dissolved, then add

Lead nitrate .... 20 grains

Again shake well and set aside to settle, pour off the clear part, and add

    Gold chloride......................... 1 grain

dissolved in half an ounce of water.

Others recommend a still more simple bath as follows :—

11. Hypo .... 1 ounce
    Water .... 8 ounces
    Gold chloride..................... 1 grain

It is said that this bath gives better results if it is prepared a few hours before use, *e.g.*, prepared in the morning and used in the evening. Meanwhile, it should be kept away from daylight, and not in a very cold place.

Drying and Glazing.—Some workers are of opinion that it is better to first "rough dry" the prints, *e.g.*, by suspending by clips, or pinning one corner to a strip of wood, etc., and then to wet again and dry on a rough or smooth surface according as a matt or glazed final effect is desired. If however, the print has been through the alum bath (No 8) this preliminary rough drying may not be necessary.

Matt Surface.—The matt paper when rough dried has a matt or slightly rough surface, but it may be desired to accentuate the effect. This may be done as follows :— Thoroughly clean with soap water and a nail brush a sheet of "fine-ground" glass similar to that used for a focussing screen. When quite dry, lightly dust it with fine talc powder (French chalk) and polish off again with a bit of clean rag. Now slip this plate rough side up into a dish of cold water, which also contains the print face downwards. Bring the print and glass into contact under water, carefully avoiding any air bubbles between them, as the two together are now raised from the water ; firmly, evenly, but lightly pass a squeegee over the back of the print now in contact with the glass. Then lightly press a sheet of blotting paper over the print to take up all adhering water, and set up in a cool airy place to dry, *e.g*, in a passage or between the door and half-open window. When quite dry, the print will very probably of itself come away from the glass, but if not, the finger nail inserted under one corner and a gently backward pull will separate it from the glass. In place of the fine ground glass, rougher glass of course may be employed. Some workers also use for the same purpose a sheet of roughened celluloid. This is more costly than glass, but being not so fragile may prove cheaper in the end.

Glazing Prints is done exactly in the same way, with the single difference, of course, that we use a *smooth* piece of glass, vulcanite, celluloid, paper maché slab, sheet of ferrotype metal, etc., etc., in place of a ground-matt, or rough surface. All the above-named substances have their partizans ; perhaps the greatest favourite being good plate glass free from scratches. In all cases it is important to attend to two points, *viz*., thoroughly cleaning the support and waxing it. Various substances and mixtures have been recommended for giving a glaze, polish to the glass, etc. Many workers adhere to the powdered talc or French chalk already mentioned. Others prefer some of the mixtures given below :—

12. Bees wax .... 20 grains
    Turpentine .... 1 ounce
13. Spermaceti .... 20 grains
    Benzole .... 1 ounce

A few drops only of the lubricant are applied to the glass plate with a bit of clean flannel, and well rubbed all over. Then a final polish is given with a clean old silk handkerchief, or clean dry wash leather. On no account attempt to strip the print from the glass until the print is *quite* dry or failure is more than likely to arise.

Mounting.—Care should be taken that the mountant does not give an acid reaction. Test with litmus paper. Clearly it is no use being at the trouble of producing a high gloss on the print if we are going to damp the print and so destroy the gloss in the operation of mounting. To avoid this, various plans have been adopted.

(1.) If a cut-out mount is used it will suffice if the print be attached to the mount by glue at the edges only of the "cut-out." (2.) Another method is to paste down on to the back of the print before it is quite dry, and while still on the glazing support, a backing of thin waterproof paper specially prepared for this purpose. This prevents the moisture of the mountant penetrating to the print. (3.) Another plan is to use a mountant which does not contain water. The following mixtures are recommended:—

14. Masticated rubber .... 10 grains
    Benzole......................... 1 ounce

A thin layer of this is applied by means of a short, stiff, flat hog's hair brush to the back of the print. It is then allowed to evaporate for a minute or so, and when tacky is applied to the mount, covered with a sheet of glazed paper, and a roller squeegee passed over the surface.

15. Saturated solution of bleached shellac in alcohol.

This must be applied as thinly as possible.

16. Le Page's fish glue applied to the edges only of the back of the print.

A fourth method is to first carefully clean the edges of the glass surrounding the print still adhering to it. Then to paste down the mount to the print and let all dry. Then strip the print from the glass now already mounted. This is, however, a process not to be recommended, because requiring a long time for the print to dry, as the evaporation has to take place through the substance of the mount.

ADDITIONAL PROCEDURES WITH P.O.P.

Development of Partially Printed Proofs.—This method of procedure is sometimes a matter of convenience in dull weather, etc. The printing is to be carried on until one can just see a very slight indication of detail in the high-lights. It is then washed in running water for about ten minutes, and then put into a ten per cent. bath of potassium bromide, and there it remains for another ten minutes or so. In this bath some of the image seems to fade away, and generally the print takes on a yellow tinge. The print is next washed in running water for about ten minutes, and then developed with ortol, metol, or preferably, hydroquinone. A considerable variation in the proportions of the constituents of the developer are possible. In general terms, one may say that a developer which gives a good black and white lantern slide when diluted with about an equal quantity of water will give a satisfactory print.

17. As an example of a thoroughly practical developer for this purpose we may give just one example:—

A

Hydroquinone	70 grains
Potassium meta-bisulphite	5 ,,
Potassium bromide	30 ,,
Water	20 ounces

B

Soda sulphite	1 ounce
Caustic soda	60 grains
Water	20 ounces

Take equal parts and mix just before use, wash for at least ten minutes in running water at once after development.

Developed prints may be toned in the combined bath 9, 10 or 11, or may first be fixed, then *thoroughly* washed, and then toned and again washed.

If good results are wanted by the development process it is important to be careful that the paper is not exposed even to weak daylight more than can be helped, and not even to strong artificial light more than is necessary. At the same time it is quite practicable to do the operation of the bromide bath and developing in fairly strong gas-light, *i.e.*, one need by no means be limited to the ordinary dark-room light as when developing plates.

Another point worth noting is that it is quite practicable to use magnesium ribbon for printing. For a rather thin negative it will be perhaps found sufficient to burn about a foot of the metal ribbon about three or four inches from the glass. The printing frame should be set up on edge in the vertical plane. The strip of metal ribbon is held by a pair of pliers, and ignited at the flame of a candle or spirit lamp. The lid of a biscuit box just in front of the frame does very well to catch the white magnesium oxide formed by burning. It is as well to move the flame of the burning metal opposite various parts of the negative during the exposure. It will be found a comfort to wear a pair of rather dark blue glasses during this operation, as the bright light of combustion prevents one seeing anything with ease for a little while.

After development the print may be fixed only, and under certain conditions it is possible to obtain a fairly satisfactory black or brown colour without toning, but there is usually a slight tendency towards rather too much yellow.

Platinum Toning.—This method of toning is a favourite with many workers. By it a considerable variety of colour tones may be obtained, from a rich red chocolate brown through sepia brown to a warm black.

The following toning baths have each their several advocates, and each worker must discover by experiment the one that gives him the particular brown colour he prefers:—

    18. Potassium chloroplatinite .... 1 grain.
        Water .... ½ ounce.

Add dilute nitric acid (one part strong acid, twenty parts water) drop by drop until the mixture just turns a bit of blue litmus paper a red tinge. Now take a glass rod and make of it a mop by tying a small bunch of clean cotton wool over one end, using for the purpose a bit of white cotton. Having thoroughly washed the print for *at least* ten minutes in running water, lay it face up on a sheet of glass, and apply the above toning solution with the cotton wool mop. Having got a tint or colour nearly what you want, but allowing for a loss of red in fixing, wash off the toning solution and immerse the print in:—

    19. Washing soda .... 1 ounce.
        Water .... 10 ,,

for three or four minutes, and then fix in the usual way in a ten per cent. hypo bath.

Here are some platinum toning baths well recommended:—

    20. Lactic acid........................ 2 drams.
        Water............................ 12 ounces.
        Pot. chloroplatinite................. 2 grains.
    21. Citric acid .... 20 grains.
        Water............................ 10 ounces.
        Table salt .... 20 grains.
        Pot. chloroplatinite................. 2 grains.
    22. Phosphoric acid .... 3 drams.
        Water............................ 10 ounces.
        Pot. chloroplatinite................. 2 grains.

The chief points to bear in mind in platinum toning are: (1) that the print must have practically all the free silver washed away before toning. To this end it is a very good plan to dip each print for a couple of minutes or so in a bath of table salt one ounce, water ten ounces, and again rinse under the tap for a minute or two.

(2) That the toning bath is acid, therefore one must either neutralize this acidity by passing through an alkaline bath, such as No. 19, or what perhaps is rather more convenient, though not quite so desirable—*i.e.*, using a fixing bath made distinctly alkaline. The following proportions are recommended :—

23. Hypo .... 1 ounce.
    Water .... 10 ounces.
    Soda sulphite .... ½ ounce.
    Washing soda.......... .... ½ „

Toning with Gold and Platinum.—A large number of experimenters have tried to find out how to produce platinotype-like effects with P.O.P. papers. Perhaps none of them have been completely successful. The following procedure, however, seems to give the nearest approach to that ideal.

The best results are obtained with a slightly matt-surfaced paper. This should be printed a shade or two deeper than the print is intended to appear finally. The print is well washed and then *partly* toned in a gold bath :—

24. Soda acetate .... 30 grains.
    Borax .... 25 „
    Water .... 10 ounces.
    Gold chloride..................... 1 grain.

It is then washed for a minute or so, and the toning continued in the following bath.

25. Phosphoric acid .... 1 dram.
    Water .... 5 ounces.
    Pot. chloroplatinite .... 2 grains.

Wash for five minutes and fix in bath 23.

Intensifying and Reducing P.O.P.—When the negative is obtainable and printable it is *very* much better, and altogether more satisfactory to make a fresh print than to attempt to intensify or reduce an unsatisfactory one.

Nevertheless, it sometimes happens that this course is not possible, and the best has to be made from an unsatisfactory print.

If the print is only very lightly printed, and comes straight from the printing frame, it is best to strengthen it by development (see formula 17 *et. seq.*). If the print has been toned and fixed, etc., the following may be tried :—

26. Make a *saturated solution* of mercury bichloride in cold water, let it settle, and use only the quite clear supernatent liquid. Immerse the print in this for 15 minutes, turning it from time to time, and see that no air bells are clinging to either side. Wash the print in running water for 15 minutes at least, and longer if convenient. Then immerse it in a bath consisting of strong ammonia one part, water ten or twelve parts· Again wash for five minutes under the tap.

Reducing P.O.P.—

27. Hypo .... 120 grains (120·)
    Uranium nitrate 4   ,,
    Water .... 2 ounces.

The advocates of this solution claim for it that it can be used either *before* or *after* toning with equal facility and advantage. Prints must be well washed both before and after its use in any case.

Another method, which is somewhat risky except in expert hands, is as follows :—

28. Dissolve metal iodine in alcohol to a rich dark port wine colour. Dilute a small quantity with cold water until the whole is a pale sherry colour. Now prepare a one in ten solution of potassium cyanide (*N.B.: a powerful poison*) and add this a *little* at a time until the pale yellow colour of the iodine solution is just discharged.

The print may be immersed in this until sufficiently reduced, or it may be applied locally with cotton wool mop (as described above under platinum toning formula 18). The print must of course be quickly washed just before the desired degree of reduction has been produced.

This solution acts somewhat quickly when once the action begins, and therefore it is well to deal with prints one at a time.

DEFECTS, ETC.

Red-orange patches are usually due to touching the gelatine surface with dirty fingers, etc. These places, being somewhat greasy, repel the various fluids and cause uneven action of the developing, toning, etc.

Brown Stains are also often produced in the same way. They may *sometimes* be removed by the application of a saturated solution of alum. If this fails one may try " chloride of lime " (" bleaching power ") one part in twenty parts of hot water. Allow to stand until cold and apply with cotton wool mop.

Yellow Stains may sometimes be removed by a dilute solution of potassium cyanide (poison) of strength one part cyanide in fifty parts water. (Yellow stains usually indicate hypo splashes.)

General Fog from Age.—This sometimes may be considerably reduced by giving the prints the bath of: Soda sulphite (one in fifteen) *before* toning, but well washing after this bath and before toning.

Very Slow Toning generally points to the fact that the toning bath is too cold, or that it has been spoilt by a small quantity of hypo or developer, or that it does not contain sufficient gold.

Uneven Toning, i.e., blue edges, generally points to a bath too strong in gold, or that there are too many prints in the bath at once, so that the edges are getting more of the metal than the central parts, or it may arise from prints sticking together or to the bottom of the dish.

Blue-Grey Tones indicate too long a time in the toning bath, or a bath too strong in gold.

Red-Yellow Tones arise from just the opposite state of affairs.

Pinking of the high-lights points to the bath being too weak or becoming worked out.

Double Toning, *i.e.*, the print shewing different colours, points to insufficient washing or uneven action of the toning bath, *i.e.*, not keeping the prints moving, or too slow toning, or that the toning bath does not suit the brand of paper.

Blisters are usually due either to using a hypo fixing bath too strong, or passing the print from one solution to another of a markedly different temperature. Hence the importance of dissolving the hypo either in tepid water or some time before use. The best all-round temperature for working this process is between the limits of 60° and 65° F.

Tinting P.O.P.—The colours to be used may be the usual moist water colours by some good maker, or solutions of aniline colours. These latter may usually be dissolved in water and applied in thin washes. The surface of the print should be rubbed as little as possible. If water colours are to be used it will be found helpful to prepare the surface of the print with one or other of the following preparations.

29. White (bleached) lac .... 1 part
    Alcohol .... 12—15 parts

Apply evenly and quickly with a spray diffuser or with a broad soft brush, and let the print become *nearly* dry before applying the colours.

30. The white of an egg in twenty ounces of water. Shake well, then add ammonia drop by drop until the mixture just very faintly smells of it. Filter and brush over the surface of the print. In mixing the water colours also use this albumen solution in place of water.

Advantages of P.O.P.—As compared with ordinary albumenized silver paper the P.O.P. class has the advantage of giving more detail with marked transparency in the shadows. The operations are more flexible and the results are as permanent, if not more so, than those on albumen paper. The paper keeps in good condition for a longer time. The negative giving the best results with P.O.P. is one having delicacy rather than vigour, *i.e.*, a long scale of gradation of delicate steps is well rendered. Printing takes place quicker with P.O.P. than with albumen papers. The cost of paper and materials is much about the same in both instances.

Notes.—In the glazed variety of paper the smooth shiny surface is the sensitive one, and, of course, goes next the negative in the printing frame. In the matt paper the sensitive side may generally be known by its tendency to curl inward, *i.e.*, the concave or hollow side is the printing side.

Formalin may be used in place of alum for hardening the gelatine. Of the usual 40 per cent. solution of formalin take one ounce and dilute with ten or twelve ounces of water.

Dark spots or specks are frequently due to metallic dust either from the fingers or in the water. Mounts having sham gold edges or bronze powders should be banished from the dark-room. Dry "pyro" floating in the air may also account for spots.

Rev. F. C. Lambert, M.A.

UNLOADING.
A. M. MORRISON.

Platinotype Printing.

AMONGST the various printing processes in common use amongst photographers, platinotype is unique in several respects.

Printing is conducted by daylight in precisely the same manner as silver printing, but the action of light only suffices to make the image partially visible. In this respect, platinotype stands, as it were, midway between what are familiarly termed "print-out" processes—that is, those in which the image is made completely visible by daylight, and those in which the action of light is latent or invisible, such as bromide paper and in the carbon process.

The distinctive character of the platinotype print, with which, probably, everyone is so familiar that a platinotype effect almost amounts to a generic term, is not so much essential to the process, but has been largely determined by the different kind of papers and the preparation of those adopted by the manufacturers of platinotype printing papers.

In the first place, the platinotype print is before anything a matt surface print, and possesses a certain kind of texture or surface which gives the finished print an appearance similar to a pencil drawing or an engraving; an appearance largely assisted by the characteristic colour of the platinum image, which is black.

The invention and production of platinotype paper is due to Mr. Willis and the Platinotype Company, and although subsequently there have been both English and foreign imitators, we may safely confine our attention to those papers made and supplied by the Platinotype Company.

As, however, the purpose of this article is to furnish the beginner with simple working instructions, rather than to describe the principles of the process, we will at once proceed to say how a platinotype print is made.

To begin with, platinotype printing is divided into cold-bath process and hot-bath process. Of the latter we shall speak later on, but for the present, as being most suitable for the amateur and beginner, we will consider the cold-bath method. The reason for this division and the meaning of the name will be abundantly evident presently.

We first of all procure a tin of paper of the quality marked AA. The paper is put up in tin cylinders containing twenty-four pieces of either ¼-plate or ½-plate sizes, or less for larger sizes. It may, if preferred, be obtained in full-size sheets 20 × 26 inches.

We have now to bear in mind that the paper is sensitive to daylight to a slightly greater degree than are the silver print-out papers, and hence, whilst handling the paper, placing it in the printing frames, or what not, we need to be a little more careful as to how near the window we bring the paper. At the side of the room furthest from the window, or with an intervening screen between the paper and the window, or yet again, with the blind drawn down, we shall be quite safe in opening our tin of paper and inspecting it.

On removing the lid of the tin we find a false top or cover hermetically sealing it, which has to be cut through in the manner becoming customary with various tinned foods and comestibles.

We then find that the paper within is yellow on one side which is the sensitive side. Within the roll of papers at the bottom of the tin we shall find a hard irregular lump of some substance wrapped round with cotton wool. Keep this in the tin and now note its use from the following:—Platinotype paper is highly susceptible to moisture and deteriorates under its influence. The air we breathe, and therefore the air enclosed within the tin case or any other vessel contains a large amount of moisture, and this moisture would be taken up by the platinotype paper to its own detriment. The presence of water or moisture in the atmosphere or in things we handle, although quite unperceived by us, would be discoverable by the platinum salts on the paper, which would thus become unfit for use, hence the only way of preserving it is by placing in the tin containing the paper some chemical which is even more susceptible to moisture than platinotype paper. Such a body is calcium chloride, and this it is which we find wrapped in cotton wool in each tin tube of paper, or to speak more accurately it is asbestos prepared in a solution of calcium chloride. So long as that little lump remains dry and hard we may be quite sure that it has left no moisture in the air around it for the platinotype paper, and it will go on drinking it up until it becomes softened by saturation, when it must be removed and a fresh piece substituted, or it may be restored to its former condition by drying it on a red-hot shovel, the asbestos remaining unconsumed.

Whilst perhaps in after practice we may find it possible to relax our precautions against damp, yet at the outset the necessity of the utmost caution being observed cannot be too strongly insisted upon. Out of a very large number of prints representing the beginner's first attempts at platinotype, by far the greatest number of failures are due to damp, and this, probably, for want of conception of the danger to which the paper is exposed. Remember then that where there is ordinary air there is also abundant moisture, and as no tin box with a movable lid is air-tight, neither is it moisture-proof, but in the case of our tin of platinotype paper when once opened will go on admitting moisture which the calcium chloride will take up until it can take no more.

After having cut through the inner sealed top of the tin, close up the little hole in the outer lid where the cutting point is with sealing wax, next cover the mouth of the tube with a piece of waxed paper or tinfoil, shut the lid down on to this, and then cover the junction of the lid with a broad indiarubber band. In this way damp may be prevented from gaining access to the inside of the tube to a great extent.

Specially constructed tubes are made which close with an air-tight stopper and have a false bottom with a perforated partition in which the calcium chloride may be kept. Such a "calcium-tube," as it is called, if not an absolute necessity, is a very desirable acquisition.

If you now take the negative to be printed from and hold it near the fire or a spirit lamp, it will on becoming

STREONSALCH.
W. J. WARREN.

warm give off perceptible moisture, thus showing that it was distinctly damp before. The negative, therefore, should be dried before being brought into contact with the platinotype paper.

The wood printing frame itself, if it has been used for printing in the open air, should be placed in an oven or held near the fire to thoroughly dry it.

Having placed the negative and the platinotype paper in the frame in the ordinary manner, there should next be placed at the back of the paper a thin sheet of waterproof cloth, vulcanized rubber of the proper size and thickness being sold for the purpose, this will prevent damp from penetrating to the paper from the back of the frame. The frame may now be closed and placed in the light for printing, and even having taken all these elaborate precautions against damp it would not be advisable to print out of doors except in dry weather, nor should the paper be left in the frame longer than need be, but if it is not proposed to finish the print off at once, it should be returned as soon as convenient to the security of the calcium tube.

GENERAL OUTLINE OF THE PROCESS.

Platinotype paper is ordinarily only available for daylight printing, though the Platinotype Company have introduced a lamp of special construction and great power, by the use of which daylight may be dispensed with, and electric light, should it be available, may be used.

As has been already said, platinotype paper is rather more sensitive to light than silver paper, and hence takes proportionately less time to print.

The duration of the 'exposure to light constitutes the only real difficulty in platinotype printing, and whilst just at first it may result in the beginner's meeting with much disappointment, yet probably, with a little care and watchfulness the trouble will be surmounted, and sufficient experience gained to secure fairly uniform success thereafter, before even the first tube of paper has been used.

The printed image shows on the yellow ground of the sensitized side as a faint grey, the darkest portions assuming an orange-grey tint, whilst the lighter parts remain all but invisible.

A little practice will enable one to judge the right depth, that is to say, how visible the image should be before printing is to be stopped, but as a rough guide to commence with it may be said that printing is complete when the image is about half as deep as we should expect it to be if it were a "print-out" process.

As we shall have occasion to return to the question of printing presently, we may now pass to the next step in the process.

In twenty-five ounces of hot water dissolve half a pound of best neutral oxalate of potash, and keep this in a stoppered bottle as stock solution. What is known as *neutral* oxalate should be used, and in order to ensure having a suitable salt it had better be obtained from a recognised photographic chemist or dealer.

As the above solution becomes cool, a good deal of the oxalate will probably settle at the bottom in the form of solid crystals, of these no notice need be taken, for as long as there are undissolved crystals at the bottom of the bottle we know we have a saturated solution.

We shall now require a dish of porcelain or enamelled iron, and if we choose the latter great care must be taken to see that the enamel is not cracked or blistered, as it will have an injurious effect if the oxalate of potash solution obtain access to the iron under the enamel.

As it will be convenient to be able to alter the temperature of the solution when in this dish at will, a spirit lamp or stove or a small gas-stove will be a useful, if not an essential addition. Over such heating apparatus the dish should be supported on an iron tripod, or by any extemporized substitute.

If a porcelain dish be used, a thin sheet of iron should be placed first on the tripod stand, and then three or four scraps of iron, large common iron nails will serve very well, and on these the porcelain dish is allowed to rest so that it does not come into direct contact with the iron plate.

The purpose of this is to save the dish from cracking, moreover the iron plate becomes hot, and retaining a good deal of heat serves as a kind of accumulator which goes far to maintain the dish and the contained solution at a uniform temperature for at least a short time. Even better than this arrangement will be an iron dish filled with clean dry sand, the porcelain dish to rest on the sand which retains much heat.

If an enamelled iron dish be employed, these precautions are not so necessary, though they may still be used with advantage.

Next we shall require another dish or similar vessel into which we pour a weak solution of hydrochloric acid, the usual proportions being :—

Water	70 parts
Pure hydrochloric acid	1 part

This constitutes the whole of the very simple apparatus needed, and we may now proceed to develop our print, which as already described is exposed to light in a printing frame in the usual manner until the image appears rather less than half-printed.

DEVELOPMENT OF THE PRINT.

If convenient it would be an advantage to have the above-mentioned apparatus set up close to the window or other situation where the printing is actually carried on in order that each print may be developed and finished off forthwith, the reason for this will, I think, appear as we proceed.

Development—that is, the changing of the print from the partially visible condition to its full degree of intensity—is practically instantaneous. The image does not gradually attain its maximum strength as in a negative or bromide print, but does so within a few seconds of its coming into contact with the oxalate of potash solution.

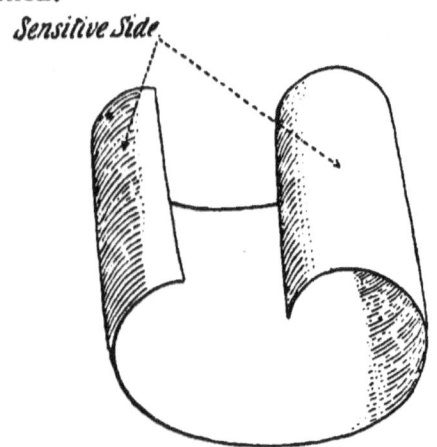

Fig. 1.

Having put into the dish on the tripod stand sufficient of the saturated solution of oxalate of potash to cover the bottom of the dish to the depth of half an inch or an inch, we light the lamp or stove and bring the solution up to a temperature of about 70° Fahrenheit. This may be tested with a thermometer or may very well be guessed by touch; we merely require the solution quite warm, but not so hot as to cause the slightest inconvenience if the fingers are placed therein. This will be a sufficiently accurate guide as to temperature.

In case any dust or scum should have accumulated on the surface of the bath, wipe the surface of the solution with a piece of clean paper, and now take the first print to be developed in both hands, giving it a decided curl, or roll it round into a cylinder *sensitive side out*, so that it naturally takes a curled-up form (Fig. 1). We now take the print to the dish containing the oxalate solution without previous washing and without exposing the paper to the influence of light or moisture, and lowering the edge of the paper held in the left hand, sensitive side downwards, until it touches the fluid quickly and smoothly bring the rest of the print down until the right-hand end finally reaches the solution, then give it a sliding sort of shake in order to set free any bubbles of air which may be imprisoned under the paper, and then on raising the paper again after five to ten seconds, the image will be found to have come out to the full degree of visibility, which the amount of exposure had paved the way for.

The paper may be returned to the oxalate bath for a minute or two longer if it be thought desirable, though only in the case of a very cold bath is any effect produced on the print by the oxalate after the first few seconds. The print is then passed *direct* to the hydrochloric acid bath, which should be ready in a dish close at hand, and the print is now practically finished.

Before placing the print in the acid bath it may be noticed that the portions of the print not affected by light still remain yellow, and this yellowness the acid bath removes almost at once.

In order to effectually remove the yellow surface (which is the unacted-upon sensitive salts and hence upon their removal the permanence of the print depends) three successive applications of the acid bath should be resorted to, the prints remaining for 5 to 10 minutes in each, and then finally washed in running water for a quarter-of-an-hour, dried between blotting paper or in any other manner preferred, and the platinotype print is finished and ready for mounting.

It should be seen from the foregoing general outline of the process that for directness, simplicity, and for the short time in which a finished print may be produced that platinotype stands alone amongst printing methods.

There are, however, some points needing careful consideration at each stage of the print's production, and to these we may now pay attention.

PRACTICAL CONSIDERATIONS AS REGARDS EXPOSURE.

As has already been stated right exposure constitutes the crux of the whole process; this once mastered the rest of the performance—development, clearing in acid and washing—is so simple that the chance of failure is remote.

Hence the greater need of paying especial attention to the question of exposure or printing.

Obviously, the duration of time of exposure cannot be fixed, not even to the extent it can be in bromide printing or any other method of printing with artificial light which may be a definite and permanent quantity.

The variable quality of the daylight and the density of the negative are both fluctuating factors in the calculation and hence some means may advisedly be resorted to for acquiring a sort of exposure index suitable for each individual negative and every variety of light.

First let it be noted that even with very great over-exposure the image will not become wholly visible, whilst to the inexperienced eye but little change takes place in the appearance of the printed image after the correct exposure has been reached.

If then the print has been over-exposed, the fact is not made evident until the print is subjected to the influence of the oxalate developing bath.

To start platinotype work trusting to chance or good fortune to secure for us good results, means that our whole course will be one of uncertainty and filled with exasperating disappointments to say nothing of the amount of paper and material which is certain to be wasted in unsuccessful efforts.

The reader will probably have learned something of this from his past experiences of negative exposure, the difficulties of which he has by now, we may hope, overcome by careful and patient study, or else if he is not even now undergoing this stage of learning he is the victim of endless mistakes, every plate exposed is a shot in the dark with no certainty attending any one of them.

Exposure, however, in platinotype is not so difficult a matter as that of a dry plate, and the correct exposure with any particular negative once ascertained, every subsequent print from the same negative can, by simple mechanical means, be made with the certainty of its being *an exact fac-simile* of the others.

PRINTING WITH AN ACTINOMETER.

Several kinds of Actinometers are made for sale, the purpose of which is either to indicate the right exposure of a plate in the camera or to tell the duration of exposure for papers such as platinotype or carbon, the image on which is invisible, or nearly so.

A simple, yet thoroughly efficient meter may be made as follows :—Cut some fine tissue paper or *papier minéral* into strips about a quarter of an inch wide and attach one to a piece of clean glass 4¼ × 3¼ with fresh starch or other colourless mountant. Upon this first strip and exactly over it place a second, but bring it to within a quarter of an inch of the end of the first, next place a third strip in like manner a quarter of an inch short of the second strip, and so on until some seven or eight strips have been fixed. The combination will now be somewhat as the following drawing (Fig. 2), thus forming a tissue band which at each quarter-inch is one thickness more opaque.

Fig. 2.

In the centre of each strip or increased thickness, paint with opaque colour, black or red, a letter or figure as in (Fig. 3). On the back or other side of the glass to which these strips are attached, paint over or cover

Fig. 3.

with opaque paper all except the space covered by the strips. Now place the whole in an ordinary ¼-plate printing frame, with the paper strips inside, next adjust a piece of silver paper, albumenized, or gelatine chloride precisely as though printing from a negative. Close the back and we then have a thoroughly efficient actinometer.

We now put out our first piece of platinotype paper to print, and alongside it so as to receive the exact same amount of light, we place our actinometer.

The first print must admittedly be guess-work.

After an interval of time, which may vary from say fifteen minutes to an hour according to the amount of light, we will withdraw the frame containing the platinotype print, and *simultaneously turn the actinometer over with its face down*, thus stopping its printing whilst examining the platinotype.

Retiring from the light we examine the progress of printing precisely as in silver printing, and we shall probably find that the image on the negative is now faintly visible on the platinotype paper, impressed in a sort of warm grey colour.

If the darkest portions are of about the tint which we might produce by shading with an H pencil on a piece of primrose yellow or pale buff paper, we may reckon that the print has been sufficiently exposed.

Now refer to the actinometer and see what has taken place on the silver paper which we put into it. Probably while the platinotype paper has been reaching the required depth of printing, the silver paper has also registered the image of the strips of paper, and has become printed through up to the fourth or fifth step of the tissue strips, showing on each strip its letter in white. Make a note of the highest letter visible and proceed to develop the platinotype print. If upon development the print is weak and grey, lacking depth or intensity in the deepest shadows, and having blank and detailless whites for the higher tones, we may reckon that our print is under-exposed. The letter visible then, *with that particular negative* is not sufficient. We then shift the paper in the actinometer so as to get a fresh portion under the tissue strips, or we substitute a new piece, We refill the printing frame and print again until the actinometer registers one, two, or three more steps and letters, and then try again. If, however, in the first case the platinotype print upon development gives a heavy dark print, with the details in shadows blocked up, and the high-lights grey, the whole possessing an overdone appearance, then in our second attempt we shall stop printing when the actinometer records some one or two letters less. But we may be more fortunate in our first attempt, and the print may be about right. In that case we mark on that negative in some way the tint or step or letter in the actinometer at which we arrested action, and henceforth, no matter the time of year, hour of the day, or latitude, that negative will give a similar print if stopped in accordance with that memorandum which it bears.

If, however, we do not hit the right exposure the first time, we are pretty certain to do so the second, or at the most the third time, and having done so, we have not only an infallible guide for all subsequent prints from that same negative, but we have also some sort of index to base our calculations on for other negatives. Thus if we at once proceed to print from another negative, that is, before any considerable alteration takes place in the light, we may by comparing the negatives at least estimate what will probably be the second negative's printing letter or step on the actinometer. Sooner or later every negative (especially those from which we anticipate wanting subsequent prints) should bear either on the negative itself, or else in a carefully kept register or note book its correct printing letter.

Although this may seem a rather laborious practice, it is not so in reality, and so great is its educational power that I anticipate that after the first dozen or so negatives we shall almost dispense with the actinometer altogether, having by then trained the eye to tell when a print is finished merely by the appearance of the half-visible image. Do not let this prospect, however, tempt the beginner to dispense with this valuable help at first, for to the inexperienced eye the appearance of the platinotype image is very deceptive, and having underexposed the first print, it will not be safe to judge the extra printing of the next print only by the eye; the beginner is nearly certain to err, and the eye must not be trusted until it has had considerable training.

After having had some considerable and varied experience in platinotype printing, one feels no little regret that an operation which has become so simple cannot be laid before a beginner in a more precise and definite manner, and I can only assure my reader that in a very little while what may now look like a very serious business, only surmountable by long and serious practice, will become a sort of intuitive faculty, and just as one feels after a little practice the precise amount of pressure which one should use when the fingers are placed on the notes of the piano, so just the right *visible* depth of print required to give a developed print of such and such intensity comes to be a matter of instinct.

It may here be stated that paper which has been affected by damp gives a slightly less visible image than dry paper. But moisture alone without oxalate will effect partial development, and if the time of exposure to light be so greatly prolonged, that despite all precautions moisture obtains access to the print during exposure, this may, as it were, start a kind of local development whilst the paper is still in the frame and printing, so that on looking at the print to watch its progress some of the deeper shadows may have sprung quite suddenly into a deep blackish-grey colour. In many cases this will quite spoil the finished result, whilst in others no harm seems to be done when the print is ultimately developed.

Remembering that the high-lights and indeed some of the lighter tints of the print are quite invisible until after development, care should be taken to look at the paper only in decidedly subdued light, or better still, artificial light, because the injury which is being done by even a short exposure to actinic light is not made manifest until after development, and as most of us know how soon a piece of silver paper will discolour in even moderately faint daylight, we should be additionally cautious with platinotype paper which is from twice to three times as sensitive to light.

Fig. 4.

SOME POINTS TO BE CONSIDERED WITH REGARD TO DEVELOPMENT.

To avoid confusion it will be well to repeat here that at present we are only considering the practice of what is known as the cold-bath paper. This term is applied only in a comparative sense. The older hot-bath process requires the developing bath to be raised to a temperature of about 170° F., whereas the best temperature for the cold process is about 70° F. or even less; nevertheless, the cold-bath paper *may* be developed in an oxalate bath of 170° or even hotter, so also it may be developed on a solution which is quite cold. The result of altering the temperature is twofold and may be stated thus :—*The colder the bath*, the *colder* the colour, that is, the *bluer* the greys and blacks, also development is slower and takes longer, and the contrasts harder. *The hotter the bath* the warmer or browner the colour of the print; the more sudden the development and the greater the amount of half-tone and consequent softer contrasts.

With these maxims in mind some amount of control may be exercised over the prints produced, especially as regards arresting development at any point desired if a cold developer be used, but in such case the print must be instantly removed to and plunged into the acid bath, until which immersion development continues, even after the print has been removed from the bath.

Development, as a general rule, should be conducted in feeble daylight or artificial light.

Development need not take place immediately, but at some subsequent time, provided the prints be meanwhile stored in a calcium tube and in every way rigorously protected from damp.

The proportions which I have given for the oxalate of potash bath represent the standard developer as given by the makers of the paper for the hot-bath papers, and they recommend that this be diluted to about half strength for cold-bath papers. Personally, I use it at full strength for the cold process, and see no reason for diluting it.

It may be said that such a course is calculated to give strong, vigorous prints, for generally speaking, the stronger the bath, the stronger the contrasts of the print. The difference, however, produced by altering the strength of the bath is not very great.

There are two alternatives to the oxalate of potash developer, both possessing certain, if not very strongly marked characteristics. The first of these is known as the " D " salts. These are sold in tins by the Platinotype Company, and consist of a loose admixture of certain salts, and hence it is essential that the entire contents of a half-pound tin be dissolved at once and kept thus as a stock solution.

The proportions to be used are as follows: Dissolve ¼ lb. of D salts in 50 ozs. water, and then take equal portions of this solution and water, in other words, dilute it to half-strength.

The "D" salts are said to give colder colours and more half-tone, but the colour derived from development on the first-named oxalate bath may be made colder by adding to 20 parts of developer 1 part of a saturated solution of oxalic acid, in like manner slightly warmer colour may be obtained if the oxalate bath be made alkaline by the addition of carbonate of potash, but only just enough should be added to turn a red litmus test paper blue.

If prints developed on D salts should appear mealy or granulated the bath should be strengthened or used at the full strength of the stock solution (salts ½ lb. to water 50oz.)

Another developer, the effect of which is to minimize half-tone and increase the vigour of the contrasts, and so give very brilliant and even hard blacks and whites, is as follows:

Oxalate of potash	16 ozs.
Phosphate of potash	4 ozs.
Sulphate of potash	½ oz.
Water	120 ozs.

This should be made with hot water, and to get the full advantage of its contrast-giving powers, used quite cold. Development will then probably take one or two minutes, but can be arrested sooner when the desired effect is attained.

It may now be as well to enumerate and describe the various kinds of platinotype paper obtainable, and whilst the general treatment of them all is the same as described in the foregoing, some special recommendations may be made in each case.

The papers for the Cold-Bath process are two called respectively AA and CC. AA is a smooth surface paper and is the kind usually employed for portraiture and general small work. CC is a heavier, stronger paper with a surface similar to stout cartridge or drawing paper. For pictorial work and for landscapes, also for large portraits or heads this paper is eminently suitable.

Next we have the papers for Hot-Bath process, to be presently described. These are firstly A and C, both precisely the same in character as the AA and CC just referred to, but intended to be developed in a bath at high temperature. These four kinds of paper all yield a picture of the normal platinotype black colour, the black tending to cooler or warmer tints according to slight modifications of treatment, but it is also possible to produce a platinotype print of a rich sepia brown by using the papers S and RS—these both in substance and character corresponding with AA or A and CC or C respectively. Thus we have a thin smooth and a thick rough paper for each Cold bath, Hot bath, and for Sepia printing.

DEVELOPMENT OF HOT-BATH AND SEPIA PAPERS.

With the Hot-Bath papers perhaps the precautions against damp should be rather more stringent than for Cold-Bath papers, certainly they may not be relaxed, and in the sepia papers, S and RS, there seems to be even greater susceptibility still, but for this, printing and development are performed precisely as already described, but the temperature of the oxalate bath should not be less than 150° to 170°, whilst in some cases it may be convenient to raise it still higher. The oxalate solution should, moreover, always be at full strength, namely, $\frac{1}{2}$ lb. in 25 ozs. of water or thereabouts, a much more diluted bath will result in granular prints.

As a general rule the colour of A and C prints is a rather browner black than their cold-bath equivalents—AA and CC—with also rather softer contrasts.

Development takes place in shorter time than with cold-bath papers, and is indeed so instantaneous that any control is next to impossible. On this account, rather more dexterity will be required in development, that is to say, between the time that one end of the print touches the developer and the rest of the print is brought into contact with it, the shortest possible time should elapse. There must be no hesitation, the whole surface must be brought down gradually but swiftly, and accompanied by a sliding movement in order to squeeze out or wipe out any air bubbles which might cling to the surface of the paper. If this be not done evenly and continuously, it is more than likely that there will be marks of unequal development on the surface.

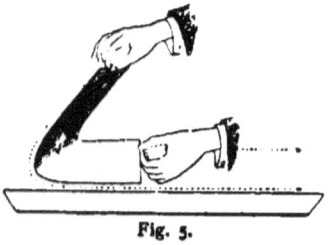

Fig. 5.

It is no uncommon thing for the tyro to let the print hover over the bath before giving it its plunge in the hot solution, but in so doing it should be remembered that he is submitting it to the direct action of the steam which the bath is giving off, and so exposing it to damp.

Whilst with prints of ½-plate size and under it may be sufficient to hold the print by one corner and wipe it across the surface of the solution, pressing it down with the fingers of the other hand, with larger sizes it will be well to cultivate a little trick in manipulation, and the accompanying figure may perhaps be suggestive (Fig. 5), in which it will be seen the left hand is bringing one end of the print into contact with the bath, whilst the right hand holds the opposite end above and well back, and the left hand will next be moved in the direction of the arrow, drawing the print with it along the surface of the bath, the right hand following but simultaneously lowering the whole of the print—thus the solution attacks the print smoothly and continuously, whilst the air is pressed out in the opposite direction. Instantly the entire print is floating on the bath it should be moved about a little, as a further means of disengaging any air bubbles.

As far as possible, prevent the developer from flowing over the back of the print, but this will be a far less evil than not bringing the whole printed surface immediately and at one stroke on to the developer. The print is next passed direct and without intermediate washing into the hydrochloric acid bath, as already described.

The sepia papers, S and RS, are both hot-bath papers, and no special instructions need to be given as regards development, except that to get the full benefit of the sepia tint and secure a fine rich bright colour, the Special Sepia Solution prepared and supplied by the Platinotype Company should be employed in the developer.

Of this, one or two drams should be added to each ounce of oxalate bath, either before heating it in the dish or afterwards and just before floating the prints. In the latter case stir the whole so as to get it equally mixed, and wipe the surface to remove any scum.

A good substitute for the bath as above prepared for sepia prints may be made by adding one part of saturated solution of oxalic acid to each ten parts of oxalate of potash solution.

P

The Sepia papers are rather more sensitive to light than the Black papers, and hence all operations should be conducted in very subdued daylight, a precaution even extending to the first acid bath.

The bath containing the special solution should be used for sepia prints only, and when done with kept in a separate bottle for future use, but the bottle must be kept from the light, and the sediment which will fall should be left undisturbed at the bottom of the bottle or filtered out, and the dish used for sepia development should be well washed before using it for black prints.

Opinions seem to differ as to the wisdom of keeping old developing baths, but as far as my own experience goes I use the oxalate solution for black prints again and again, taking no heed of its discoloured condition.

After developing, the bath is poured into the stock bottle, and so long as undissolved crystals remain at the bottom of the bottle hot water may be added from time to time to make up the loss occasioned by spilling and waste, thus the stock solution is always a combination of old and freshly-dissolved oxalate, and I have had one large jar of solution thus in very frequent use for over twelve months, a greenish-black encrustation gradually accumulating at the bottom without detriment.

CONCERNING THE HYDROCHLORIC CLEARING OR FIXING BATH.

Little needs to be said as to the Hydrochloric Acid bath into which the prints are passed immediately after development. The purpose of the acid bath is to dissolve out the sensitive salts which have been unaffected by light and which are still light-sensitive, the removal of these making the paper white and clean. Thus the acid bath is both fixing and clearing in its action.

Into the first acid bath the prints will carry a good deal of the oxalate solution in which they have been developed, and it therefore soon becomes very much discoloured, wherefore after a lapse of about five minutes the print should be removed to a second acid bath of the same strength as the first (pure hydrochloric acid 1 part, water 70 parts) and after five or ten minutes into a third.

After the prints (many may be done at the same time) have been in the third acid for five minutes, the bath should be examined, and if it is quite colourless, that is if the prints have not discoloured it at all, we may rest satisfied that clearing and fixation are complete, but if not, yet another acid bath should be given.

Whilst five or ten minutes in each acid bath is long enough, probably no harm to the print itself, yet no good, will follow a longer immersion. There may, however, be a danger of softening or rotting the paper, a danger which is increased should the bath be made stronger in acid.

If a number of prints are being made, or if numerous dishes for acid constitute a difficulty or inconvenience, we may modify procedure as follows :—

Make up the first acid bath to about half the prescribed strength, say hydrochloric acid one part to water 120 to 140 parts. Into this each print may be flung as soon as developed, until the entire batch is thus far finished. In this weak acid bath the prints will take no harm if left for several hours, when an acid bath (one to seventy) of full strength having been prepared, the first weak solution may be poured off and the fresh poured on. In this the prints should be separately turned over, so that each receives thorough treatment, when the second bath may be thrown away and a third substituted. One dish thus serves for the whole series of acid baths.

If adopting this course, it will be safer not to mix sepia and ordinary black prints in the same *first* acid bath, after which, however, they may be treated altogether.

Sufficient washing to rid the paper of acid is all that is required to complete operations; but acid does not cling to the print as does hypo, moreover, we have not an absorbent gelatine surface to deal with, so that if prints were dealt with individually and washed by hand, probably a few minutes sluicing under a tap would suffice, but in a properly constructed print-washer, or even a large dish, twenty minutes to half-an-hour should be ample. If any doubt is felt, the last washing water may be tested with blue litmus paper.

MODIFICATIONS IN DEVELOPMENT.

To impart a warmer and richer tone to prints on CC (cold-bath) paper, the following slight modification may be resorted to, but it must be regarded merely as an exception for definite purposes, being in violation of the instructions and rules already laid down. It consists of developing CC paper as though it were hot-bath paper, using a bath of about 170° F and submitting it to the influence of damp to a slight degree. This latter very heterodox course may be effected by leaving the paper laid out all night in a room where there has been no fire to dry the air, or by using paper which has been kept for a week or so in its tube without calcium chloride and without sealing the lid, or yet again, the print may be held over the steam of the developer for a few minutes before developing it.

It must be remembered that in doing this we are taking liberties with the process, and if poor, "muddy" prints result, we can only blame ourselves, but as a rule this will not be the case, the effect being rather to impart a slight creamy tone to the whites without otherwise degrading their brilliance, whilst the use of a hot bath gives the whole a distinctly brown-black image, which combined with the cream tint of the high-lights has a very luminous and warm effect.

Another method of development which must also be taken as an exceptional one, only to be used in special cases to attain special ends, is local development with a brush, using glycerine as a medium.

As may have been seen from the foregoing descriptions, the development of a platinotype print, even with a cold bath, is so rapid that there is not a possibility of developing one portion more than another, or if such could be done, still it would be done with the certainty of leaving a mark where development had been stopped. These difficulties, however, may be overcome by the use of glycerine, the effect of which is to retard development to almost any degree, and by its soft, viscid character to soften and blend the line of demarcation where greater or less development ceased. The method of applying it is as follows: On removing the print from the frame it should be fastened to a board with pins, print side upwards. Next pour on to the surface a small pool of *pure* glycerine, and with the finger tip, a brush or soft pad, spread it *evenly* and thinly over the print. It must not be allowed to remain on the surface in irregular patches of unequal depth, but after spreading it had better be wiped with a fresh pad of cotton wool, so as to remove any superfluous glycerine. Now have four small vessels at hand, and into No. 1 place an ounce or two of the ordinary oxalate developing solution; in No. 2 put equal parts of oxalate solution and glycerine, in No. 3 one part oxalate solution and two parts glycerine, and in No. 4 pure glycerine.

With a broad, soft hair brush apply the contents of No. 3 to the less printed portions of the image and wait results. These portions will presently begin to gain in depth and to slowly develop up, now spread the No. 3 mixture to the rest of the print and apply the contents of No. 2 to the portions first treated with No. 3. The most obstinate parts may be touched with No. 1, plain oxalate solution, whilst any spots which have come up too quickly may be promptly arrested from further progress by the application of pure glycerine.

Here we have a method of developing up any one part, and restraining or entirely stopping any other.

I do not think any good will be done by a more detailed description of its working, even if there be anything more to tell. It is essentially a method of development in which the individual worker will invent modifications and dodges for himself, and when all is said for it, it must be admitted only as a means of improving a subject when ordinary procedure fails.

THE CHARACTER OF THE NEGATIVE FOR PLATINOTYPE.

In the earlier days of platinotype printing it was generally insisted upon that the most suitable negatives were such as we should describe as somewhat vigorous or "plucky." Whether it is that some alteration has been made in the manufacture of the paper or that taste as regards what constitutes a good print has changed, I cannot say. Certain it is that in the experience of a good many, a "plucky" negative is by no means essential to the production of a good platinotype print.

The soft, delicate negatives, of which the best professional portrait negatives are a good sample, yield the best possible results, whilst with the CC paper, negatives so thin and delicate as to be suitable for hardly any other printing process, give all that can be wished for.

Much, of course, will depend on the kind of print desired and the paper used, and here it may be remarked that from a given negative the different kinds of platinotype paper give different results.

From a given negative the hot-bath papers yield the greatest amount of half-tone, the hot development tending to yield flatter results. Next comes the smooth, cold-bath paper, and finally as yielding the maximum amount of vigour is the CC paper. Hence if we make our negatives specially for our chosen printing process, a stronger negative will be needed for S, RS, A and C than for the AA and CC, whilst for the latter a negative distinctly erring on the side of extreme thinness will be best.

If a negative gives prints which are too weak and flat for our purpose, a great improvement may be effected by printing through blue glass. If on the other hand the prints are too hard and harsh in contrast, it is advisable to print through "signal" green glass.

TONING PLATINOTYPE PRINTS.

Several formula and methods have been published from time to time, the object of which is to change the colour of the platinotype print by subsequent staining or toning, and whilst by such methods pleasing colours may sometimes be obtained, they possess an element of uncertainty, and must not be too much relied upon. An exception in this respect must, however, be made in the case of what is known as Packham's method, the effect of which is to change the black platinotype to a sepia brown, or a brown slightly tinged with green. The necessary "tinctorial powder" must be obtained from Mr. Packham or through a dealer. To prepare the bath a packet of this powder is dissolved by boiling for three or four minutes in five fluid ounces of water, to which when cold add one ounce methylated spirit. This forms the stock solution and will keep for a long time if well corked. For use add thirty or forty minims of the stock solution to one pint of water, and in this steep the prints, turning them over frequently. Toning may occupy several hours. To expedite matters, the dilute solution should be made with water of 150° F., and the bath maintained at this temperature as in the case of hot-bath development. As soon as the desired tint is secured, remove the prints and wash well in three changes of cold water.

Prints may be so treated at any time after they have been made.

Glycerine developed prints are not suitable. Prints must have been very thoroughly washed, so as to free them from every trace of acid, also thoroughly fixed in acid if they are to be "toned" by Packham's method. If after "toning" and washing the whites of the print appear to have suffered, the prints should be placed for five or ten minutes in the following bath, which should be kept at a temperature of 180° F.

Castille soap	40 grains
Bicarbonate of soda	80 grains
Water, hot (180° F.)	1 pint

This will clear the whites and intensify the colour generally.

Platinotypes may be toned to a red-brown by uranium nitrate, or to a bluer colour with chloride of gold. They may also be intensified by pyrogallic acid or hydroquinone, but as the purpose of this article was merely to give simple working instructions for platinotype printing for the beginner, he may defer the consideration of such side issues until he has become *au fait* in the production of a good platinotype print.

A. Horsley Hinton.

Contact Printing on Bromide Paper.

IT is well to bear in mind at the outset that bromide paper is extremely sensitive to light, almost as much so as is a rapid dry plate. For this reason, it is obvious that it must not be carelessly exposed to actinic light. All manipulations except the actual printing must be conducted by red or yellow light, such as is allowed to pass through glass of these colours.

For evenness of result, it is better to use a lantern than daylight, because the fluctuation in intensity of the latter is very misleading and liable to lead to failures through over or under development.

The actual colour of the light, also, is of far more importance than one would suppose: ruby light tends to give one the impression that development is complete long before that is the actual case; it is also somewhat more difficult to handle the paper satisfactorily by this light than by a good yellow.

For these and other reasons I strongly recommend the use of yellow light, a thoroughly safe one being given by gas or lamplight passing through one sheet of yellow glass and one thickness of "canary medium."

This light, while being absolutely safe, gives such perfect illumination that it is as easy to control and estimate results as it would be by ordinary unfiltered gaslight.

If a ruby glazed lantern is already in use for negative work, it can readily be prepared for bromide printing by merely removing the ruby glass and substituting the yellow and canary medium. With these brief hints as to illumination, let us consider the entire process in its various stages.

Unpacking the Paper.—The sensitive paper is generally packed in envelopes sufficiently opaque to protect it from the admission of light. The packet must be opened in the dark-room from which *all* light (even stray streaks beneath the door) is excluded, excepting only that given by the yellow glazed lantern. The outer envelope being carefully undone, an inner cover will be found and these wrappers should be placed on a dry table while a sheet of the paper is removed.

It is a good plan to have a "light-tight" box (obtainable from any dealer) in which to put the paper after unpacking it; this prevents loss of time and awkwardness of handling in having to replace the paper in its wrappers each time a piece is withdrawn for use.

When several prints from one or more negatives are required, it is an excellent thing to have two of these boxes, one for the unexposed paper and one in which to put the prints as made until all are ready for development.

The Class of Negative.—Bromide paper gives us a great command over results ; in fact, so vast is the control we may exercise that it is possible to secure good results from almost all classes of negatives, from mere ghosts to those with density almost equal to that of a brick wall. But there is, of course, a class of negative that gives a good result with the least expenditure of skill, such a one is generally known as of average density, having a full scale of gradation with high-lights dense, yet not so opaque as to prevent you seeing a window clearly defined when looking towards it *through* the densest parts of the film, such as the sky, for instance. Another way to test the density is to put the negative, film side down, on some large print on white paper, the large letters should be just visible through the sky, but the smaller print should not be readable.

That is the class of negative usually considered in Instructions for Use, as an "average" negative.

The Sensitive Side of the Paper.—A difficulty sometimes occurs in telling which is the sensitive side of the paper : this may be easily ascertained by the appearance of the edge, which turns slightly inwards *towards* the sensitive side. This is quite apparent to the sense of touch as well as sight. Some people moisten their finger and thumb and squeeze the paper and see which sticks (the sensitive side), but that is a dirty method and quite unnecessary.

Printing from the Negative.—Having unpacked the paper, after making sure that all but the yellow (or ruby) light has been excluded from the room, we are ready to print.

For this purpose, different workers favour different classes of light : one prefers gaslight, another swears by magnesium ribbon, and some even prefer the light of day.

Personally, I favour ordinary gaslight passed through a No. 5 Bray's burner, because it is quite rapid enough for all practical purposes and is perfectly under control and free from serious variation.

The burner should be within easy reach of the worktable and should be fitted with a byepass to obviate the necessity of continually striking matches. Several years ago I had my bromide printing rooms fitted with an excellent lantern of this class in which the byepass was connected to two jets (one inside and the other out-

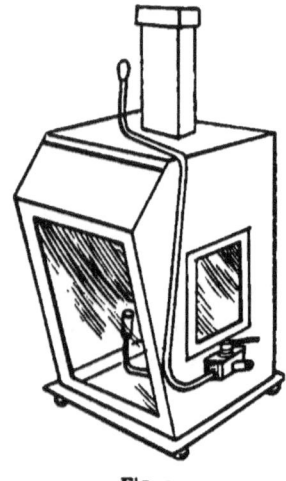

Fig. 1.

side the lantern) in such a way as to turn down the white light with the same movement that raised the coloured light, and *vice versa*. By this means no gas was wasted and the simple action of pulling or pushing a lever operated either light at will. By placing the same lever "amidships," both jets were lowered to the point of invisibility and could so remain for days at a time, yet always ready at a moment's notice. The accompanying sketch (fig. 1) will give some idea of its construction.

CONTACT PRINTING ON BROMIDE PAPER.   229

If the dark-room is small, and space is an object, the sink may be fitted with a wooden cover and this may be used as a table for printing the paper, but care must be observed to avoid the slightest moisture upon it or satisfactory work is impossible and the negatives may be ruined. In a large room, it is much better to have an ordinary kitchen table removed some distance from the sink; with this and a comfortable chair bromide printing is a very pleasant occupation. The following sketch (fig. 2) will explain the arrangement of the table, and it applies equally well to the movable top of the sink.

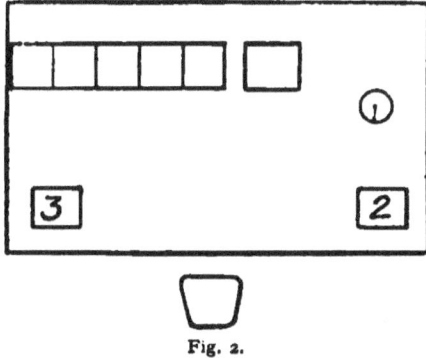

Fig. 2.

Supposing that some arrangement of this sort is devised, we must unpack some bromide paper and put it in its box and then put a negative of "average" density in an ordinary printing frame. On the film side of the negative we must now place a sheet of bromide paper with its sensitive side in contact, replace the back of the frame and it is ready for exposure. Before exposing it, *make sure that both boxes are shut* or their contents will be ruined the moment the white light is turned up.

Upon reference to the instructions that accompany each packet of bromide paper, you will observe a certain number of seconds' exposure is advised at a certain distance from the light; in the case of the Barnet extra rapid paper the time is given as about four seconds at a distance of eighteen inches.

When all is ready for exposure, place the printing frame upright opposite the lantern at the mark indicating eighteen inches (see fig. 2), note the time on the seconds hand of the clock and throw the lever over for white light for four seconds and then reverse it. Remove the paper and if many are likely to be required from that negative, it would be well to develop the first print in order to judge as to the accuracy of the exposure. If over or under-exposed, the time must be reduced or lengthened as required. When the best time and distance has been ascertained for a certain negative, mark it with a narrow strip of paper bearing full particulars for future guidance, such as: "4 sec., 18 in., No. 5 Bray;" in this way absolute correctness of future exposures is assured. Of course, if gas is not obtainable, magnesium ribbon may be used instead. In this case the negative would be marked " 1 inch (or more) ribbon, 3 ft. distant," as the case may be.

Using Masks and Discs.—Prints are sometimes required with an oval (or square) centre and white margins: this is effected by interposing a black mask of the desired size and shape (obtainable from all dealers) between the negative and the sensitive paper. The black paper prevents the passage of light and leaves white margins to the print. If grey margins are required, a disc (to fit the mask) is attached to a sheet of glass the same size as the negative and arranged so that registration is easily effected; the print is first made with a mask and is then placed in contact with the disc and plain glass (the negative being removed from the frame), and again exposed for a second to the light. If a black border is required the exposure of the margin must be extended three or four seconds.

Vignetting.—To vignette bromide prints, the printing frame must be covered with a piece of cardboard in which a small hole (about 1½ inches by 1 inch for a cabinet head and bust) is pierced. The hole *must* be covered with a sheet of white tissue paper which will diffuse the light and cause it to travel without harsh lines beneath the opening, and make the print with perfectly gradated edges. It is sometimes an advantage to move the negative while printing vignettes; but it is not absolutely essential if the hole in the cardboard is not too large and if the card is removed some little distance from the negative. If the card is too close to the negative, the gradation will be abrupt and the vignette will not look well.

Cloud Printing.—This requires some care in order to avoid harshness and sharply defined lines. If the sky of the negative prints white, the addition of clouds from another negative is not difficult; but if it is at all thin, the entire sky must be carefully painted out with a deeply opaque pigment in order to make it quite dense and unprintable.

As a bromide print cannot be examined while in progress: that is, cannot be seen at all before development, careful registration is desirable in order to prevent printing the clouds across the landscape instead of above it. To do this an opaque mask should be made thus: Make a print from the negative on P.O.P. and, without fixing or toning it, cut it carefully in two parts following the horizon line as nearly as possible, then expose to light, until quite black, that part representing the landscape. Attach this to the glass side of the cloud negative (with the paper side of the P.O.P. in contact) and see that the bottom edge and the right corner of the paper and glass (viewed from the glass side of the negative) exactly coincide. To make use of this arrangement, you first make a print from the landscape negative, making sure that the negative and paper are firmly pressed against the bottom and left-hand side of the printing frame when looking towards the film side of the negative; mark the registered corner with lead pencil thus L in order to prevent mistakes in the second printing.

To print the clouds, you put the negative in the frame and press it well home to the left-hand corner and the base of frame (looking at the film side, of course), and then put the print in contact with the same precaution and replace the back. Now take a piece of brown paper with one edge roughly torn in shape of the horizon line of the mask and cover the entire negative on the glass side. Hold the covered frame in your hands at a distance of (say) four feet from the gas and turn on the white light. Directly the light is up, draw the paper slowly downwards until the horizon line is just passed, and then *immediately* begin to slowly push it upwards towards the top of the sky. Do this steadily and slowly for (say) four to six seconds, according to the density of the cloud negative. With a good thin cloud, four seconds should be quite enough, but you can easily settle this point on developing the first print.

Printing from Dense Negatives.—Dense negatives require much longer exposures than those of " average " (or ideal) density. This may often be prolonged to twice or three times the normal exposure at the same distance. A yellow coloured negative increases the exposure greatly, as much as ten to thirty times the normal frequently being requisite to get a decent print. An over dense negative that gives very harsh prints by other printing processes can be made to yield prints of exquisite softness on bromide paper by giving a full exposure at a *short* distance from the gas.

Printing from Thin Negatives.—Thin negatives on the other hand, require quite different treatment. In order to get plucky prints from very thin negatives, useless in other processes, we must give a very brief exposure at some distance from the gas; and here it may be well to note that removing the negative to a greater distance from the light is equal to decreasing the actual time of exposure and has other advantages in connection with thin negatives with which theory does not seem to agree. To print from a very thin negative, then, instead of four seconds at eighteen inches, let us cover it with a sheet of tissue paper and give it four seconds at a distance of three or four feet and note the result on development. If it appears to be over-exposed, we may reduce the time of exposure to three seconds at the same distance and modify the developer, as will be explained later on.

Development of Prints.—All my remarks in this article apply equally to most commercial brands of bromide paper; but it is only fair to state that they are particularly intended for that made by the firm of manufacturers publishing this book. Development, and so on, is very similar with all makes of paper, but most of my recent experiments have been made on the " Barnet " matt surface bromide.

I shall presently describe the use of several well-known developers, but it must be well understood that, whatever formula is adopted, a preliminary soaking of the print before development must be done.

When we are about to develop a number of prints we must first soak them in plain cold water until quite flaccid, otherwise the application of the developer would cause the dry print to cockle and curl, and the development would not be regular. This rule applies equally in the case of one print only as when a hundred are ready for development; a prolonged soaking in plain water having no ill effect.

The Iron Developer.—This is one of the developers most frequently recommended for bromide work, but personally I never advise its use (especially by a novice) because the use of the acid clearing bath, which is an essential part of the process, is so frequent a cause of disaster and yellow prints. The Barnet formula is as follows:—

A.
Potassium oxalate....	1 lb.
Potassium bromide	5 grains
Hot water	48 ozs.

B.
Iron sulphate......................	1 lb.
Citric acid	4 drams.
Hot water	32 ozs.

To six ounces of A, add one ounce of B; this order of mixing must be observed or a dense precipitate of ferrous oxalate will be formed.

Place one of the soaked prints face (which may be distinguished by its "slippery" surface) upwards in a clean porcelain dish and pour the developer over it as evenly as possible. With this developer, the image comes up very rapidly, so that it is not advisable to try and develop more than one at a time. If the first print of a batch appears to be over-exposed, that is, if it flashes out instantly and the high-lights become rapidly clouded, add to each ounce of mixed developer from 10 to 30 drops of a ten per cent. solution of potassium bromide which will act as a restrainer, retard development, and keep the high-lights clear while the shadows acquire density. Under-exposed prints can rarely be made to give passable results with ferrous oxalate. The addition of a trace of hypo to the developer has been recommended for bringing up their detail, but the result is far from good.

As soon as development is complete the prints must *not* be put in clean water, but must be transferred direct from the developer to the following acid bath:—

    Acetic acid .... 1 drm
    Water .....,............ .... 32 ounces

After an immersion of one minute, the operation must be twice repeated in similar baths that have not been previously used; this is to remove the iron from the print. A thorough washing must next be given to remove the acid and the print may then be fixed for at least fifteen minutes in

    Hypo .... 2 ounces
    Water .... 20 ounces

After fixing (no matter what developer has been used) the prints must be thoroughly washed in several changes of water for at least two hours.

The chief reasons against the use of ferrous oxalate are lack of control over development and the necessary use of an acid bath. Unless the acid bath is used, the prints will be yellow because of the iron in them, and if the acid is not entirely removed before fixing the prints will be yellow owing to the decomposition of the hypo by the acid in the print which causes deposition of sulphur.

Metol Developer.—With this, and the other developers I shall mention, an acid bath is not necessary and so one cause of failure (and extra work) is obviated. I have somewhat amended the Barnet formula to meet the needs of workers on a small scale and have also arranged A and B to balance each other without disturbing the relative proportions of the ingredients.

                        A.
    Metol .... 120 grains
    Water (cold) .... 24 ounces

Dissolve *completely* and then add

    Sodium sulphite .... $2\frac{1}{2}$ ounces
    Potassium bromide ...,............ 15 grains

Shake until completely dissolved but do not apply heat.

B.

 Potassium carbonate .... 350 grains
 Water .... 8 ounces

For use, mix three parts by measure of A and one part of B.

With this developer and a normal exposure, the image should appear in a few seconds and development should be complete in about two minutes. As fast as the prints are developed they should be immersed in

 Salt .... 2 ounces
 Water .... 20 ounces

to stop development. When all are developed, they must be rinsed for a minute or two in clean water and then fixed. Over-exposure is remedied by the addition of potassium bromide solution (as in the case of ferrous oxalate); under-exposed prints should be developed in a weak solution such as

 A .... 3 parts
 B .... 1 part
 Water .... 4 parts

Development will take longer, but the weaker solution will help to bring up the detail without the harshness of the shadows that would be the case if the normal developer was used.

Hydroquinone and Eikonogen.—The advantage of combining eikonogen with quinol lies in the fact that one provides what the other lacks, the eikonogen tending to give detail without density and the quinol (in inexperienced hands) giving density without detail. The following formula will be found very satisfactory:—

A.

 Quinol .... 40 grains
 Eikonogen .... 120 ,,
 Sodium sulphite .... 480 ,,
 Citric acid .... 20 ,,
 Water to .... 20 ounces

Dissolve the sodium sulphite and citric acid in 15 ounces of water, then add the other ingredients and enough water to make a total bulk of 20 ounces.

B.

Sodium carbonate	60 grains
Sodium hydrate	30 ,,
Potassium bromide	5 ,,
Water to	20 ounces

For use, mix one part of A, one part of B and two parts of water. The same remarks as to over and under-exposure apply as in the case of metol.

Toning Bromide Prints.—The " tone " or colour of the deposit depends largely upon the accuracy of exposure and the developer employed. Ferrous oxalate gives a rich black deposit, but to my mind metol and the combined eiko-quinol give tones at least as beautiful with pretty gray half-tones.

But some people prefer warmer colours, brown and red for instance, and some get brownish blacks (through over-exposure and the use of bromide) which they would like to change.

The colour of the deposit may be changed in various ways by treating the print in baths of different metals. I will give a brief outline of the methods employed, leaving readers to modify them to suit each particular case.

Black and Blue-black Tone.—Brownish black prints can be much improved after fixing by immersion in a strong bath of gold chloride; the following is the strength used by me :—

A.

Ammonium sulphocyanide	20 grains
Water	1 ounce

B.

Gold chloride	2 grains
Water	1 ounce

When quite dissolved add B very gradually to A, shaking almost continuously. The fixed print should be washed for at least fifteen minutes before toning and should then be placed in a clean tray while the toning bath is poured over it. The solution must be kept moving and the print must be removed and washed directly the desired tone is reached. Prolonged immersion will cause the print to acquire a deep blue tone.

Brown and Red Tones with Uranium.—Prints immersed in the uranium toning bath gradually become warmer in tone, changing from black to brown and brownish red until they assume a deep red nearly approaching the well-known Bartollozzi chalk.

Prints to be toned by this process must be *thoroughly* free from hypo or stains will be the inevitable result. The toning bath should be made up as follows, and it must be used at once as it will not keep after mixing A and B :—

A.

Potassium ferricyanide	20 grains
Water	20 ounces
Glacial acetic acid	1 ounce

When quite dissolved add

B.

Uranium nitrate	20 grains
Water	1 ounce

Immerse the print and keep the solution in motion until the desired colour is produced, then wash the print for half an hour in several changes of water acidulated (1 dram in 30 ounces) with acetic acid. Weak, under-developed prints are much improved by this method of toning.

At the end of half an hour, if the whites are at all yellow they may be cleared by immersing the print for a minute or two in the following bath :—

Ammonium sulphocyanide	20 grains
Water	10 ounces

After immersion, rinse the print for five minutes and dry.

Intensification.—It sometimes happens (especially when too little light has been used to properly judge development) that one acquires a collection of prints that, owing to under or over-development, are useless; let us see how they may be rendered serviceable.

An under-developed print, though weakly looking and "washed out," simply needs intensification to give it the requisite pluck. The foregoing uranium bath acts as an intensifier while conferring a ruddy tone on the deposit. A black deposit can be obtained by intensifying the well-washed print with mercury. The print must first be immersed in a saturated solution of mercuric chloride until the image disappears; it must then be again thoroughly washed to remove all traces of free mercury and may then be redeveloped by flowing over it an old ferrous-oxalate developer. If ferrous oxalate is not at hand, an old metol developer may be substituted, but the former is the more reliable.

When the image is sufficiently intense, the print must once more be thoroughly washed. All the toning and intensifying operations may be conducted by daylight.

Reduction of Density.—Over dense prints can be made fit for many purposes by means of a "reducer" capable of dissolving part of the deposit. The best for the purpose and the one least liable to cause stains is know as the Belitzski's; it is prepared thus :—

Water	60 ounces
Potassium ferric oxalate	3 "
Sodium sulphite	3 "

Dissolve and add to the red solution so obtained.

Oxalic acid	1 ounce

Shake until the solution turns green and then immediately pour off the solution from any crystals remaining undissolved. To this solution add

Hyposulphite of soda	15 ounces

and shake until dissolved, when it is ready for use.

The print to be reduced need not be free from hypo, but should be rinsed for a few minutes after fixing (or soaked until limp, if previously dried) and may then be placed in a tray and flooded with the reducer. The tray must be well rocked and the print, when sufficiently reduced, must be removed without delay and rapidly washed in running water.

Some Cheap and Useful Trays.—If large-sized prints are made, the cost of suitable trays becomes a very serious item. The expense of these may be reduced to a mere nothing, without loss of effectiveness, by the substitution of home-made ones. All that is required to make a tray of any size is a thin wooden confectionery box (or the bottom part of a larger case) lined with the shiny white marbled oilcloth known as "American moleskin." This is fitted inside the box (the corners being turned under) and secured by a row of tacks around the top edge. No further lining or preparation is required and the tray will stand all sorts of ill-treatment. As for durability: I had three such trays made out of old herring-boxes picked up at Calgary and lined with moleskin that had already seen service as cover to a wash-handstand and chest of drawers in a Canadian boarding-house. For upwards of a year those trays were used daily and travelled many hundreds of miles by mule and dog train, and were not worn out when I returned home. My porcelain trays were smashed by a fall from a refractory mule, but the rough and ready makeshifts were a priceless boon.

It seems to me that by practising economy of this kind and in various similar ways (*i.e.*, where economy is necessary as, unfortunately, it sometimes is) the cost of practising our pet recreation is very materially reduced.

W. Ethelbert Henry, C.E.

The Gum-Bichromate Process.

PICTORIAL photography is answerable for the revival of this, one of the almost forgotten methods of printing. Results unacceptable to bygone requirements have been re-introduced with advantage, where suggestive individuality and artistic effect have been desired.

The gum process has an unlimited range of possibilities, it would be impossible to describe them all. The minutest details, or the broadest diffusion together with the power of working from the highest to the lowest keys of *chiaroscuro* are values that can only be realized when the infatuation consequent on successfully working the process is experienced.

This method of printing, as with the so-called "carbon process," is dependent upon the characteristic behaviour of the chromic salts when in combination with organic substances, such as gelatine, gums of various kinds, starch, etc.

When any of these mixtures are submitted to the action of actinic light, they become more or less insoluble.

This property was partially discovered as far back as 1798, by Vauquelin. Professor Sucrow, Mungo Ponton, Beauregard and others advanced its application to photography up to about 1840, but it was not until some ten years later that its great value as a photographic agent was definitely established.

Hunt, Fox Talbot and Poitevin, each worked indefatigably to bring the application of the chromic process to a successful issue; but to Poitevin must be accredited the honour of being the original inventor of the chromated pigment or carbon process. This brings us up to about 1855.

None of these investigators appear to have been remarkably successful, beyond having established definite, but valuable facts of the changes produced.

This want of success may possibly be accounted for by the general employment of gelatine and direct printing. It was not until Pouncey and others, about 1859, employed gum as the colloid medium, that any great advance was made.

About this time an important commission of inquiry decided that to Pouncey, Garnier and Salmon, and Beauregard the honour of producing permanent prints must be equally credited, and accordingly divided the Duc de Luyue's prize between them, giving to Poitevin the credit of the priority of invention.

Pouncey appears to have followed up the process with some considerable success, as some of his existing examples are excellent; it is much to be regretted that we have not more detailed particulars of his methods of working; but he evidently was before his time and met with but little encouragement.

To Alfred Maskell and M. Demachy must be accredited the revival of this long neglected process, and during the last three years much advancement has been made towards perfecting it.

Serious workers, both at home and abroad, are industriously exhausting the possibilities of the process, and crude as some of the earlier examples of this revival have been, improvements and simplicity of working are giving us productions of every description, of such excellent quality that it may soon be expected to satisfy even the caustic criticism that has so persistently opposed its re-introduction.

Dexterity in the various stages of practical manipulation is necessary before skilful efficiency can be secured, and in order to arrive at this, due consideration must be given to the selection of the paper the colour most suitable to the subject and the effect desired.

Almost any kind of paper will be found workable, if it be of fairly good quality. Those that are thickly coated with soluble sizing media are unsuitable, for although they may give clear whites they sometimes produce harsh prints, the half-tones are also liable to be lost in development unless very deeply printed. Several of the continental kinds are well adapted to the process and work in an excellent manner, giving soft and even results; of course, it will be understood that for definition and fine detail the finer grained descriptions are the best, but where diffusion is desired those of a coarser texture may be advantageously used, they give a granulation that tends materially to secure the peculiarities of gradation characteristic of this process.

A few of the continental papers that will be found to work with ease to the beginner, are as follows :—

Michallet paper is rather coarse, but takes the gum coating easily, it has a series of lines running in both directions, which are rather objectionable for some subjects; but it is an excellent paper for first experiments.

Ingrés, is also a paper of similar character, and can be worked with equal facility. Lallane is another paper of the same class, but much finer.

Allongé paper is entirely free from the markings peculiar to those previously mentioned. This paper is best worked on the reverse side, which can be distinguished by examining the name marked in one corner.

Among the English papers the ordinary cartridge, Whatman's drawing papers and many others are adaptable, but it must be borne in mind that those with a toothed or grained surface are preferable.

There are two methods of working, and results of equal excellence have been produced by either. Some of the most proficient workers of the process adopt the easier one of coating the paper, without previous preparation, with a mixture of gum, bichromate of potass and pigment. Others adopt the precaution of first saturating the paper with a strong solution of bichromate, and when dry coating it with a mixture containing only gum and pigment.

Experience is in favour of the previous saturation of the paper, this is recommended especially for beginners, as there are several kinds of paper that will not work efficiently by the first method; but when skill and practical knowledge of the special behaviour of the materials employed is acquired, either method can be adopted.

We may presume that the advantage of the previous saturation of the paper with the chromic salt is, that should there be any inequality in its structural character, or should it be unequally sized, the bichromate appears to act as a kind of resist to the penetration of the pigment, thereby securing an increased range of tone and a corresponding purity of the whites.

The process may be divided into the following operations:—

>Saturation or sensitizing of the paper.
>Preparation of the gum mucilage
>Mixing and preparing the pigments.
>Coating the paper.
>Printing and exposure.
>Development.

For working by the previously chromated paper method, the sensitizing solution is made up of one part of bichromate of potassium dissolved in ten parts of water. This strength will not keep at all temperatures. Should the salt crystallize out, it is necessary to warm a portion of the solution and re-dissolve the crystals. The solution may be used repeatedly, but it will be necessary to filter it occasionally.

Before saturation it is convenient to cut the paper into the most useful sizes—quarter sheets are handy. Having decided which is to be the working side, mark the back distinctly. Into a dish of sufficient depth pour in the one in ten bichromate solution to a depth of about one inch, and immerse your paper sheet by sheet, until you have in it all you intend to sensitize. As each sheet is placed in the solution, remove air bells and turn it over and repeat this precaution. The time necessary for immersion is of no importance so that the saturation is absolute, about five minutes being generally sufficient for the thickest of papers. By removing the bottom sheet to the top and passing through the whole in this manner, turning over each sheet and removing all air bells, even saturation is secured. Each sheet is carefully and slowly removed from the solution and dried in the dark. The paper is now very sensitive to actinic light, which must during all future operations be carefully guarded against.

After the paper is dry, it will—if kept so—be in good condition for a long time.

To prepare the gum mucilage, take two ounces of Soudan or Turkey gum and dissolve it in five fluid ounces of cold water, strain out the floating impurities through fine muslin, and allow others, and finer to subside. This mucilage will keep in good condition in a well-corked bottle, for a considerable time. M. Demachy employs gum mucilage of twice this density.

Pigments in powder are more suitable than in any other form, if in cakes or paste. The medium in which they are prepared, does not work kindly with the gum, and it is also difficult to accurately measure quantities. No advantage is gained by using expensive colours, they can all be purchased at a good colourman's, and at a small cost.

Lamp or any carbon, black, red ochre, yellow ochre, burnt sienna, and raw sienna, all work well; there is some uncertainty with the umbers and sepias. It will be found that much time will be saved if a combination of these dry colours is made up in bulk, as for instance— one hundred and seventy-five grains of vegetable black and one hundred of burnt sienna, give a rich soft brown colour. These must be finely and intimately mixed with each other, which is conveniently accomplished by grinding with a small pestle and mortar; after which the mixture may be kept in a wide-mouthed bottle. Another advantage in thus keeping combinations of dry colours in bulk, is the absolute certainty of repeating the actual tint when required.

Various combinations of similar mixtures can be made. Of course it will be understood that any or all of the above-named colours may be used singly.

The grinding of the pigment with the mucilage is easily done on a stone slab with a palette knife. Take half a fluid ounce of the two in five gum mucilage, to which add the same quantity of water and thoroughly mix. Weigh out fifteen grains of the mixed pigment and place in a heap on the slab, add a few drops of the diluted mucilage, grind and regrind the mixture until it is completely smooth, then remove it to a cup, and clean the stone with another portion of the reduced mucilage, finally adding the whole of the ounce, intimately mix, and it is then ready for coating the paper.

For extra fine work on smooth paper, and in fact for all classes of work, the fine grinding of the colours adds materially to extend the range of gradation, and although the trituration may be carried out fairly well with a palette knife, when the finest possible grades are desired, recourse must be had to the muller and stone. Mullers are obtainable of any artist's colourman, they are made in glass, and a convenient size is about one inch in diameter.

The most convenient brush for applying the mixture of combined gum and pigment to the paper, is of the description known as bear's hair, these are usually set in tin ; a flat one about two inches wide is a useful size.

In order to coat the paper evenly, pin it down to a drawing board by each corner with a double layer of blotting paper an inch or two larger than the paper to be coated. The blotting paper will absorb the excess of colour at the margins and enable you to secure an even coating up to the extreme edge.

Take a fairly full brush of the mixture after thoroughly incorporating the colour and spread it evenly over the paper, crossing and recrossing it with the brush. Allow the mixture to lie upon the paper for a second or two so that the paper may expand; now release each of the corners and pin the paper down again. Upon the next operation depends the evenness of the coating.

Take a four inch wide artist's badger's hair softener, hold it vertically and lightly by two fingers and the thumb about an inch and a half from the top of the handle, and pass it rapidly over the whole surface of the paper as quickly and evenly as possible. The motion producing the best effect is not the usual sweeping action, but a series of sudden short jerks, difficult to describe but easily acquired. Continue this softening down until the paper has an even semi-transparent surface without uneven cloudy spots. Allow it to dry spontaneously, but before it is stored for future use dry it carefully by the fire, but avoid overheating.

Uncertainty of result is a defect often brought into argument against this process; but absolute uniformity is not difficult if strictly accurate quantities only are employed. With constant strength of bichromate and gum, uniform weights and combination of pigment, similarity of repeats are obtained: but these can only be secured when each sheet of paper is coated identically with its fellow. To get this evenness the badger hair softener must be washed out and dried after coating each sheet. This is very quickly accomplished by an energetic shaking and drying upon a smooth towel. If the paper has been coated properly, it has an even semi-transparent surface slightly glassy.

Failures often occur from using an excess of pigment and allowing the gum to become too thick in consequence of evaporation. Excess of pigment gives dense heavy shadows and increases the difficulty of printing; excess of gum gives clear high-lights, tending to hardness and easy solubility endangering the half-tones.

The paper, if it has been correctly coated will work satisfactorily, if on steeping a small piece of it downwards upon cold water, the pigmented gum dissolves and drops from the surface leaving the paper nearly clean. From ten to fifteen minutes should complete this test.

The method of working without previously chromatizing the paper is as follows:—Take half a fluid ounce of four-in-ten gum mucilage and add to it an equal quantity of saturated solution of bichromate of potass; to this, with all care as to grinding and mixing, add the pigment; coat the paper as before directed. This method will be considerably slower in printing than that in which the paper had been previously saturated with the bichromate; neither are the whites as a rule quite so clear; but it will possess a peculiar grain and softness not otherwise obtainable, which is much approved by some workers of the process.

Exposure is so much dependent on circumstances that it is difficult to give precise directions, being governed by the density of the negative, the thickness of the coating and the intensity of the light. Even and not too dense negatives are the more suitable, for if the intermediate and high-lights are over dense the shadows are considerably over printed before the lighter parts can be brought out. Skill in development can do much to overcome these defects, but they may be considerably modified by the judicious employment of matt varnish, and by other methods of locally retarding printing.

The greatest assistance in obtaining uniformity in printing is the employment of a reliable actinometer, Wynne's print meter is probably the most useful for this purpose, with ordinary gelatino-chloride paper as a register; from twelve to sixteen numbers will be mostly sufficient for an ordinary negative, on not too thickly coated paper. Another method of judging exposure is by the appearance of the shadows; they may frequently be seen by transmitted light, and when well out printing may be judged to be correct, but this is a slovenly method and only approximately correct at the best.

If the bichromate is used only in the pigmented gum, without previous saturation of the paper, exposure must be much more prolonged.

By no other process is it possible to obtain such diversity of effect as by this; much will, however, depend on the skill which is exercised in development. Should the printing exposure have been fairly correct it is a simple procedure. The print is floated face downward upon cold water contained in a deep dish; see that all parts are equally acted upon by the water, and that no air bells exist; if any, they may be easily removed by gently raising the print and immersing it again once or twice. After it has been soaking some five or ten minutes it may be examined; if all is going well, and the exposure has been approximately correct, the pigmented gum on the unexposed margins will have left the paper, and possibly some of the high-lights and half-tones may be making an appearance, if so, the treatment must be of a gentle character, and the print may be safely left for some time longer in the same position face downward; never allow it to lie either in or out of the water face upwards for any long time, or unremovable stains will be developed. Many prints will develop almost entirely without assistance, or with only an occasional laving of water if allowed to lie in this position for a long time. On the other hand some may, even when only slightly over-printed, give no indication of development. When this is the case remove the print from the water and place it face upwards upon a thin, smooth board, fix it in position with one drawing pin on the extreme margin, then gently lave cold water over it; should some of the darker parts still resist this action, longer soaking will be found advantageous. If there are still parts on which the colour will not move, recourse must be had to the brush, and for this purpose nothing is better than a large camel's hair mop. Keeping the brush always full of water, touch where necessary very softly; do not sweep it up or down, but just dab here and there as may be required, constantly flowing over the surface a copious supply of water.

If there are still parts in the shadows, or even in the high-lights that will not move, a jet of water from an enema syringe or from the household service pipe is very useful.

As a last resource a prolonged steeping in water of varying degrees of temperature, even up to the boiling point, may be resorted to, but the application of increased temperature requires judicious management.

When the print is sufficiently developed, if the creamy yellowness of the chromate stain is not desired, the print must be cleared or bleached, either in a solution of alum, sulphite of soda, or hypo-sulphite of soda, strength being immaterial with a careful after-washing. If the print is only just sufficient or only slightly over-printed, care must be taken that the clearing bath is not acid, neither must the washing be too prolonged, but if the print is first dried and submitted to light, this precaution is unnecessary.

Always allow the prints to dry spontaneously. It will not do to use any kind of pressure or blotting paper, for the surface of the colour is very tender and delicate.

Jas. Packham, F.R.P.S.

An Introduction to Carbon Printing for Beginners.

IN the article that follows next will be found a complete exposition of the carbon process, with its various adaptations from the preparation of the paper and material forwards.

Whilst at the present time carbon printing is more largely used by professional photographers, yet its simplicity, the absence of chemical formulæ and complications combined with the beauty of the results, makes it eminently suitable for amateur workers, and hence it has been thought desirable that as an introduction to the subsequent article, a brief and simple outline of the process should be given for the benefit of those who have not hitherto made its acquaintance.

In the first place then let it be understood that in carbon printing instead of depending on light to make a visible alteration of the sensitive salts as in silver printing, we expose the prepared paper or "tissue," as it is called, under a negative and secure a positive in insoluble gelatine, the gelatine having combined with it a pigment, and hence we get an image in pigment, not in platinum, or silver, or gold, but in a simple pigment which may be of any colour.

If bichromate of potash is mixed with an organic substance such as gelatine, that gelatine becomes insoluble after exposure to light, and if that gelatine carries with it a pigment, then on becoming insoluble it holds the pigment with it. If now, paper or other material be coated with bichromate, gelatine, and pigment, and exposed to light under a negative in the usual way, the thin portions of the negative will admit of the light acting on this coating and making it insoluble, whilst the parts which are protected from light, as for instance the sky or white objects, will remain unchanged and soluble, and on being washed in water will dissolve away, leaving white paper, whilst the light-affected portions which have become insoluble remain in proportion as the light has penetrated the various densities of the negative. This then is how we obtain our print.

For fuller explanation of the paper or "tissue" and its manufacture the reader is referred to the next article.

The beginner will certainly first obtain his tissue ready made, and he can purchase it ready sensitized or otherwise. The former will be best at the outset, but it must be borne in mind that it should not be kept longer than can be helped before use, and never more than ten to fourteen days at the utmost. Various shades of blacks, browns, and reds are the usual colours, also grey, green, and blue. The tissue is rather more sensitive to light than silver paper, and should therefore be opened and handled in subdued light. It must be kept as dry as possible. A rather vigorous negative is best for carbon printing, one not too strong in contrasts. Before placing the negative in the frame, we must give it what is termed a "safe edge." This is done by making a narrow border, say of about a quarter of an inch or less, round the negative, either on the glass or film side, with opaque black varnish, or it may be done by gumming on narrow strips of paper, such as lantern-slide binders. If binders and not black varnish are used, they must be applied to the glass side.

The Carbon printing paper which will hereinafter be called the "tissue" will be found to present an unpromising appearance, and as the coating is the full colour of the pigment in which the print is eventually to appear, it follows that the progress of printing will not be visible, and a mechanical means of gauging the exposure must be resorted to. An actinometer, similar to that described in the article on Platinotype, will do, and another and simpler form is described in the next article.

Printing will occupy about one-third of the time occupied by gelatino-chloride of silver paper.

Development is conducted in daylight, but not too close to a window.

The absence of chemical solutions has been suggested as an advantage, in this process the developer being merely hot water.

It is not necessary to have this laid on, a can of hot water close at hand and a kettle on the fire or gas stove not far off are all that are required.

We shall require four or five dishes, one at least of which should be a good deal larger than the size of the prints we are to develop and several inches deep—a good-sized pie-dish or a basin will do.

Development merely consists of washing away the unaffected and therefore soluble coating, but it must be remembered that the less affected portions representing the half-tones have received their modicum of light on the surface, and therefore the soluble part of the film is underneath the part that has like a surface skin become insoluble. This necessitates the printed film or tissue being transferred to another paper or "support," so that we may develop or wash away from the back.

In procuring your carbon tissue order at the same time a packet of Single Transfer Paper, which is paper with a thin coating of hard gelatine. Now to proceed. Place a piece of single transfer paper into a dish of cold water, and in three or four minutes the coated side will feel slimy, then place in the same dish a piece of the printed tissue face upwards. This will probably curl up at first and afterwards flatten out again. When this has happened or in a few minutes after immersion bring the piece of single transfer paper and the print together, film to film, so that they may be in contact, and square one with the other. Now holding them by one edge, withdraw them together by sliding them out of the dish on to a sheet of thick glass, a large cutting glass serves well, or stout sheet of zinc.

This should be supported in readiness at the rim of the dish.

Having the transfer paper and print now on the glass or zinc, hold them firmly and with a rubber squeegee press them closely into contact, squeezing as much water out as possible.

A better way perhaps is, if the dish is large enough, to place the glass or zinc under the two papers whilst in the water and so raise them out.

The squeegeeing must be done thoroughly, firmly, and all over—several strokes being given in each direction.

Next lift the papers, now in firm contact and sticking together, and place them between blotting paper on which is a heavy weight. The next print may now be proceeded with and so on.

The print should be between blotting paper and under pressure for about twenty minutes, after which it is removed to a dish of hot water—almost as hot as the hands can comfortably bear, say 100° to 120° F.

After lying in this for a few moments the dark pigment will be seen to be oozing out from between the two papers. When this has begun to come pretty freely take one corner of the print and pull it away from the transfer paper. It should come quite easily, and on being peeled off entirely it is thrown away. We have now the transfer paper bearing the printed film reversed, that is, the side which was previously at the bottom and next the original paper support, is now uppermost and can therefore be got at.

If we splash it or lave it with the hand, using the hot water, we shall soon see what happens. The smudgy mass of pigment begins to wash away and the picture gradually appears.

This constitutes development and we continue working it with hot water until the whole is clear and bright, being careful not to touch the film with fingers or anything but water, for being in a very delicate and soft condition it would be certain to sustain injury.

The hotter the water the greater its washing-off action, and hence in cases of over-exposure very hot water may go far to recover the print. When the desired result is secured, transfer the print to a dish of cold water, this instantly tends to slightly harden the film by cooling it, and after two or three minutes it is passed into a dish of alum and water, which further hardens it and also "clears" the print of any bichromate salts which may still remain. In the alum bath the print should remain until any sign of yellow stain has disappeared, when after a final rinse of a few minutes in cold water to remove the alum, the print may be hung up to dry.

It will be seen that there is no prolonged washing as with those processes in which hypo is employed, and the print is absolutely permanent.

It must be remembered, however, that in the finished picture we are looking at the back of the printed film as it received the light impressions from the negative, and hence the image is reversed, that is, the left is on the right and the right on the left. For landscape and views this reversed position will probably be of no importance, but if it is desired to have things right way round—in portraits it will be essential—we must either work from reversed negatives, or we must again transfer the film which will then constitute a *double* transfer. We shall now understand why previously we called the paper to which the film was transferred *single* transfer.

Inasmuch as it will be seen that the print is not on paper, but consists of a transferable film of pigmented gelatine, it will be understood that the paper employed is merely a support to that film, hence it is customary to speak of the paper as the support, whilst moreover it may be, and as often as not is ivory, glass, textile fabrics, wood, or other substances.

If now we wish to again transfer the film so as to correct the lateral reversal, we substitute for the single transfer paper a " *temporary* support."

The temporary support which is to receive the film merely whilst it is being developed, and with the intention of its being subsequently transferred again to a *final* support, may be paper or many other things.

Moreover, remembering that the film is mainly gelatine, it should be clear that whatever the nature of the surface of the temporary support, the soft glutinous film will take that surface just as we may make the impression of a seal in sealing-wax.

The normal carbon print is shiny, due to the gelatine, and so, if as a temporary support we were to use ground glass or matt "opal," the carbon print film would receive the fine granulated surface and give a matted print as a result. This merely by the way as suggesting an additional advantage offered by the double transfer process as a set-off against the slight extra trouble.

If double transfer is determined upon, and it is not intended to experiment with ground glass, etc., then when purchasing the carbon tissue, some *temporary* support (sheets of paper coated with gelatine and shellac) should be procured, also some pieces of *final* support.

Whatever the temporary support, it must receive an application of waxing solution. This also may be bought, or can be made of:—

>   Yellow resin .... 36 grains.
>   Yellow wax........................... 12   ,,
>   Ether .... 2 ounces.

Melt the wax, add the resin, stir together and then add the ether.

Pour a little of this mixture on to the temporary support and spread with a tuft of cotton wool, and rub over to make it even.

The final support for double transfer may be purchased, and is made ready for use by soaking for ten minutes in alum.

The temporary support, after being waxed and the waxing solution having become dry, is to take the place of the single transfer paper in every respect, and the film developed as already described. When it has reached the final washing, after the alum clearing bath, it is brought into contact with the final support (which has been for ten minutes in alum bath as just described) and is removed to the glass or zinc plate and squeegeed.

It is now hung up to dry, and when quite dry the blade of a knife should be inserted at one corner and the temporary support gently pulled off.

Such is the carbon process, neither difficult nor lengthy, and with this brief outline to form an introduction, the reader who is a tyro will the better appreciate the fuller description which follows.

Whilst the article that follows is more comprehensive than the beginner may require at first, he is nevertheless advised to read it carefully through, and some points which may not seem clear at first will explain themselves after a very little experience.

The Carbon Process.

BEFORE proceeding to practical details of working, it may be as well to realize what a piece of carbon tissue is, and what takes place in the process of exposing such tissue to light. Mr. J. W. Swan, who is to be regarded as the inventor of carbon process as we now know it, was justified in giving the name "tissue" to the film of pigmented bichromatized gelatine, as at first it was a tissue unsupported by paper backing and containing pigment practically, if not entirely, carbon. The terms "carbon" and "tissue" have been generally accepted as describing a pigmented paper containing permanent colour, therefore little if any misunderstanding is caused by such general description. The carbon process, like other kindred methods, is based upon the well-known hardening action of light upon a bichromate salt in combination with organic matter. When paper is coated with a mixture of gelatine pigment and a bichromate salt, dried under favourable conditions and exposed to light under a negative it naturally follows that a positive image is produced. The negative acting as a screen, prevents any undue hardening of such portions of the picture as are intended to form the highlights, only slightly interfering with what are to be the middle tints, and practically permitting full play in the shadows. The latent image is imprinted on and into the film of tissue compound with the most delicate portions on the surface, and means must therefore be adopted to protect the surface during the washing away of all parts of the film not intended or desired to form any part of the finished picture.* In Swan's process this object was secured by cementing the surface of the printed tissue to its temporary support with rubber solution, but after J. R. Johnson discovered that the printed tissue would adhere without any cement to any surface impervious to air and water simply by atmospheric pressure, the same end was gained by soaking the undeveloped print in water until about *half saturated*, then bringing it into contact *under water* with either its temporary or permanent support, slightly squeegeeing or sponging to remove as much water as possible without

---

*It is generally asserted by non-practical carbon printers that all portions of the film behind that which finally forms the print, are unacted upon by light. That is to say, unchanged and quite as soluble as if not printed at all. The upholders of such a theory should try the following experiment:—Take a piece of tissue, cut it through the centre, expose one piece, then mount both under precisely similar conditions and wash in the same warm water bath. Paying special attention to the backing papers, they will find the one unacted upon by light will have parted with its load of coloured material in much less time than the piece that formed the backing of the print.

injury to the print; as to *air, there ought not to be any present* if care is taken to exclude it before lifting from the water bath. The half-soaked tissue after mounting absorbs every particle of water from between the surfaces, and thus secures optical contact.

The squeegee, handy tool as it is, ought to be used with great care, in no case with any degree of force, or serious injury will result, particularly to the finer kinds of work, such as double transfer prints of all kinds, either on paper, ivory or opal. The rubber edge of the squeegee should be free from notches, often caused by contact with the sharp edges of glass plates. The notches can be removed by rubbing on a sheet of glass paper placed on a plane surface.

TISSUE MAKING.

The tissue compound consists of a mixture of the following ingredients:—Gelatine, sugar, pigment and water. The proportions are of infinite variety according to season, the nature of the pigment used, and the purpose for which the tissue is intended. For convenience it is the rule for tissue makers to prepare what is termed stock jelly by dissolving, by the aid of a water bath, gelatine and sugar in water, in varying proportions —roughly speaking :—

Gelatine	2 parts.
Water	4 to 7 ,,
Sugar*	$\frac{3}{4}$ to $1\frac{1}{4}$,,

The pigments are made up into what are termed jelly colours, which are ground either by hand on a slab of glass, marble or granite, using a suitable muller for the purpose, or when large quantities are required a paint mill driven by steam or other power is employed. In

---

*For some purposes (instead of sugar), glycerine, sugar of milk, or treacle may be substituted.

hand grinding the colour is kept moist by syrup on greatly reduced stock jelly. After grinding by hand the pigment is lifted from the slab with a palette knife and stirred into melted stock jelly. When the mill is used, the pigment is mixed with the jelly before grinding. The proportion of pigment to jelly varies enormously according to the nature of the pigment, and may be anything between 2½ per cent. and 25 per cent. Having prepared stock jelly and jelly colours, and allowed both to set, they are weighed out in proper proportions, the jelly being dissolved in a tin vessel placed in a water bath. The colour, generally speaking, is dissolved in a small proportion of the stock jelly placed in the mill and again ground into the bulk of the jelly. In some cases the pigment is dissolved in warm water and filtered through cotton wool, fine felt or flannel. After adding powdered recrystallized bichromate, the jelly compound is ready for coating or spreading on the paper. The coating may be done by hand or machine. Several forms of machine are in use, including the first form invented by Mr. Swan. When only a small quantity is required, it is the general practice to coat by hand.

In hand coating, the tissue compound may be strained through fine muslin into a flat tin dish placed on a water bath; the surface cleared of air bubbles by dragging over it a strip of stiff paper. The sheet of paper to be coated is held in an upright position at the further end of the dish with its bottom edge just touching the surface of the solution, gently lowered until the whole surface of the sheet is in contact with the solution. If the lowering is properly done there will not be any default in contact, but if allowed to rest on the solution a few moments, the presence of air bubbles, if any, will be detected by the presence of little lumps on the back

AT THE FOUNTAIN.
J. W. WADE.

of the paper, these may be removed by raising a corner and touching the spots with a finger tip. The sheet is then raised with a rather slow and steady motion, allowed to drip, then clipped to a line by its top corners and left to dry in a warm dry room from which white light has been excluded. When this method of coating is adopted it is best to have the sheets of paper an inch longer than the dish; the blank edge prevents contamination of the fingers and distortion of the sheet caused by contraction in drying. Another method of hand-coating is to roll the sheet into a tube shape, placing the roll on the surface of the jelly compound one and a half inches from the top of the free end, raising with rather slow and steady motion as before. When the second method is chosen an oblong and somewhat deep dish will be found better than the flat shape; the flat dish may be used if tilted to give greater depth of solution in a corner.

In the manufacture of tissues the greatest care must be taken to avoid over or long-continued heating of the gelatine solution. Either a too high temperature or a lower temperature, long continued, destroys the solution by rendering a considerable portion of it soluble in cold water and to a great degree reducing its gelatinous character.

The samples of gelatine used in tissue making are of two kinds, although both of good quality they differ in solubility, in hot weather a larger proportion of the "hard" sample is used, in cold weather *vice versa*.

INSENSITIVE TISSUES.

All insensitive tissues are made with a single sample of hard gelatine. They are stocked by dealers and must of necessity be fit for use at any season of the year, to say nothing of those exported to hot climates.

TRANSFER PAPERS.

Papers of many kinds are necessary for single transfer prints, the tint of the paper must blend and harmonize with the tone of the tissue or by contrasting help to produce a pleasing effect. For prints of warm tones such as red chalk, terra cotta and the various tints of sepia, a yellowish or cream-toned paper forms the most harmonious basis; the various tints of black, blue, and purple look best on a slightly bluish-tinted paper. For instance, a copy of an old engraving in tissue, of the brown tone of the original would be utterly spoilt by a blue-tinted basis. The above remarks apply only in a limited degree to double transfer papers which in general use are confined almost exclusively to portraiture. Such papers are sometimes modified by tinting mauve, rose, opal, etc., etc. Such tints are only in small demand and are in all cases confined to papers coated with enamel preparations. The best and most durable form of double transfer paper is that prepared on fine chemically pure paper with colourless gelatine and made insoluble by the smallest possible quantity of chrome alum, entirely without white or tinted pigment of any kind. The best variety of double transfer paper only differs from the finest form of single transfer paper in having on its surface a rather thicker and softer coating of colourless gelatine.

All transfer papers, either for single or double transfer, may be coated in the same way as tissue, with the exception of those having a very rough surface. All drawing papers and in fact all papers of very rough surface are prepared by brushing over their surfaces several coatings of a very thin solution of gelatine containing a larger proportion of chrome alum or formalin than is used in making ordinary single transfers. A flat camel-hair brush is best for this form of coating, care must be taken to avoid air bubbles.

FLEXIBLE TEMPORARY SUPPORT.

Is paper coated with a gelatine solution in the first instance, and after drying, again coated with an aqueous solution of shellac.

SENSITIZING THE TISSUE.

Pour the bichromate solution into a deep flat dish (porcelain, ebonite, zinc, wood or tin) to the depth of half an inch to an inch; place a sheet of tissue in it face upwards, remove air-bubbles with a camel-hair brush or soft sponge, using as little pressure as may be; turn the sheet and remove bubbles formed on the paper, turn the sheet again face upwards, and passing brush or sponge gently over the surface, keep it evenly wet until it is fairly limp; remove from the solution, place face downwards on a perfectly clean glass or zinc plate, squeegee to remove excess of solution, blot or wipe with a soft cloth, remove any solution from the fingers, lift from the plate, handle by edges only, clip to a line, small sizes by one corner only, larger sheets by two corners, leaving a little slackness between the two clips to allow for contraction in drying, otherwise the sheet will be distorted and difficult to press into contact with the negative.

The sensitizing *may* be done in ordinary daylight. The drying *must* take place in a room from which actinic light is excluded, and in a current of warm dry air, free from impurities, such as the products of combustion from burning gas, or an escape of sewer gas, etc., and at a temperature not higher than 120° F. The drying should be done as quickly as possible, otherwise the tissue's keeping property will be greatly reduced, and in all probability a thin film formed on the surface, of insoluble gelatine, known to printers as "decomposed tint," degrading the high-lights, and, except in the case of very "hard" negatives, spoiling the work.

It will be evident to anyone that the fancy forms of sensitizing have been carefully avoided—floating on the back, floating on the face, etc., etc. All the results desired can be obtained by immersion. If a hard negative has to be dealt with, a stronger solution, or longer soaking in the bichromate solution, is all that is needed; for weak negatives *vice versa*.

Note.—In the dry frosty air of winter, sensitized tissue will dry without heat, and continue soluble for a considerable length of time, often as long as a month, or even longer.

In hot weather it is recommended that the solution of recrystallized bichromate be made immediately before using, as in dissolving the crystals a considerable reduction of temperature is produced. Should the temperature then be over 60° F., ice must be used, not in the solution, but roughly broken up and mixed with salt in an outer vessel. If ice is placed in the bichromate bath allowance must be made by keeping out part of the water. The ice should be encased in several thicknesses of fine muslin to prevent the solid impurities it generally contains getting into the solution. When recrystallized bichromate is not procurable, a few drops of liquid ammonia added to solution of crude bichromate is recommended. As bichromate is cheap, a fresh solution should be made for each large batch of tissue.

PRINTING THE NEGATIVE.

Any negative that will yield a thoroughly good albumen print is suitable for carbon work. The thinner negatives now made for P.O.P. and similar processes are less satisfactory for direct prints in carbon, for enlargements and reproductions such negatives can be made to yield most satisfactory results by modifying the transparency and the enlarged or reproduced negative. The latitude in this direction is great. No matter how flat the original negative may be, *if all the grades are present* it can be manipulated in such a way that the most brilliant result will be produced.

PREPARATION OF THE NEGATIVE FOR PRINTING.

The negative is prepared for printing as in all other processes by removing all defects such as pin-holes, streaks, etc. For the carbon process the negative requires to be further provided with what is termed a "*safe edge*;" this is a line of black varnish, from one-eighth to half an inch in width according to the sizes of the negatives, painted on its margin, either on the film or glass side. In the case of original negatives masks of opaque paper are used instead of the painted edge, the masks having openings cut in them slightly less than the size of the negative. The purpose of the safe edge is to secure a margin on which light has not acted, as such a margin gives greater freedom to the operator in the process of development by preventing the more deeply printed portions of the picture leaving the support when the backing paper is removed.

DOUBLE TRANSFER PRINTING.

It may be explained in a few words why an ordinary (non-reversed) negative must be printed by double transfer. In all other solar processes when the print is removed from or taken off the face of the negative, it is turned over to view, it therefore follows that the details on the left side of the negative are found on the right side of the positive print; with the carbon print no such turning occurs, it is mounted upon its support in the same position as it lay on the negative, developed in that position from the back and leaving the position of objects the same as in the negative. In some cases this reversal of the position of details is unimportant.

We will first consider the double transfer. In all double transfer processes a temporary support must be provided. Such supports are of two kinds, flexible and rigid. When a matt-surface print on paper is required, finely grained opal glass is used. For the enamelled surface patent plate, for intermediate or only slightly glazed surface, a flexible support is used. Flexible support yields a surface similar to an albumen print without special preparation. When the higher glaze of the double-albumenized print is desired, the printed tissue is coated with thin collodion before mounting on the flexible support. Rigid supports, zinc or ground-glass plates, have been used, but owing to the difficulty of seeing the details during development their use is practically discontinued. Flexible temporary support is always used in transferring to canvas, wood panel, opal, ivory, etc., etc. In the case of canvas, the double transfer process has two great advantages. First, staining is avoided, the bichromate has been thoroughly got rid of in the process of development. Secondly, the canvas is prepared to receive the print by a substratum that allows the carbon image to expand and contract with the expansion or contraction of the canvas and not in opposition to it. There are also two advantages in adopting the double transfer process for the production of pictures on ivory. The first, is freedom from bichromate stains. Secondly, the ivory is not distorted by washing in hot water, such distortion generally takes place when the single transfer process is adopted. Wood panels are prepared in a similar way to canvas. Stains are avoided, and as there is not the expansion and contraction of canvas to provide against, the substratum is modified in composition and greatly reduced. The stains above alluded to are caused by the chemical combination of bichromate with the lead of the paint, forming chromate of lead or chrome yellow. In the case of opal, opaque celluloid, and similar substances, no staining takes place, the double transfer is only required to restore the image to its proper position.

SINGLE TRANSFER.

The single transfer process is practically the only method in use when large sizes or large numbers of prints are required. For large sizes the negatives are reversed in the process of enlargement. For small sizes one or more reproduced reversed negatives are made, either in the camera from a carbon transparency, or by contact printing from a carbon transparency on a dry plate. With reasonable care, little if any loss of quality occurs in reproduction. As the single transfer process is the most simple form of carbon printing, it is generally recommended to beginners. Probably the most simple form of all is single transfer on opal. The opal plate does not require any preparation beyond cleaning Neither soap nor grease of any kind must be permitted to contaminate the surface, otherwise the print will fail to adhere. Opal plates are cleaned by scrubbing with fine graining sand and water, and a muller or a small plate, either of ordinary or opal glass, placed upon the wetted sand and moved over the surface with a circular motion until soiled or discoloured markings are ground off.

THE ACTINOMETER.

An actinometer must be used to gauge the amount of exposure, as only a faint image, and in some tissues none at all, is visible during or after exposure. The simplest form of instrument is the best. That in general use is known as Johnson's Actinometer, a square tin box containing a long strip of sensitive albumen paper, and provided with a glass lid painted to the colour of printed albumen paper, an opening in the paint in the form of a slit three-sixteenths of an inch in width, from which the paint has been removed. The strip of sensitive paper is made to pass between the top of an inner lid and the painted side of the glass lid underneath the clear slit with the end of the strip protruding at one side of the box. On exposure to light the sensitive silver paper gradually discolours until it closely resembles the colour of the paint, that is called one tint; the tint is changed by pulling the slip forward just the width of the slit, and so on until the requisite number of tints have been printed for the strongest or densest negative in the batch exposed, those negatives requiring less exposure are turned down or removed when the requisite number of tints are registered in each case.

EXPOSURE.

For double transfer from opal the materials required are opal plates, sensitive tissue, French chalk, collodion, double transfer paper, pressure frame, flat camel-hair brush, chamois leather. Before placing the negative in pressure frame, carefully clean from both sides all finger marks, etc., with the leather, place negative in frame on a paper mask, or provided with a safe edge. After exposure to light, remove from frame and develop on plate prepared as follows :—Rub the whole surface with French chalk on a pad of muslin, afterwards removing loose particles by gentle brushing. Coat with collodion made as follows :—Enamel collodion, 1 part; ether, 1 part; alcohol, 1 part. Filter and coat by pouring a pool on centre of the plate, and, by tilting it, force the collodion to flow into the top right corner, then to the left, then to bottom left, and finally drain off at bottom right corner, rocking the plate the while. The collodion must be allowed to set until it will bear the gentle pressure of a finger in its thickest part, but must not be permitted to dry in any part before plunging into clean cold water to remove the solvents by washing. The time required in washing is variable according to time of year. When the collodion ceases to repel water it is ready to receive the printed tissue. Soak the tissue for the requisite time, but not so long as to become quite saturated, bring it into contact with collodionized side of plate, remove to squeegeeing board, place over it a piece of wet rubber cloth, or a piece of wet thick single transfer paper, coated side up, to prevent injury to exposed margin of collodion and to facilitate the smooth passage of squeegee over the surface in removing excess of water. If, on removing the covering from the plate, the back of tissue is found to be unevenly wet, blot or place plate in a rack to drain; in a few minutes develop in warm water, temperature 90° to 100° F. Be careful to remove the backing paper *under water, and as soon as possible after immersion* in the warm bath. Finish development by laving or pouring warm water over the print from jug or other vessel, until all details are brought out. When washing is finished the print should look rather light, as in drying a decided increase in strength is obtained; rinse *slightly* in alum solution to stop bleeding only, place in clean cold water to wash out any remains of bichromate, thoroughly rinse by dashing water upon the print to remove any particles of solid matter that may have stuck to its surface; place in a rack to dry, and transfer as soon after drying as possible. The transfer paper is cut a trifle larger than the net size of the print, but less than the opal support; it is soaked in warm water until the surface is slimy to the touch, but not soft enough to break under pressure between finger and thumb. The softened transfer paper is placed in clean cold water into which the dry print is plunged, water dashed upon its surface to remove air; the two surfaces are brought into contact under water, and squeegeed into contact as in first mounting before development. When thoroughly dry, the print may be removed from the opal plate by inserting the point of a knife at the edge.

Double transfer prints with enamelled surface are produced precisely as above, only substituting patent plate for ground opal, and by adding a second thickness of paper to the back of the finished print before removal from its temporary support.

DOUBLE TRANSFER FROM FLEXIBLE SUPPORT.

The flexible temporary support is prepared by waxing. The waxing solutions are :—

No. 1.
Benzol.............................. 1 oz.
Pure beeswax (natural not bleached) .... 3 grs.

No. 2.
Turpentine........................... 1 oz.
Yellow resin .... 10 grs.

After dissolving, mix the two solutions, pour a little of the mixture on fine flannel, rub it over so as to evenly moisten the surface of the flexible support, wipe off with a second flannel using only slight pressure but rubbing briskly and with circular *motion*. When finished, the waxed surface should be perfectly even and quite free from streaks or other markings. The waxing should be done some considerable time before the support is required for use, and exposed to the free action of air to remove all trace of the solvents.

PAPER PRINTS WITH ORDINARY OR SLIGHTLY GLAZED SURFACE.

After removal from the pressure frame, the tissue is plunged into cold water with a piece of support slightly larger. After soaking the necessary time, the prepared surfaces are brought into contact under water, removed from the bath and placed upon any even plane surface, such as zinc, glass, etc., squeegeed into contact, blotted or otherwise treated to remove uneven dampness, and developed in warm water as in double transfer from rigid support, then slightly rinsed in alum solution and washed in clean cold water until all traces of bichromate are removed. After the transferring is done as before described, only the print on flexible support must be soaked in water until quite flat before bringing into contact with its final support.

PAPER PRINTS WITH HIGHLY GLAZED SURFACE.

The printed tissue after removal from the pressure frame is coated with collodion, for this coating allowance must be made in printing. A considerable reduction in temperature takes place and any moisture present in the air is condensed on the tissue, bringing into action the well-known effect of continued moisture, *i.e.*, considerably increasing the depth of the print. Great care must be taken to coat evenly and to prevent the collodion running in streaks on the back of the print. When such streaks or unevenness of any kind are present, a corresponding dark line or lines will be found on the face of the finished print. Transfer same as for prints with ordinary surface. All prints from flexible support on paper with a highly glazed surface as well as those intended for transfer to ivory or opal are coated with thin collodion:—

Enamel collodion	2 parts
Ether	4 ,,
Alcohol	4 ,,

DOUBLE TRANSFER TO OPAL AND IVORY.

After development the print is allowed to dry, and as soon after drying as possible it is transferred to its final support, whether opal or ivory, by a solution of gelatine composed of the following ingredients:—

Gelatine (fairly hard)	1½ ozs.
Water	20 ,,
Chrome alum solution (30 grs.)	2 ,,

Soak the gelatine in the water until quite limp, dissolve by heat, then add the 30 grain chrome alum solution; roughly filter through two or more thicknesses of fine muslin into a flat dish on a water bath. After cutting the print to a size a trifle less than opal or ivory, place both print and final support in gelatine solution, allow print to stretch until quite flat, then bring them into contact under solution, squeegee and place on edge to dry. When quite dry, remove temporary support by inserting the point of a knife between the surfaces at the edge, wash with benzol or ether to remove all traces of the waxing solution. The print is now ready for the artist.

DOUBLE TRANSFER PRINTS ON CANVAS.

For double transfer prints on canvas, as a basis for oil painting, there is not at the present moment a large demand. A strong prejudice exists, and deservedly so, against such prints, for the following reasons. Some thirty years ago, in the principal establishment in which carbon work was done, a process of printing on canvas was in vogue. It was roughly this:—A stretched artist's canvas without other preparation was coated with dammar varnish; after drying, the canvas was used in pretty much the same way as single transfer paper is now—that is to say, a piece of printed tissue was squeegeed into contact with its surface, developed by floating on hot water, and practically in that crude condition placed in the hands of artists for oil-colour painting or finishing as it is sometimes prudently called. The natural result followed—*viz.*, in a dry warm room the canvas stretched, the film of unmodified gelatine contracted; hence cracks, peeling, etc., until the work, valuable or otherwise, was utterly ruined. The method of preparing the canvas for the reception of the carbon image introduced by the writer is based upon opposite principles, as mentioned in the preceding general remarks, and may be described as follows:— A yielding and elastic substratum of gelatine forms a crust, so to speak, that expands and contracts according to the corresponding behaviour of the canvas support.

Ordinary painted canvas, such as is used by artists, or strong linen may be used with special treatment.

PREPARATION OF PAINTED CANVAS.

The canvas is first stretched tightly on a drawing board, same size as picture required, the greater part of paint removed by scrubbing with soda solution (either nail brush, sponge or a piece of flannel will answer the purpose) until the surface of the fabric is exposed and little of the paint remains beyond the priming. After drying, the canvas is coated with the following solution, applied with a flat camel-hair brush. Several coats (three in cold, four in warm weather) are given, drying between each and rubbing with fine sand paper if at all uneven.

Coating Solution.

Cooking gelatine (Cox's soup answers perfectly)	4 oz.
Sugar	2 ,,
Glycerine	2 ,,
Water	30 ,,
30 grain chrome alum solution	1 ,,

The print is exposed in the ordinary manner, developed on temporary support, allowed to dry and transferred to the canvas as follows:—The canvas is placed face upwards, on a level surface by preference, on a broad board over a large tank. The dry print is placed face upwards in a flat dish, the warm coating solution poured over it, air bells removed with the brush, the surface of the canvas brushed over with the solution. The bulk of the solution is then poured on the canvas and before it has had time to run off the print is lowered carefully and quickly upon it and squeegeed to remove excess of solution. After thorough drying, the temporary support is removed, the surface of the print cleaned with benzol or ether or a mixture of both to remove every trace of the waxing compound, and mounted on a stretcher in the usual manner. A print on canvas prepared as above, is perfectly reliable, it will neither crack nor peel, and can be used with perfect confidence as a basis for the most costly form of artistic finishing, as the carbon image rests upon an elastic substratum in actual contact with the fibrous substance of the canvas.

TO PREPARE ORDINARY STRONG LINEN OR CALICO.

Proceed precisely as for painted canvas (of course without scrubbing), using the same coating solution with half-a-pound white pigment added, sulphate of baryta answers perfectly. Sand or glass paper must be used pretty freely as the surface of the unpainted fabric washes up roughly when the gelatine coatings are applied.

WOOD PANELS.

Wood panels are prepared by removing the surface of the paint only with soda solution. After drying, a tooth is given by rubbing with fine sand paper and coating with solution as under:—

Gelatine (Cox's soup)	3	oz.
Sugar	1	,,
Glycerine	½	,,
Water	30	,,
30 grain chrome alum solution	¾	,,

Note.—Before transferring to either kinds of canvas or wood panel in cold weather, it is absolutely necessary to thoroughly warm the final support, otherwise the gelatine solution will gelatinize before the excess can be removed from between the surfaces.

THE SINGLE TRANSFER PROCESS.

The single transfer process may be briefly described as follows:—The sensitive tissue is exposed under a negative and the exposure gauged by actinometer as for double transfer printing. After removal from the pressure frame the printed tissue is plunged into clean cold water along with a piece of transfer paper of any desired surface or quality, cut a little larger than the tissue (to provide a margin by which the picture may be handled without injury during development). After soaking the requisite time, the two prepared surfaces are brought into contact under the water, removed to a squeegeeing board, plate of glass or zinc, and squeegeed into contact; care must be taken to use only as much pressure as is needed to remove the superfluous water from between the surfaces. A sponge may be used instead of a squeegee, or both may be dispensed with, if care is taken to remove every trace of air from surfaces before lifting from the cold water bath. When neither squeegee or substitute for it is used, the print must be handled with greater care, as undue bending before atmospheric pressure comes into operation would destroy contact. The print is hung up to drain, and more time allowed between mounting and development. Development is the same as in double transfer, with one or two rather important exceptions. 1st. The single transfer print is developed upon the material on which it is to remain. 2nd. There is no preparation of the supports, neither in the case of paper or opal. 3rd. The developed print can be soaked for a considerable time in a saturated solution of alum without injury, the alum solution greatly assisting in removing bichromate.

CARBON TRANSPARENCIES.

Carbon transparencies, either for projection, enlargement, or reproduction, are printed in a special tissue known as transparency tissue, and developed on glass plates prepared with a thin coating of fine hard gelatine. The coating solution is composed as follows:—

Gelatine	¾ oz.
Water	40 ,,
Bichromate potash	1 dram.

The glass plates are carefully selected, free from bells, scratches, and other defects; thoroughly cleaned, either by acid or rubbing with plate powder to remove every trace of grease, and then coated with the gelatine solution, and placed in a rack to dry; when dry, exposed to light to render the film somewhat insoluble. It is not desirable to print until the film is absolutely hardened throughout. The print adheres firmly to the plate when the substratum is not over-printed.

A positive intended for projection should show clear glass in the highest lights without undue density in the shadows, all details plainly seen—in a word, quite transparent.

Positives intended for enlargement must be fully exposed—that is to say, every detail on the highest lights brought out, but no more; beyond that point there is nothing to be gained. Over-printing in the transparency tends to bury detail in the shadows of the enlarged negative, and to blend the highest grades in the highlights, reducing the roundness or modelling of the picture.

In the case of very hard negatives intended for enlargement, the usual treatment is to sun the whole surface of the transparency in order to secure detail in the high-lights. A moment's consideration will convince any practical printer that nothing but injury to the final print can result from such treatment of the transparency. The high-lights are degraded, the details in the shadows further buried. The better method is to make an extra special transparency tissue, for the printing of such hard negatives, containing a greatly reduced proportion of pigment to gelatine. Such a tissue permits greater depth of printing, retains all details in the shadows and high-lights, and, in fact, enables the enlarger to produce a negative that will yield a thoroughly satisfactory print.

REPRODUCED NEGATIVES.

In making reproduced negatives from hard originals, ordinary transparency tissue will serve every purpose. The transparency is printed in the usual way, and developed on a prepared glass plate; when dry a negative is printed from the transparency without special treatment and also developed on glass, when a decided reduction of density will be found to have taken place. The reproduced negative will possess all the good qualities of the original, plus improved printing quality. It is only in the case of extremely hard negatives that the extra special tissue is required.

T

If a perfect reproduction of an original negative is required, the transparency must be printed either in very weak light or in direct sunlight. Either method gives a brighter image than that produced in ordinary diffused daylight. The same method must be adopted in printing the negative.

Note.—Care must be taken when direct sunlight is used to see that the pressure frame and everything in and about it is thoroughly dry, otherwise the tissue may stick to the negative, spoiling the print and probably the negative also. It must also be noted that two tints, printed in direct sunlight, although of apparently the same depth, mean quite as much as three such tints printed in diffused light.

FAILURES AND DEFECTS: THEIR CAUSES AND CURE.

As a rule, failures in working the carbon process are caused, as in most other cases of failure, by imperfect *knowledge of the substances and nature of the ingredients used in the process.* Before going into further detail, it may be as well to point out that a great deal of misunderstanding has been caused, by writers on this subject—that may be fairly termed " blind leaders of the blind." With only slight knowledge of the subject they have misled beginners by assuring them that the process is simplicity itself, in fact the most simple photographic printing process extant. Up to a certain point, and to that certain point only, is such description true. There are no subtle chemical combinations, no mixing and maturing of toning or other solutions. But—and in this case there is great virtue in the *but*—the greatest care is not only required, it is absolutely demanded, in manipulation. A carbon print from start to finish is probably subject to more chances of injury than any other form of print in existence. When this fact has been fully grasped by the novice, and he has been thoroughly prepared for the difficulties before him, the rest is plain sailing. Care, and care only; nothing beyond. He who wishes to succeed in carbon work must pay infinite attention to every small matter of detail as far as such detail relates to manipulation, otherwise he will only succeed in achieving failure.

FRILLING AND RETICULATIONS.

Frilly reticulations are generally caused by oversoaking the tissue before development, or failing to provide protection of the clear portions of the margin of the negative by a safe edge.

SPOTS ON THE FINISHED PRINT.

Spots are generally caused by solid particles of grit or other impurities being allowed to find their way into the water in the process of development, or, as in the case of certain peculiar circular spots that often deface the carbon print, such spots are caused by small fragments of tissue broken from the edges in cutting, which, being of the same colour as the prepared surface of the tissue and exceedingly small, often escape notice. They adhere most tenaciously to the surface of the tissue, and if not removed before the print is mounted upon its temporary or final support, cause the mischief referred to; being confined between two surfaces they cannot escape, but are dissolved by the water used in developing the print, swell and make a circular patch, often greatly injuring the picture.

Spots of a different character are produced in quite an opposite direction. Instead of being black they are light, in groups each spot having a dark rim on the outside. They generally occur in under-exposed prints, and are formed by fine particles of air imprisoned between the coating of gelatine and the paper support. When the tissue is mounted for development and placed in warm water, the fine particles of air swell, and not being able to escape from between the surfaces, impress themselves into the yielding portions of the printed tissue and make the marks above referred to, unless the printing has been deep enough to allow of their removal before development is completed.

CAUSE OF FAILURES IN THE SECOND TRANSFER.

Other causes of failure refer particularly to prints by double transfer, either to paper, opal, ivory, canvas or wood panel or any similar surfaces.

Such failures are generally produced by *soap*, *fat*, or *any kind* of greasy substances being permitted to find their way into the water in which such prints have been manipulated previous to their final transfer. Another point should be mentioned : the sooner a print intended for second transfer is finished the better the result will be.

PRESSURE MARKS.

Pressure marks are caused by using damp tissue or damp pads in the pressure frame. It is recommended that a piece of waterproof material, such as mackintosh cloth, be placed between the tissue and the padding, and that the pads be as smooth and free from grain as possible. It will be found on close examination that the mottled, spotty appearance, known as pressure marks, closely resemble the texture of the pads behind the tissue.

Thos. S. Skelton.

INDEX.

A.

	PAGE
Alpine Photography	9
,, Outfit for	9
,, Lens for	10
,, Carrying camera in	12
,, Plates for	14
,, Carrying Baggage for	15
,, Outfit for Developing	16
,, Exposures	17
,, Development	18
,, ,, Formulæ	20
,, Light (tables)	21, 22
Accelerator	24
Alum Bath, Formula	41
Aberration, Spherical	60
,, Chromatic	61
Astigmatism	62
Aplanat Lens	64
Astigmat Lens	64
Aperture of Lens	68
Angle of Image	70
Accessories in Portraiture	79
Architectural Photography	117
,, Camera for	118
,, Lenses for	119
,, Plates for	122
Actinometer for Platinotype	208
,, for Carbon Process	271

B.

Backing Mixtures	49
Background in Portraiture	78
Breadth in Pictorial Work	93
Blisters on P.O.P.	194
Bromide Printing	225
,, Safe light for	226
,, Negative for	227
Bromide Paper, sensitive side of	227
,, Printing	232, 233, 227
,, ,, Lamp for	228
Bromide Printing, masks and discs	230
,, ,, Vignetting	231
,, ,, Cloud Printing	231
Bromide Paper, development of	233
,, ,, Iron developer for	234
,, ,, Metol	235
,, ,, Hydrokinone for	236
,, ,, Eikonogen for	236
,, ,, Clearing Bath	235
,, ,, Fixing Bath	235
Bromide Prints, toning with gold	237
,, ,, Toning with Uranium	238
,, ,, Intensifying	238
,, ,, Reducing	239
,, ,, Cheap Trays for	240

C.

Camera, Carrying in Alps	12
Caramel for Backing	49
Curvature of Field of Lens	62
Cooke Lens	65
Composition in Pictorial Work	95
Clearing Bath for Platinotype	203, 218
Cloud Printing on Bromide Paper	231
Clearing Bath for Bromides	235
Clearing Bath for Gum-Print	251
Carbon Process, outline of	253
,, Safe Edge for	269, 255
Carbon Process, Negative for	255
,, Transfer Paper for	266, 256
,, Temporary Support	258
,, in Detail	261
,, Squeegee for	263
,, Stock Jelly	263
,, Coating Paper for	264
,, Transfer Papers for	266
,, Flexible Support	267
,, Sensitizing Tissue for	267
,, Drying Tissue	267
,, Negative for	268
,, Reasons for Transfer	269
,, Transfer to Opal	271
,, Actinometer	271
,, Exposure	272
,, Transfer from Opal	272
,, T'sfer. from Flex. Spt.	274
,, Glazed Surface Prints	275
,, Transfer to Ivory	276
,, Transfer to Canvas	276
,, Preparation of Canvas	277
,, ,, Linen	278
,, ,, Wood	279
,, Single Transfer	289
,, Transparencies by	280
,, Reproduced Negs. by	281
,, Failures and Defects	282
,, Frilling of Print	283
,, Spots, etc.	283
,, Pressure Marks	284
Canvas, Carbon Prints on	276

D.

Development	23
,, Dishes for	25
,, Effect of Temperature on	28
,, Light for Developing Room	28
,, with Pyro-Ammonia	29
,, ,, Formulæ	30
,, with Pyro-Soda	33
,, ,, Formulæ	34
,, with Ortol, Formulæ	35
,, with Hydroquinone (Quinol)	36
,, ,, Formulæ	36
,, with Ferrous Oxalate	36
,, ,, Formulæ	37
Drying Plates	41
Dark-Room Light, Testing	44
Defects of Negative	43
Dallmeyer's Portrait Lens	64
,, Stigmatic Lens	65
Depth of Definition (Focus)	71
Distortion of Lens	72
Development of Portrait Negative	81
,, ,, Formulæ	83
Detail in Pictorial Work	110, 93
Development in Hand Cam. Exps.	137
,, Formulæ	138
,, of Lantern Slides	149, 147
,, of Enlargements	168
,, of P.O.P.	188
,, Platinotype Paper	221, 204
,, of Bromide Paper	234-6, 233
,, of Gum Print	250

E

Exposure, Over	27, 32
,, Under	27, 32
,, Table with Pinhole	76

	PAGE
Exposure of Lantern Slides	146
Enlargements	155
„ Light for	156, 162
„ Daylight	156
„ Apparatus for	157
„ Lens	164
„ Direct	167
„ Development of	168
Enlarged Negatives	171
„ „ Transparency for	172
Exposure in Carbon Printing	272

F.

Fixing	37
„ Formula	38
Frilling	41
Flat Image	44
Fog on Negative	44
Fog-Green	45
Focal Length of Lens	66
„ „ Comparison of	67
Focussing Interiors	127
Finders for Hand Cameras	134
Focussing Scale for Hand Camera	135
Fixing Bath for Bromide	235
Frilling of Carbon Print	283
Failures in Carbon Printing	282
Flexible Suppt. Carbon Process	267, 274

FORMULÆ:—

Development, Pyro-amm. (Abney)	30
„ „ (Bothamly)	30
„ Pyro-soda „	34
„ Ortol „	35
„ Hydrokinone „	36
„ Ferrous Oxalate „	37
Fixing, Hypo. „	38
Clearing, Alum „	41
Reduction, Ferricyanide „	50
Belitzski Reducer	51
Intensification, Mercury „	52
„ Uranium „	54
Development, Metol (Baker)	83
„ Pyro-Soda „	83
„ Quinol and Rodinal „	83
„ Amidol (Thomas)	138
„ Hydrokinone „	138
„ Eikonogen „	138
„ Metol (Pringle)	150
„ Ortol „	151
„ Hydrokinone „	151
„ Amidol (Hodges)	169
Fixing, Hypo. „	171
P.O.P. Toning, Gold (Lambert)	180
„ „ „	181
„ „ „	182
„ „ Alum Bath „	184
„ Combined Bath (gold) „	184
„ „ (lead) „	184
„ „ (gold) „	185
P.O.P. Glazing	186
„ Mounting	187
„ Development, Quinol „	188
„ Toning, Platinum „	190
„ Fixing „	191
„ Toning (gold) „	191
„ Reducing „	192
„ Tinting „	194
Platinotype Clearing (Hinton)	203
„ Developing „	202
„ „ „	214
„ Toning „	223
Bromide Devlping., Iron, (Henry)	234
„ Clearing „	235

	PAGE
Bromide Fixing (Henry)	235
„ Developing, Metol „	235
„ Quinol & Eikonogen „	236
„ Toning (gold) „	237
„ Reducing „	238
„ „	239
Carbon Process Waxing, (Skelton)	259
„ „ Tissue Jelly „	263
„ „ Waxing „	274
„ „ Collodion „	276
„ „ Substratum „	276
„ „ „	278
„ „ „	279
„ „ „	280

G.

Green Fog	45
„ „ Cure for	46
Glazing P.O.P.	185, 186
Gum Bichromate Process	241
„ „ Paper for	243
„ „ Outline of Process	245
„ „ Gum Solution	246
„ „ Colours	246
„ „ Brushes for	247
„ „ Development	250
„ „ Clearing Bath	251

H.

Hypo.—Test for	40
Hard Image	44
Halation	48
Head-rest in Portraiture	78
Hand Camera, Photography with	131
„ Lens for	133
„ Finders for	134
„ Shutter for	134
„ Focussing Scale for	135
„ Development of Exposures	137
Hardening P.O.P.	195

I.

Intensification of Negatives	51
„ with Mercury formulæ	51
„ with Uranium formulæ	53
Image Formation	58
Image Angle	70
Isochromatic Plates for Pict. Work	115
Interior—Focussing	127
„ Exposure for	127
Intensification of Lantern Slides	153
„ of P.O.P.	191
Intensifying Bromide Prints	238
Ivory, Carbon Prints on	276

J.

Jena Glass for Lenses	64

L.

Latent Image	23
Local Development	20, 32
Lens	57
„ Function of a	59
„ Aberrations of a	60
Lenses, Comparison of	73
„ Testing	73
Lens for Pictorial Work	113
„ for Architectural Work	120
Levels	121
Lens for Hand Camera	133
Lantern Slides	141
„ „ Various Processes	143
„ „ Camera for Making	144
„ „ Exposure of	146
„ „ Development	147, 149
„ „ Warm Tones on	148, 152
„ „ Reducer for	153
„ „ Intensifier for	153

INDEX. 287

	PAGE
Linen, Prints on by Carbon Process	278
M.	
Mountain Photography see Alpine do.	
Monocles	75
Moving Objects & Architect. Work	129
Mounting P.O.P.	187
N.	
Negative Making	23
,, Washing	39
,, Drying	40
,, Defects of the	43
,, too Thin	43
,, too Dense	43
,, Image too Flat	44
,, Image too Dense	44
,, Fog on	44
,, Green Fog on	45
,, Black Spots, Marks, Bands on	46
,, Transpnt. Bands, Spots on	47
,, Stains on	47
,, to Intensify	51
,, to Reduce	49
,, to Varnish	54
,, for Platinotype	222
,, for Bromide Printing	227
,, Reprodn. by Carbon Process	281
,, for Carbon Printing ... 268,	255
O.	
Optics—see Lenses	57
Opal for Carbon Print 272,	271
P.	
Preservative	25
Pinhole Image 75,	58
Portrait Lens 64,	63
Planar Lens of Zeiss	65
Pinhole Table of Exposures	75
Portraiture	77
,, Shutter for	77
,, in Ordinary Rooms	79
Portraits Out-of-Doors	80
Portraiture, Lenses for	80
,, Development in	81
,, ,, Formulæ	83
Pictorial Photography	87
Plates for Architectural Work	122
P.O.P., Print-out Paper	177
,, Care of the Paper	178
,, Printing	178
,, Washing	179
,, Toning	180
,, Fixing	183
,, Combined Bath for	184
,, Alum Bath for	184
,, Drying	185
,, Glazing 186,	185
,, Matt Surface	185
,, Mounting	187
,, Development of	188
,, Platinum Toning	189
,, Toning with Gold & Platnm.	191
,, Intensifying	191
,, Reducing	192
,, Defects of	193
,, Stains on 195,	193
,, Blisters	194
,, Tinting	194
,, Hardening	195
,, Spots on	195
Printing P.O.P.	178
Platinotype Printing	197
,, Paper to Preserve	199
,, Outline of Process	201
,, Development 220,	204
,, Exposure of........206,	202

	PAGE
Platinotype, Print'g. with Act'meter.	207
,, Temperature of Develmt.	212
,, Developing Salts	213
,, Papers, various kinds	214
,, Sepia Paper	215
,, Clearing Bath, ...203	218
,, Devpmt. by Glyc. method	221
,, Negative for	222
,, Prints Toning	223
Printing Bromide Paper, 232, 233	227
Papers for Gum-Bichro. Process..	243
Pressure Marks in Carbon Prints..	284
R.	
Restrainer or Retarder	24
Reducer	24
Reduction of negative	49
,, Formulæ 50,	51
Reduction, local	50
Refraction of Light	60
Rapid Rectilinear, Symmetrical, Lens	64
Rapidity of Lens	68
Rembrandt Effects in Portraiture	79
Retouching Portrait Negative	83
Reducer for Lantern Slides	153
Reducing P.O.P.	192
Reducing Bromide Prints	239
Reticulation of Carbon Prints	283
Reproduction of Neg. by Car. Pro.	281
S.	
Satz-Anastigmat Lens	65
Stigmatic Lens of Dallmeyer	69
Stops, Value of	69
Stops, Comparative Value, Table	70
Spectacle Lens	75
Selection in Pictorial Work	95
Shutter for Hand Camera	134
Stains on P.O.P. 193,	195
Sepia Platinotype	215
Spots on Carbon Prints	283
Single Transfer Carbon Process..	289
Safe Edge for Carbon Printing 255,	269
Sensitizing Carbon Tissue	267
T.	
Tripod on Ice, a caution	14
Test for Hypo	40
Testing Dark-room Light	
Tele-photo Lens	70
Truth in Pictorial Photograph	91
Tone Value	107
Toning P.O.P. 180, 189,	191
Tinting P.O.P.	194
Toning Platinotypes.......... 223,	224
Toning Bromide Prints (gold)	237
,, ,, (uranium)	238
Trays for Bromide Printing	240
Transparency by Carbon Process	280
T'sfer. Paper for Carbon P'cess. 256,	266
Temporary Support, Carbon Process	258
TABLES:—	
Light	21
,,	22
Stops	70
Pinholes	75
V.	
View Finder	13
Varnishing Negatives	54
Vignetting Bromide Prints	231
W.	
Washing Plates after Development	38
Wood, Carbon Prints on	279
Z.	
Zeiss-Planar Lens	65
,, Lens for Architecture ... ,,	120

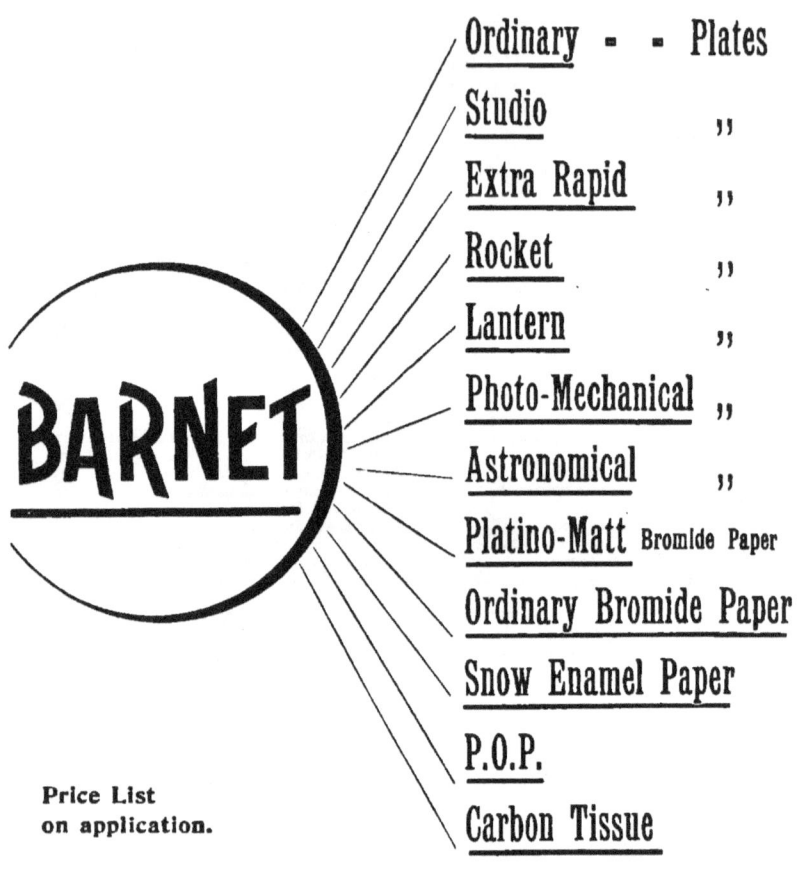

www.ingramcontent.com/pod-product-compliance
Lightning Source LLC
Chambersburg PA
CBHW022054230426
43672CB00008B/1175